The Reference Shelf®

The United States Supreme Court

Edited by Paul McCaffrey and Lynn M. Messina

The Reference Shelf
Volume 77 • Number 5

The H. W. Wilson Company
2005

The Reference Shelf

The books in this series contain reprints of articles, excerpts from books, addresses on current issues, and studies of social trends in the United States and other countries. There are six separately bound numbers in each volume, all of which are usually published in the same calendar year. Numbers one through five are each devoted to a single subject, providing background information and discussion from various points of view and concluding with a subject index and comprehensive bibliography that lists books, pamphlets, and abstracts of additional articles on the subject. The final number of each volume is a collection of recent speeches, and it contains a cumulative speaker index. Books in the series may be purchased individually or on subscription.

Library of Congress has cataloged this title as follows:

The United States Supreme Court / edited by Paul McCaffrey and Lynn M. Messina.
    p. cm.—(The reference shelf; v. 77, no. 5)
  Includes bibliographical references and index.
  ISBN 0-8242-1050-6
  1. United States. Supreme Court. 2. United States. Supreme Court—History. 3. Courts of last resort—United States. 4. Constitutional history—United States. I. McCaffrey, Paul, 1977– II. Messina, Lynn. III. Series.
  KF8742.Z9U55 2005
  347.73'26—dc22

                                     2005019579

Cover: Supreme Court Building, Washington, D.C.

Visit H.W. Wilson's Web site: www.hwwilson.com

Printed in the United States of America

Contents

Preface

As the final arbiter of constitutional disputes, the U.S. Supreme Court wields enormous influence in national affairs. Indeed, given the magnitude of some of its decisions over the last half-century or so, the Court has, perhaps more than any other governmental body, shaped the social landscape of modern America. In terms of their transformative impact, few presidential initiatives or pieces of congressional legislation can compare to Supreme Court rulings like *Brown v. Board of Education*, which struck down the "separate but equal" provisions that permitted racial segregation; *Roe v. Wade*, which declared that women have the constitutional right to an abortion; or *Bush v. Gore*, which paved the way for George W. Bush's assumption of the presidency by halting the Florida recount during the disputed 2000 election.

Furthermore, the Supreme Court's true influence is often greater than the sum of its decisions: At times the unintended consequences of a particular verdict have been every bit as substantial as the verdict itself. *Brown*, for example, struck a blow against racial injustice, but it also radicalized certain segments of the white population, particularly in the South, where segregation was most prevalent. Paradoxically, by legalizing abortion, *Roe* may have cultivated the seeds of its own destruction, galvanizing abortion opponents, particularly among evangelical and religious populations, and spurring their entry into the electoral arena in order to overturn the decision.

But the Court has not always played such a decisive role. Though the framers of the Constitution envisioned a system of checks and balances whereby the three co-equal branches of the federal government—the legislative, executive, and judicial—would rein in one another, thus preventing any single branch from exercising too much power, this hoped-for interplay did not develop immediately. In fact, in the decade after the ratification of the Constitution in 1789, the Supreme Court—and the judiciary as a whole—was quite demonstrably eclipsed in influence and prestige by both Congress and the president, the titular heads of the legislative and executive branches. In 1803, however, in *Marbury v. Madison*, the Supreme Court under Chief Justice John Marshall established its authority over judicial review, declaring that the judiciary alone has the power to determine the constitutionality of federal legislation or executive actions.

Since *Marbury*, the Supreme Court has remained a more or less equal partner in the federal government. At times, the Court's decisions—in the *Dred Scott* case, for example, which strengthened the institution of slavery—have fared poorly in the eyes of history, while at other moments the Court has bucked the popular will, as in *Brown*, to right a historic wrong. Still other rulings have had more mixed results: *Roe*, for example, continues to divide the country more than 30 years after it was decided, calling to mind Justice Robert H. Jackson's famous quote about the Court: "We are not final because we are infallible, but we are infallible only because we are final."

The first chapter of this book provides an overview of the composition, function, and history of the Court. Among the topics addressed are the Court's bureaucratic procedures and overall culture. Specific articles chart the evolution of the Court over the centuries and describe the various luminaries who have served on the bench and helped shape the Court as an institution.

Some of the more renowned and influential cases decided by the Court during its history are examined in the second section. Along with *Marbury*, certain politically incendiary verdicts—*Brown*, *Roe*, and *Bush v. Gore*, among them—are analyzed, as are various equally weighty if less-explosive verdicts, like *Gideon v. Wainwright*, which established a defendant's right to legal counsel, and *Miranda v. Arizona*, which declared that law enforcement officers must inform arrestees of their legal rights when taking them into custody.

Like the country as a whole, the Supreme Court is frequently divided along partisan lines, and a stable consensus has yet to emerge on a number of controversial topics. Abortion, gay rights, and the war on terror, for example, all raise significant legal issues that have yet to be fully and definitively addressed. These unsettled areas of Supreme Court jurisprudence are examined in the third chapter.

The late Chief Justice William Rehnquist, who was elevated to his post in 1986 after 14 years as an associate justice, was known for his conservative inclinations, particularly for his espousal of federalism, a judicial philosophy that champions states' rights. Selections in the fourth chapter examine his personal history and legacy. Dubbed the "Lone Ranger" during his early tenure for often coming out on the wrong end of 8–1 verdicts, Rehnquist oversaw an ideological revolution on the Court, which, through the appointments of such conservatives as Antonin Scalia and Clarence Thomas, was remade in his image.

The Court's future forms the thematic framework of the final chapter. With the death of Chief Justice Rehnquist and the pending resignation of Justice Sandra Day O'Connor, who frequently cast the deciding vote in 5–4 verdicts, President George W. Bush will have the opportunity to reshape the ideological makeup of the Court. With the nomination of John G. Roberts Jr. to succeed Rehnquist and Harriet Miers to replace O'Connnor, Bush let it be known that he would seek to maintain the Court's conservative tenor.

In closing, we would like to thank the authors and publishers of the articles contained in this volume. We would also like to express our gratitude to the colleagues and friends whose advice and assistance helped make this compilation possible, particularly Sandra Watson and Michael A. Messina.

Paul McCaffrey and Lynn M. Messina
October 2005

I. Heritage and History

Editors' Introduction

Since its first inauspicious meeting in the winter of 1790, the U.S. Supreme Court, like the nation it serves, has weathered periods of both profound crisis and relative tranquility. It has survived wars, both foreign and civil, fended off challenges from the legislative and executive branches, and opined on the most divisive issues facing the country. Its rulings have not always been greeted with universal praise; indeed, its decisions on aspects of slavery, civil rights, women's rights, and government programs have at times incited deep national discord. Nevertheless, today, according to opinion polls, the public holds the Court in greater esteem than either the president or the Congress. Yet, among the highest federal offices in the nation, the Supreme Court is in some ways the most obscure and least understood.

The articles in this chapter—and this book as a whole—will endeavor to address this deficit. Together the entries selected for this section provide a general overview of the Supreme Court, from its constitutional origins to its current status. The first piece, "About the Supreme Court," from the official Web site of the Court, lays the foundation for the book as a whole, addressing four essential topics in particular: "The Court As an Institution," "The Court and Constitutional Interpretation," "The Court and Its Procedures," and "The Court and Its Traditions." In "A History of the Supreme Court," from the Find-Law Web site, the themes touched on in the first article are expanded upon with a particular emphasis on procedure.

In "The Supreme Court in the Nineteenth Century," the late Chief Justice William H. Rehnquist charts the history of the Court during this tumultuous period. He discusses the various luminaries—John Marshall, Salmon P. Chase, and Roger B. Taney, for example—who served on the bench, as well as some of the more weighty and difficult cases decided by the Court. In conclusion, Rehnquist points out that though certain issues and decisions were deemed extremely important and highly divisive during their time, history often has the habit of causing them to fade into irrelevance: "These questions have long since either been solved or disappeared," he observes, "just as many of the questions that now perplex this Court will meet a similar fate a century from now."

In the "The Once and Future Supreme Court," the chapter's final selection, David J. Garrow takes a close look at appointments to the Supreme Court during the 20th century, including how they have influenced particular decisions and, by extension, the country as a whole. He notes that, in the past, presidents would frequently tap their counselors or other seasoned politicians to serve on the bench. This practice has given way to the elevation of largely independent career jurists who, Garrow argues, are often intent on preserving or creating judicial prerogatives. This, he concludes, "may . . . represent a redistribution of political power that has occurred by quiet accretion rather than robust debate or explicit decision."

From About the Supreme Court

SUPREME COURT OF THE UNITED STATES, 2005

The Court As an Institution

The Constitution elaborated neither the exact powers and prerogatives of the Supreme Court nor the organization of the Judicial Branch as a whole. Thus, it was left to Congress and to the Justices of the Court through their decisions to develop the Federal Judiciary and a body of Federal law.

The establishment of a Federal Judiciary was a high priority for the new government, and the first bill introduced in the United States Senate became the Judiciary Act of 1789. The act divided the country into 13 judicial districts, which were, in turn, organized into three circuits: the Eastern, Middle, and Southern. The Supreme Court, the country's highest judicial tribunal, was to sit in the Nation's Capital, and was initially composed of a Chief Justice and five Associate Justices. For the first 101 years of the Supreme Court's life—but for a brief period in the early 1800s—the Justices were also required to "ride circuit," and hold circuit court twice a year in each judicial district.

The Supreme Court first assembled on February 1, 1790, in the Merchants Exchange Building in New York City—then the Nation's Capital. Chief Justice John Jay was, however, forced to postpone the initial meeting of the Court until the next day since, due to transportation problems, some of the Justices were not able to reach New York until February 2.

The earliest sessions of the Court were devoted to organizational proceedings. The first cases reached the Supreme Court during its second year, and the Justices handed down their first opinion in 1792.

During its first decade of existence, the Supreme Court rendered some significant decisions and established lasting precedents. However, the first Justices complained of the Court's limited stature; they were also concerned about the burdens of "riding circuit" under primitive travel conditions. Chief Justice John Jay resigned from the Court in 1795 to become Governor of New York and, despite the pleading of President John Adams, could not be persuaded to accept reappointment as Chief Justice when the post again became vacant in 1800.

Consequently, shortly before being succeeded in the White House by Thomas Jefferson, President Adams appointed John Marshall of Virginia to be the fourth Chief Justice. This appointment was to

Courtesy of the Supreme Court of the United States and the Supreme Court Historical Society.

have a significant and lasting effect on the Court and the country. Chief Justice Marshall's vigorous and able leadership in the formative years of the Court was central to the development of its prominent role in American government. Although his immediate predecessors had served only briefly, Marshall remained on the Court for 34 years and five months and several of his colleagues served for more than 20 years.

Members of the Supreme Court are appointed by the President subject to the approval of the Senate. To ensure an independent Judiciary and to protect judges from partisan pressures, the Constitution provides that judges serve during "good Behaviour," which has generally meant life terms. To further assure their independence, the Constitution provides that judges' salaries may not be diminished while they are in office.

The number of Justices on the Supreme Court changed six times before settling at the present total of nine in 1869. Since the formation of the Court in 1790, there have been only 16 Chief Justices*and 97 Associate Justices, with Justices serving for an average of 15 years. Despite this important institutional continuity, the Court has had periodic infusions of new Justices and new ideas throughout its existence; on average a new Justice joins the Court every 22 months. President Washington appointed the six original Justices and before the end of his second term had appointed four other Justices. During his long tenure, President Franklin D. Roosevelt came close to this record by appointing eight Justices and elevating Justice Harlan Fiske Stone to be Chief Justice.

The Court and Constitutional Interpretation

"Equal justice under law"—These words, written above the main entrance to the Supreme Court Building, express the ultimate responsibility of the Supreme Court of the United States. The Court is the highest tribunal in the Nation for all cases and controversies arising under the Constitution or the laws of the United States. As the final arbiter of the law, the Court is charged with ensuring the American people the promise of equal justice under law and, thereby, also functions as guardian and interpreter of the Constitution.

The Supreme Court is "distinctly American in concept and function," as Chief Justice Charles Evans Hughes observed. Few other courts in the world have the same authority of constitutional interpretation and none have exercised it for as long or with as much influence. A century and a half ago, the French political observer

---

* Since five Chief Justices had previously served as Associate Justices, there have been 108 Justices in all. This included former Justice John Rutledge, who was appointed Chief Justice under an interim commission during a recess of Congress and served for only four months in 1795. When the Senate failed to confirm him, his nomination was withdrawn; however, since he held the office and performed the judicial duties of Chief Justice, he is properly regarded as an incumbent of that office.

Alexis de Tocqueville noted the unique position of the Supreme Court in the history of nations and of jurisprudence. "The representative system of government has been adopted in several states of Europe," he remarked, "but I am unaware that any nation of the globe has hitherto organized a judicial power in the same manner as the Americans. . . . A more imposing judicial power was never constituted by any people."

The unique position of the Supreme Court stems, in large part, from the deep commitment of the American people to the Rule of Law and to constitutional government. The United States has demonstrated an unprecedented determination to preserve and protect its written Constitution, thereby providing the American "experiment in democracy" with the oldest written Constitution still in force.

The Constitution of the United States is a carefully balanced document. It is designed to provide for a national government sufficiently strong and flexible to meet the needs of the republic, yet sufficiently limited and just to protect the guaranteed rights of cit-

---

The Supreme Court is "distinctly American in concept and function."—Chief Justice Charles Evans Hughes

---

izens; it permits a balance between society's need for order and the individual's right to freedom. To assure these ends, the Framers of the Constitution created three independent and coequal branches of government. That this Constitution has provided continuous democratic government through the periodic stresses of more than two centuries illustrates the genius of the American system of government.

The complex role of the Supreme Court in this system derives from its authority to invalidate legislation or executive actions which, in the Court's considered judgment, conflict with the Constitution. This power of "judicial review" has given the Court a crucial responsibility in assuring individual rights, as well as in maintaining a "living Constitution" whose broad provisions are continually applied to complicated new situations.

While the function of judicial review is not explicitly provided in the Constitution, it had been anticipated before the adoption of that document. Prior to 1789, state courts had already overturned legislative acts which conflicted with state constitutions. Moreover, many of the Founding Fathers expected the Supreme Court to assume this role in regard to the Constitution; Alexander Hamilton and James Madison, for example, had underlined the importance of judicial review in the *Federalist Papers*, which urged adoption of the Constitution.

Hamilton had written that through the practice of judicial review the Court ensured that the will of the whole people, as expressed in their Constitution, would be supreme over the will of a legislature, whose statutes might express only the temporary will of part of the people. And Madison had written that constitutional interpretation must be left to the reasoned judgment of independent judges, rather than to the tumult and conflict of the political process. If every constitutional question were to be decided by public political bargaining, Madison argued, the Constitution would be reduced to a battleground of competing factions, political passion, and partisan spirit.

Despite this background the Court's power of judicial review was not confirmed until 1803, when it was invoked by Chief Justice John Marshall in *Marbury v. Madison.* In this decision, the Chief Justice asserted that the Supreme Court's responsibility to overturn unconstitutional legislation was a necessary consequence of its sworn duty to uphold the Constitution. That oath could not be fulfilled any other way. "It is emphatically the province of the judicial department to say what the law is," he declared.

In retrospect, it is evident that constitutional interpretation and application were made necessary by the very nature of the Constitution. The Founding Fathers had wisely worded that document in rather general terms leaving it open to future elaboration to meet changing conditions. As Chief Justice Marshall noted in *McCulloch v. Maryland*, a constitution that attempted to detail every aspect of its own application "would partake of the prolixity of a legal code, and could scarcely be embraced by the human mind. . . . Its nature, therefore, requires that only its great outlines should be marked, its important objects designated, and the minor ingredients which compose those objects be deduced from the nature of the objects themselves."

The Constitution limits the Court to dealing with "Cases" and "Controversies." John Jay, the first Chief Justice, clarified this restraint early in the Court's history by declining to advise President George Washington on the constitutional implications of a proposed foreign policy decision. The Court does not give advisory opinions; rather, its function is limited only to deciding specific cases.

The Justices must exercise considerable discretion in deciding which cases to hear, since more than 7,000 civil and criminal cases are filed in the Supreme Court each year from the various state and federal courts. The Supreme Court also has "original jurisdiction" in a very small number of cases arising out of disputes between States or between a State and the Federal Government.

When the Supreme Court rules on a constitutional issue, that judgment is virtually final; its decisions can be altered only by the rarely used procedure of constitutional amendment or by a new ruling of the Court. However, when the Court interprets a statute, new legislative action can be taken.

Chief Justice Marshall expressed the challenge which the Supreme Court faces in maintaining free government by noting: "We must never forget that it is a *constitution* we are expounding . . . intended to endure for ages to come, and consequently, to be adapted to the various *crises* of human affairs."

The Court and Its Procedures

A Term of the Supreme Court begins, by statute, on the first Monday in October. Usually Court sessions continue until late June or early July. The Term is divided between "sittings," when the Justices hear cases and deliver opinions, and intervening "recesses," when they consider the business before the Court and write opinions. Sittings and recesses alternate at approximately two-week intervals.

With rare exceptions, each side is allowed 30 minutes argument and up to 24 cases may be argued at one sitting. Since the majority of cases involve the review of a decision of some other court, there is no jury and no witnesses are heard. For each case, the Court has before it a record of prior proceedings and printed briefs containing the arguments of each side.

During the intervening recess period, the Justices study the argued and forthcoming cases and work on their opinions. Each week the Justices must also evaluate more than 130 petitions seeking review of judgments of state and federal courts to determine which cases are to be granted full review with oral arguments by attorneys.

When the Court is sitting, public sessions begin promptly at 10 A.M. and continue until 3 P.M., with a one-hour lunch recess starting at noon. No public sessions are held on Thursdays or Fridays. On Fridays during and preceding argument weeks, the Justices meet to discuss the argued cases and to discuss and vote on petitions for review.

When the Court is in session, the 10 A.M. entrance of the Justices into the Courtroom is announced by the Marshal. Those present, at the sound of the gavel, arise and remain standing until the robed Justices are seated following the traditional chant: "The Honorable, the Chief Justice and the Associate Justices of the Supreme Court of the United States. Oyez! Oyez! Oyez! All persons having business before the Honorable, the Supreme Court of the United States, are admonished to draw near and give their attention, for the Court is now sitting. God save the United States and this Honorable Court!"

Prior to hearing oral argument, other business of the Court is transacted. On Monday mornings this includes the release of an Order List, a public report of Court actions including the acceptance and rejection of cases, and the admission of new members to the Court Bar. Opinions are typically released on Tuesday and Wednesday mornings and on the third Monday of each sitting, when the Court takes the Bench but no arguments are heard.

The Court maintains this schedule each Term until all cases ready for submission have been heard and decided. In May and June the Court sits only to announce orders and opinions. The Court recesses at the end of June, but the work of the Justices is unceasing. During the summer they continue to analyze new petitions for review, consider motions and applications, and must make preparations for cases scheduled for fall argument.

The Court and Its Traditions

For all of the changes in its history, the Supreme Court has retained so many traditions that it is in many respects the same institution that first met in 1790, prompting one legal historian to call it, "the first Court still sitting."

Recent Justices have perpetuated the tradition of longevity of tenure. Justice Hugo Black served for 34 years and one month prior to his retirement in 1971. In October 1973, Justice William O. Douglas surpassed the previous longevity record of Justice Stephen J. Field, who had served for 34 years and six months from 1863 to 1897. When Justice Douglas retired on November 12, 1975, he had served a total of 36 years and six months.

As is customary in American courts, the nine Justices are seated by seniority on the Bench. The Chief Justice occupies the center chair; the senior Associate Justice sits to his right, the second senior to his left, and so on, alternating right and left by seniority.

Since at least 1800, it has been traditional for Justices to wear black robes while in Court. Chief Justice Jay, and apparently his colleagues, lent a colorful air to the earlier sessions by wearing robes with a red facing, somewhat like those worn by early colonial and English judges. The Jay robe of black and salmon is now in the possession of the Smithsonian Institution.

Initially, all attorneys wore formal "morning clothes" when appearing before the Court. Senator George Wharton Pepper of Pennsylvania often told friends of the incident he provoked when, as a young lawyer in the 1890s, he arrived to argue a case in "street clothes." Justice Horace Gray was overheard whispering to a colleague, "Who is that beast who dares to come in here with a grey coat?" The young attorney was refused admission until he borrowed a "morning coat." Today, the tradition of formal dress is followed only by Department of Justice and other government lawyers, who serve as advocates for the United States Government.

Quill pens have remained part of the Courtroom scene. White quills are placed on counsel tables each day that the Court sits, as was done at the earliest sessions of the Court. The "Conference handshake" has been a tradition since the days of Chief Justice Melville W. Fuller in the late 19th century. When the Justices assemble to go on the Bench each day and at the beginning of the private Conferences at which they discuss decisions, each Justice shakes hands with each of the other eight. Chief Justice Fuller instituted the practice as a reminder that differences of opinion on the Court did not preclude overall harmony of purpose.

The Supreme Court has a traditional seal, which is similar to the Great Seal of the United States, but which has a single star beneath the eagle's claws—symbolizing the Constitution's creation of "one Supreme Court." The Seal of the Supreme Court of the United States is kept in the custody of the Clerk of the Court and is stamped on official papers, such as certificates given to attorneys newly admitted to practice before the Supreme Court. The seal now used is the fifth in the Court's history.

A History of the Supreme Court

FINDLAW, 2005

Article III, Section 1 of the Constitution provides that "[t]he judicial Power of the United States, shall be vested in one Supreme Court, and in such inferior Courts as the Congress may from time to time ordain and establish."

Under this section and the Judiciary Act of 1789, the United States Supreme Court was created. The Act organized the Supreme Court, the federal circuit courts, and the federal district courts, established the Office of the Attorney General, and reserved the president's right to nominate justices for appointment to the United States Supreme Court with the advice and consent of the Senate.

When the Supreme Court was unveiled on February 2, 1790, six justices shared the bench. One justice was appointed as the Chief Justice and held additional administrative duties related both to the Supreme Court and to the entire federal court system. The other five were associate justices. At its creation, the judicial branch was by far the weakest and most timid of all three government branches, holding back from strongly upholding and deciding controversial issues. However, in 1801, Chief Justice John Marshall joined the Supreme Court and boldly asserted the judicial branch's authority and judicial rights.

In *Marbury v. Madison*, Chief Justice Marshall asserted that the doctrine of judicial review permitted the Court to review the constitutionality of congressional legislation. Before the end of his 34 years, he succeeded in strengthening the central government and making the Judiciary branch, in some respects, the strongest branch of the national government.

Congress holds the power to set the number of Associate Justices sitting on the Supreme Court and that number has gradually changed over time. The current Court composition of one Chief Justice and eight Associate Justices was established under an act passed on June 25, 1948 (28 U.S.C. 1). William H. Rehnquist, who entered duty on September 26, 1986, presides as the Chief Justice. The current Associate Justices are John Paul Stevens, Sandra Day O'Connor, Antonin Scalia, Anthony M. Kennedy, David H. Souter, Clarence Thomas, Ruth Bader Ginsburg, and Stephen G. Breyer. Each justice is also assigned to one of the Court of Appeals for emergency response purposes.

Article from the FindLaw Web site, *supreme.lp.findlaw.com/supreme_court/supcthist.html*. Reprinted with permission.

Justices are appointed for life and Article III, section 1, of the Constitution further provides that "[t]he Judges, both of the Supreme and inferior Courts, shall hold their Offices during good behavior, and shall, at stated times, receive for their services, a compensation, which shall not be diminished during their continuance in office." A Justice may, if so desired, retire at the age of 70 after serving for 10 years as a Federal judge or at age 65 after 15 years of service.

To assist in the performance of its functions, the Supreme Court appoints several clerks, a Reporter of Decisions, a librarian, and a marshal to service. Each Justice usually appoints four law clerks, many of whom are the cream of Ivy League law school graduates. The Chief Justice appoints the other Court officers, which includes the Administrative Assistant, the Court Counsel, the Curator, the Director of Data Systems, and the Public Information Officer, to assist him with his administrative duties. The library is open to members of the bar of the Court, attorneys for the various Federal departments and agencies, and members of Congress.

Each year, the Supreme Court receives 7,000 or so writs of certiorari, which are petitions from parties seeking review of their cases. These petitions do not result in automatic appeals. Just because a party wants to take its case "all the way to the Supreme Court," the Court will not necessarily hear the case. Instead, such a case must pass through the Court's screening process.

The screening process begins with the Court's law clerks, who sift through the petitions and settle upon a select few that they deem worthy of consideration by the justices. Next, inside a closed conference room, the Chief Justice leads the meeting in which the Justices discuss the petitions and vote aloud on which cases they find more significant and deserving of deliberation. Voting begins with the Chief Justice and is followed by the Associate Justices according to seniority. The most junior Justice, now Stephen G. Breyer, takes the handwritten notes that will be passed to a clerk for public announcement of their disposition of the petitions. To be considered, a case must receive at least four votes. Whether or not a case is accepted "strikes me as a rather

Joyce Naltchayan/AFP/Getty Images

Associate Justice Stephen G. Breyer, the most junior member of the Court.

subjective decision, made up in part of intuition and in part of legal judgement," Rehnquist wrote in his book, *The Supreme Court: How It Was, How It Is.* In deciding whether to review a case, the Court will generally consider whether the legal question was decided differently by two lower courts and needs resolution by a higher court, whether a lower court decision conflicts with an existing Supreme Court ruling, and whether the issue could have broader social significance beyond the interests of the two parties involved. However, not all cases of significant social issues needing resolution are accepted by the Supreme Court. For example, last June, the Court declined to hear a case on the legality of college affirmative action programs; the case did not garner the required four votes.

The Court also receives another 1,200 applications of various kinds each year that can be acted upon by a single Justice.

> *Not all cases of significant social issues needing resolution are accepted by the Supreme Court.*

Once the Court accepts a petition, it then schedules the case for oral arguments. While the Court discreetly reviews petitions, it hears each party's oral arguments before the public—anyone may sit in as an audience member in the Supreme Court's stately, burgundy draped, gold-trimmed courtroom. Cases are heard *en banc*, which means by open court, when a quorum of two-thirds of the Justices is present. Therefore, six Justices are currently required. The public audience will view a 30-minute argument given by one lawyer from each side, and intense, vigorous questioning, including hypothetical inquiries, from the seated Justices. Questioning can be directed at the lawyers or at another Justice to bolster or sway opinions. The hypothetical questions are opportunities to pose slightly different factual situations to which a decision may have implications upon in the future. While a lawyer's appearance before the highest court often can be a tense, dramatic affair, it also can be a career highlight. Lawyers have been known to hang and frame the white quill pens they receive as a souvenir from the Court. The Court usually hears between one and three cases each day, on the Monday, Tuesday, and Wednesday of each week. The Court's term begins, by law, the first Monday in October of each year and continues as long as the business before the Court requires, which is usually until about the end of June.

After oral arguments, the Justices will vote. Sometimes more than one round of voting will take place because the Justices may switch sides during the process, often turning a minority into a majority and vice versa. The first vote on a case is taken during the week of oral arguments. For cases heard on Monday, the Justices will vote on it on Wednesday afternoon. For oral arguments heard on Tuesday and Wednesday, the Justices will vote on Friday. After the vote, the most senior Justice in the majority assigns the task of writing the majority opinion. Likewise, the most senior Justice in the minority also decides who will write the dissenting opinion. In addition, each Justice may write his or her own statements if they wish, but the majority opinion speaks for the final decision of the Court. Throughout this process, the clerks are intimately involved, researching past cases that may support a ruling and even strategizing to sway opinions in one direction or another.

Each year the Court decides about 150 cases of great national importance and interest, and about three-fourths of such decisions are announced in fully published opinions.

The Supreme Court is the highest court within the United States courts system and the powers allotted to the judicial branch of the government are vast. As stated in the Constitution (Art. III, sec. 2), "[t]he judicial Power shall extend to all Cases, in Law and Equity, arising under this Constitution, the Laws of the United States, and Treaties made, or which shall be made, under their Authority; to all Cases affecting Ambassadors, other public Ministers and Consuls; to all Cases of admiralty and maritime Jurisdiction;—to Controversies to which the United States shall be a Party; to Controversies between two or more States; between a State and Citizens of another State; between Citizens of different States; between Citizens of the same State claiming Lands under Grants of different States, and between a State, or the Citizens thereof, and foreign States, Citizens or Subjects." "In all Cases affecting Ambassadors, other public Ministers and Consuls, and those in which a State shall be Party, the Supreme Court shall have original Jurisdiction. In all the other Cases before mentioned, the Supreme Court shall have appellate Jurisdiction, both as to Law and Fact, with such Exceptions, and under such Regulations as the Congress shall make."

Each year the Court decides about 150 cases of great national importance and interest.

While Congress has no authority to change the Supreme Court's original jurisdiction, it does control the Court's appellate jurisdiction. The basic statutes effective at this time in conferring and controlling jurisdiction of the Supreme Court may be found in 28 U.S.C. 1251, 1253, 1254, 1257-1259, and in various special statutes. Congress also has from time to time conferred upon the Supreme Court power to prescribe rules of procedure to be followed by the lower courts of the United States. Pursuant to these statutes, the Court has promulgated rules governing civil and criminal cases in the district courts, bankruptcy proceedings, admiralty cases, appellate proceedings, and the trial of misdemeanors before U.S. magistrate judges.

The Supreme Court is located across the street from the U.S. Capitol Building in Washington, D.C. The mailing address for the Court is One First Street, N.E., Washington, D.C. 20543

History by the Numbers

U.S. Supreme Court Justices

Since **1789** there have been **108** justices who have served on the Supreme Court of the United States. There have been **16** chief justices, **5** of whom were also among the **97** persons to have served as associate justices. There have been **28** nominated justices who have failed to win confirmation.

Among the Justices there was ONE

President. William H. Taft, seven years after serving as the 27th U.S. president, was appointed chief justice in 1921.
Impeached. Samuel Chase was impeached by the House of Representatives but acquitted by the Senate in 1805.
Pictured on Currency. Salmon P. Chase on the now-defunct $10,000 bill in 1918.
Who served two separate terms. Charles Evans Hughes resigned in 1916 to run for the presidency and was then reappointed in 1930.

Among the Justices there have been

2 Females. Sandra Day O'Connor (1981*) and Ruth Bader Ginsburg (1993*).
2 African Americans. Thurgood Marshall (1967*) and Clarence Thomas (1991*).
6 Appointed to the first U.S. Supreme Court under the Judiciary Act of 1789.
7 Jews. The first was Louis Brandeis, confirmed in 1916.
9 Who have comprised the Supreme Court every year since 1869, when Congress fixed the number of justices.
10 Roman Catholics. The first was Roger Taney, confirmed in 1836.
14 From New York, the most of any state.
17 Resigned their seats for reasons other than retirement.
48 Died while serving an active term.

Days & Years

436 days: Shortest tenure of any justice, Thomas Johnson, from 1791 to 1793 • **36 years, 209 days:** Longest tenure of any justice, William O. Douglas, from 1939 to 1975 • **34 years:** Longest tenure of a chief justice, John Marshall, from 1801 to 1835 • **126 days:** Shortest tenure of a chief justice, John Rutledge, sworn in as a recess appointment in August of 1795 but rejected by the Senate in December • **32:** Age of the youngest justice appointed, Joseph Story in 1812 • **65:** Age of the oldest justice appointed, Horace Lurton in 1910 • **90:** Age of the oldest serving justice, Oliver Wendell Holmes.

The Supreme Court and the President

9 Presidential oaths of office administered by John Marshall (1801*), the most by any justice
7 Different presidents sworn in by Roger Taney (1836*), the most by any justice
11 Justices appointed by George Washington, the most of any president
5 Presidents William H. Harrison, Zachary Taylor, Andrew Johnson, Jimmy Carter, and George W. Bush(**) did not make a single appointment to the court

Votes by the numbers of some well-known decisions

9–0: *Brown v. Board of Education* (1954)
7–2: *Dred Scott v. Sandford* (1857); *Roe v. Wade* (1973)
5–0: *Marbury v. Madison* (1803)

---

*Judicial oath taken
**As of March 2004

The Supreme Court in the Nineteenth Century*

By WILLIAM H. REHNQUIST
JOURNAL OF SUPREME COURT HISTORY, 2002

At the beginning of the 19th century, we find a Court which has not yet found its role, and whose principal impact is deciding which litigant wins in a particular lawsuit. Chief Justice John Marshall, appointed in 1801, changes that; he and his successor, Roger B. Taney, are the dominant figures in the Courts over which they preside. From 1801 until 1864—sixty-three years—the nation had only two Chief Justices; during the same time, it had 15 presidents. In the latter part of the 19th century, the Chief Justices are less dominant and influential, sharing their authority with several notable Associate Justices. By the end of the century, the Court is beginning to wrestle with the many problems facing the nation after a little more than a century of existence.

Today, the federal judiciary, headed by the Supreme Court, is regarded as a co-equal branch of the federal government, along with Congress and the Executive Branch. But in the first decade of the new republic—from 1790 to 1800—the judiciary was very much a junior partner. The Supreme Court's present-day status is due in large part to John Marshall, who served as Chief Justice for 34 years, from 1801 until 1935.

During the first decade of the new republic, the Supreme Court got off to a very slow start. It decided a total of 60 cases in this 10-year period—not *60* cases per year, but about *six* per year, because there was so little business to do. The Justices met in the national capital for only a few weeks each year. They spent the rest of their time riding circuit and sitting as trial judges in their respective circuits, from Portsmouth, New Hampshire, to Savannah, Georgia.

John Jay, the first Chief Justice, was a rather elegant New Yorker. He was appointed by George Washington in 1789. In the East and West conference rooms at the Supreme Court, there are portraits of each of these early Chief Justices, and only Jay is shown wearing a red robe. He had held most of the important positions in the state government of New York, and was half English and half Dutch—just the right combination for political success in New York at that time.

---

* This article is an adaptation of the Supreme Court Historical Society's Annual Lecture delivered by the Chief Justice on June 4, 2001.

In 1794, Washington decided that he needed a special ambassador to go to the Court of St. James and negotiate with Great Britain various disputes that had come up as a result of the Treaty of Paris of 1783, which had ended the Revolutionary War. He picked John Jay. Jay sailed for England in the spring of 1794, and did not return until the summer of 1795. There is no indication that he was greatly missed in the work of the Supreme Court during this time. When he returned, he found that he had been elected Governor of New York *in absentia*, and resigned the Chief Justiceship to assume what he regarded as the more important job.

The next Chief Justice who actually served was Oliver Ellsworth of Connecticut, who had been a delegate to the Constitutional Convention and the chairman of the Senate Judiciary Committee in the First Congress. But Ellsworth, too, was selected for a special mission—to France—by President John Adams, who succeeded George Washington. He left for France in the fall of 1799, and fell ill while there. He submitted his resignation to President Adams in December 1800.

Thomas Jefferson had defeated John Adams in the presidential election of 1800, but in those days the term of the outgoing president expired not on January 20, as it does today, but on March 4, and the terms of members of Congress were similarly longer. Thus, for several months after they knew the outcome of the election, John Adams and the Federalists continued to control the Presidency and both houses of Congress.

Adams first wanted to reappoint John Jay as Chief Justice, but Jay declined. Adams ultimately chose as Ellsworth's successor John Marshall, a Virginia Federalist of considerably different stripe than Jefferson. In his "Autobiographical Sketch," Marshall recounted the circumstances of his appointment:

> When I waited on the President with Mr. Jay's letter declining the appointment he said thoughtfully "Who shall I nominate now"? I replied that I could not tell, as I supposed that his objection to Judge [Paterson] remained. He said in a decided tone "I shall not nominate him." After a moment's hesitation, he said, "I believe I must nominate you."

Confirmation hearings in those days not being what they are today, Marshall was quickly confirmed by the Senate on January 27, 1901.

To illustrate the low estate of the Supreme Court at this time, the federal government was in the process of moving from Philadelphia, which had been the capital for 10 years, to the new capital of Washington in the District of Columbia. The White House—then called the President's House—was, finished, and John Adams was the first president to occupy it. The Capitol building had been constructed on Capitol Hill, and was ready for Congress, though it was not nearly the building we know today as the Capitol. But no provision whatever had been made for housing the Supreme Court. Finally, at the last minute, a room in the basement of the Capitol was set aside for the third branch. The Court would sit in that rather undistinguished environment for eight years.

John Marshall was born in the Blue Ridge foothills of Virginia, about 50 miles west of present-day Washington. He had very little formal education. However by the time he reached 25 years of age, he had served as a captain commanding a line company of artillery in the Battles of Brandywine and Monmouth during the Revolutionary War. He had also suffered through the terrible winter at Valley Forge with George Washington and the rest of the Continental troops. It was this experience that led him to remark that he looked upon "America as my country, and Congress as my government." This is not an unusual sentiment today, to be sure, but quite an unusual sentiment for a Virginian at that time.

After mustering out of the service, Marshall studied law very briefly, attending the lectures of George Wythe in Williamsburg, and was admitted to the Virginia Bar. In 1782 he was elected to the Virginia legislature, serving for two years before he resigned to

---

> *[Marshall] turned what otherwise would have been an obscure case into the fountainhead of all of our present-day constitutional law.*

---

return to his law practice. He was again elected to the Virginia legislature in 1787, where, despite the tide of Anti-Federalist sentiment in Virginia, he was an ardent supporter of ratification of the Constitution.

During the next several years, Marshall continued in the Virginia assembly and with his law practice. He turned down President Washington's offer to become Attorney General, but in 1797 agreed to President Adams' request that he serve as a member of a delegation sent to France to resolve the mounting tensions between the two countries. This episode, of course, came to be known as "the XYZ Affair."

After returning, to Richmond, Marshall agreed to run for Congress at the urging of George Washington. During Marshall's election campaign, President Adams offered him a seat as Associate Justice of the Supreme Court. Marshall declined and Bushrod Washington, President Washington's nephew, was appointed instead. Marshall was elected to Congress in 1799, and at the time of his appointment as Chief Justice he was serving as Adams' Secretary of State. He was much better known as a politician than as a legal scholar.

When he became Chief Justice in 1801, the Supreme Court of the United States was very much like other courts of last resort, finally deciding cases between litigants but otherwise contributing very little to the manner in which the country was governed. Marshall's principal claim to fame as Chief Justice—though by no means his only one—is his authoring the Court's opinion in the famous case of *Marbury v. Madison*. When it was decided in 1803, two years after he became Chief Justice, he turned what otherwise would have been an obscure case into the fountainhead of all of our present-day constitutional law.

The case arose out of a suit by William Marbury, who had been nominated and confirmed as a Justice of the Peace in the District of Columbia, against James Madison, whom Thomas Jefferson had appointed as his Secretary of State. Although Marbury had been nominated and confirmed, his commission had not been issued by the time of the change in administration, and James Madison refused to issue it.

Marbury contended that once he had been nominated by the president and confirmed by the Senate, the issuance of his commission was simply a ministerial task for the Secretary of State who had no choice but to issue it. He brought an original action in the Supreme Court, relying on a provision of the Judiciary Act of 1789 that said that the Supreme Court could issue writs of mandamus to any federal official where appropriate; he said that James Madison was a public official, which no one denied, and that a writ of mandamus—a recognized judicial writ available to require public officials to perform their duty—was appropriate in his case.

Marshall's opinion for the Court is divided into several parts. He first addresses the question of whether one nominated and confirmed by the Senate is entitled to receive his commission without further ado, so to speak. He concluded quite reasonably that Marbury is entitled to his commission, and goes on to say that if Marbury has this right, surely the law must afford him a remedy. And, says Marshall, that remedy is a writ of mandamus, which exists just for this purpose.

But now comes the hidden-ball play. The next question Marshall asks in his opinion is whether it is proper for the Supreme Court to issue a writ of mandamus in this case. He agrees with Marbury that Congress in the Judiciary Act of 1789 authorized the Supreme Court to issue writs in such a case. But wait a minute, he says: Look at Article III of the Constitution. It says that the original jurisdiction of the Supreme Court—that is, cases that may be brought in the Supreme Court in the first instance, without ever having gone to another court—is limited to lawsuits between the states and lawsuits involving ambassadors and other foreign ministers. Clearly this suit is not within the original jurisdiction provided by Article III of the Constitution.

So, Marshall goes on to say, we have an act of Congress saying the Supreme Court may do a particular thing, and the Constitution saying it may not. What is a court then to do under a system like ours? Marshall says that, unlike the British Parliament, which is supreme, no branch of the federal government—whether it is the legislative, the executive, or the judiciary—is supreme. The Constitution is supreme, because it has been adopted by the people in the various states, and it delegates particular powers to each of the three branches. If any of these three branches may exceed their delegated authority, the whole idea of a written constitution is meaningless. So the Constitution must prevail over an act ot Congress that is inconsistent with the Constitution.

But who will have the final say as to what the Constitution means in a situation like this? Marshall says that the Constitution is a written agreement among the several states and the people in those states and the courts have always had the final say in interpreting the provisions of a written agreement. Therefore it is the federal courts, and particularly the Supreme Court, which is the ultimate arbiter of the meaning of the Constitution. The Court ruled that the federal judiciary had the authority and responsibility to strike down those laws that violate the Constitution.

The opinion in *Marbury v. Madison* is a remarkable example of judicial statesmanship. The Court says that Marbury is entitled to his commission, and Madison is wrong to withhold it. It says that this is the sort of ministerial duty of a public official such as Madison that can be enforced by a writ of mandamus. But it concludes by saying that Congress—in granting the Supreme Court the power to issue a writ of mandamus in a case like this—has run afoul of the original jurisdiction provision of the Supreme Court contained in Article III of the Constitution. Madison and Jefferson are verbally chastised, but it turns out that there is nothing that the Supreme Court can do about it because Congress tried to give the Supreme Court more authority than the Constitution would permit. The doctrine of judicial review—the authority of federal courts to declare legislative acts unconstitutional—is established, but in such a self-denying way that it is the Court's authority that is cut back.

During the 34 years he served as Chief Justice, Marshall wrote most of the important opinions that the Court decided. In *Gibbons v. Ogden*, decided in 1824, he wrote the opinion adopting a broad construction of the power of Congress under its authority to regulate interstate commerce contained in Article I of the Constitution. In the *Dartmouth College* case, he gave a generous interpretation to the prohibition in the Constitution against state impairment of the obligation of contract. One cannot name all of the significant opinions authored by Marshall. Suffice it to say that by the time of Marshall's death in 1835, the Supreme Court was a full partner in the federal government.

What was the secret of John Marshall's success? It was not that he was "present at the creation," because he was not; he was not the first Chief Justice, but the fourth. John Jay and Oliver Ellsworth were both able jurists by the standards of their time, but neither of them had the vision of constitutional government that Marshall did.

> *"The proudest act of my life was the gift of John Marshall to the people of the United States"*
> —President John Adams

Marshall was certainly no more "learned in the law" than his colleagues on the Court, and there were probably several of those who would have been thought more learned than he was. He also faced a built-in headwind against his views for the first 24 years of his tenure as Chief Justice: during this period the "Virginia dynasty" of presidents—Thomas Jefferson, James Madison, and James Monroe—were in office, and these presidents had quite a different view of the relationship between the federal and state governments than Marshall did. But the Justices they appointed tended eventually to side with Marshall rather than to express the views of the Virginia dynasty. Surely exhibit A in this category is Joseph Story of Massachusetts, who was appointed by James Madison in 1811 but became Marshall's right bower during his long tenure on the Court.

I think Marshall's success arose from several sources. He had a remarkable ability to reason from general principles, such as those set forth in the Constitution, to conclusions based on those principles. And in a day when legal writing was obscured and befogged with technical jargon, he was able to write clearly and cogently.

But—every bit as important—I think Marshall probably had an outgoing personality and was very well liked by those he moved among. Here his service in the military probably made him a more engaging personality than someone who had simply drafted writs of replevin for his entire adult career. The familiar story of the dinner ritual when the Justices were in Washington perhaps illustrates this point. The Justices all stayed at the same boarding house, and had their meals together during their few weeks in Washington. If it were raining, they would have a glass of wine with dinner. They looked forward to this ritual, and one day were expressing regret that the weather outside was fair and sunny. But Marshall said "somewhere in our broad jurisdiction it must surely be raining," and from then on they had a glass of wine with dinner everyday.

One occasionally hears the expression that an institution is the lengthened shadow of an individual. It may be risky to suggest that any institution which has endured for 210 years, the way the Supreme Court of the United States has, could be the lengthened shadow of only one individual; but surely there is only one individual who could possibly qualify for this distinction, and that individual is John Marshall. After his retirement from the Presidency, John Adams said that "the proudest act of my life was the gift of John Marshall to the people of the United States."

At the time of Marshall's death, Andrew Jackson was serving his second term as President of the United States. He appointed his loyal lieutenant Roger B. Taney of Maryland to succeed Marshall as Chief Justice. Taney had a first-rate legal mind and was a clear, forceful writer. Like Marshall, he did not believe in legal learning for its own sake, and he realized that constitutional law required not only legal analysis, but also vision and common sense. The Taney Court, over which he presided for 28 years, was less nationalist in its orientation than was the Marshall Court. The principal doctrines of the Marshall Court remained in place, but they were tempered by a greater willingness to uphold state authority. In the *Charles River Bridge* case, for instance, decided in 1837, the Court, in an opinion by Taney, limited the scope of the earlier Marshall Court decision in the *Dartmouth College* case, saying that implied covenants would not be read into state contracts for purposes of the impairment of the Contracts Clause. In *Cooley v. The Board of Wardens*, the Court held that some activities, even though within the scope of congressional authority over commerce, could nonetheless be regulated by the states until Congress had acted. There were dissents on both ends of this case; Justice John McLean of Ohio would accord no such power to the States, and Justice Daniel of Virginia—surely one of the most extreme champions of states' rights ever to sit on the Court—would have allowed the state regulation even though it was contrary to an act of Congress.

Taney's long and otherwise admirable career is, unfortunately, marred by his opinion in the ill-starred *Dred Scott* case in which he opined that even free blacks could not be citizens for purposes of diversity jurisdiction, and that Congress lacked the constitutional authority to ban slavery in territories that had not yet been admitted as states. Charles Evans Hughes rightly described the *Dred Scott* decision as a "self-inflicted wound" from which it took the Court at least a generation to recover.

Towards the end of Taney's tenure, Abraham Lincoln became president and appointed several new Justices to the Court whose opinions would have little in common with those of Taney. But one of them, Samuel F. Miller, left this memento of his feeling for the aged Chief Justice:

> When I came to Washington, I had never looked upon the face of Judge Taney, but I knew of him. I remembered that he had attempted to throttle the Bank of the United States, and I hated him for it. I remembered that he took his seat upon the Bench, as I believed, in reward for what he had done in that connection, and I hated him for that. He had been the chief spokesman of the Court in the *Dred Scott* case, and I hated him for that. But from my first acquaintance with him I realized that these feelings toward him were but the suggestions of the

worse elements of our nature: for before the first [T]erm of my service in the Court had passed I more than liked him: I loved him And after all that has been said of that great, good man, I stand always ready to say that Conscience was his guide and sense of duty his principle.

Taney was in his mid 80s, and looked feeble, when he swore in Abraham Lincoln as president in 1861. But he continued to serve as Chief Justice until his death in 1864. His long tenure prompted Ben Wade, an abolitionist Senator from Ohio, to remark that he had prayed every night during the Buchanan administration that Chief Justice Taney's life might be spared until a new president could appoint a successor. But eventually the Senator worried that he had overdone it, because Taney lived well into the next administration as well. Actually, Taney remained on the job because he needed the income to support himself; at that time, no provision was made for pensions for federal judges.

For most men, the Chief Justiceship would have been enough, but not for Salmon P. Chase.

Lincoln now had an opportunity to appoint a successor, and he pondered several different choices. Finally, in an act that epitomizes his absolute magnanimity, he nominated his former Secretary of the Treasury, Salmon P. Chase. While in that office, Chase had committed the unpardonable sin of seeking to wrest the Republican nomination away from Lincoln by use of the extensive patronage of the Treasury Department. Lincoln chose him because he thought he would vote to uphold the Greenback Laws, passed during the Civil War to make paper money legal tender in order to finance the war. But he added a cautionary note—Chase would be a good Chief Justice if he could just give up his presidential ambitions.

For most men, the Chief Justiceship would have been enough, but not for Salmon P. Chase. He was an able man, a devoted foe of slavery, but an egotist through and through. One of his detractors said that there were four persons, rather than three, in his trinity. During his rather brief tenure on the Court from 1864 until his death in 1873, his ambition for the presidency never left him. He authorized the submission of his name as a presidential candidate to the Republican convention in 1868, and when that convention turned to U.S. Grant, he authorized the submission of his name to the Democratic convention. There he actually received a few votes before losing to Horatio Seymour of New York, who in turn lost the election to Grant. In 1872, Chase made inquiries not only of the Republican convention, but also of the Liberal Republican convention in Cincinnati, a small splinter group of the party. Neither one was interested.

Salmon Chase was not a great Chief Justice, and from his time until the end of the 19th century, the Court would be as much influenced by several of its abler Associate Justices as by its Chief Justice. Three of these come to mind.

Samuel Freeman Miller, already mentioned, was born in the bluegrass country of Kentucky in 1816. For 10 years he practiced medicine, but then tired of his work as a doctor, studying law while continuing to practice medicine. He was admitted to practice in Kentucky in 1847, but three years later moved to Keokuk, Iowa, because he wanted to live in a free state rather than in a slave state. He became active in Republican politics and played a part in securing Iowa's votes for Lincoln in 1860. Lincoln appointed him to the Supreme Court in 1862.

Stephen J. Field was born in Connecticut in 1816, and grew up one of nine children, several of whom were to achieve fame. His older brother, David Dudley Field, was a New York lawyer who obtained prominence by drafting the Field Code, which codified the common law in New York and was adopted in other states. Another brother, Cyrus Field, laid the transatlantic cable from Ireland to Newfoundland in 1866. Field began the practice of law with his brother in New York in 1841, but contracted the well-known "gold fever" in 1849 and journeyed to California by means of the Isthmus of Panama. He became active in California politics and legal affairs, serving as Chief Justice of the state supreme court before Lincoln appointed him to the Supreme Court of the United States in 1863.

After the Civil War, cases began reaching the Supreme Court involving the Civil War amendments to the Constitution—the Thirteenth, Fourteenth, and Fifteenth Amendments. The first important case of this kind to be decided was the so-called *Slaughterhouse* cases in 1873. Justice Miller wrote for a majority of five, giving the Fourteenth Amendment a narrow construction and saying that it was doubtful that it would have any application to individuals other than the newly freed slaves. Justice Field wrote in dissent that if this were so it was "a vain and idle enactment" that accomplished nothing. Though Field lost this round, it was his broader view of the Fourteenth Amendment, rather than Miller's narrow one, that would ultimately prevail with the Court.

The third of this triumvirate of Associate Justices was Joseph P. Bradley. He was born in upstate New York, near Albany, the oldest of 12 children of a subsistence farmer. Deciding that he needed some formal education, he dressed in a homespun suit and walked from near Albany to Rutgers University "on the banks of the old Raritan" in New Jersey, a distance of about 200 miles. He got his education, studied for the bar, and successfully practiced law in New Jersey. He was known as a "railroad lawyer" because of his clients, and was appointed to the Supreme Court by President Grant in 1870. He authored the opinion of the Supreme Court in the Civil Rights Cases, one of its more important decisions of this era, saying that the Fourteenth Amendment applied only to government discrimination, and that Congress could not prohibit merely private discrimination.

Chief Justice Chase's presidential ambitions were not the only ones among members of the Court at this time. Stephen Field wanted to be considered for the Democratic presidential nomination on at least one occasion, and David Davis had always been more interested in politics than in law. Lincoln had practiced before Davis when the latter was a state court judge of a circuit in downstate Illinois, and when Lincoln became president, he appointed Davis to the Court.

> *Chief Justice Chase's presidential ambitions were not the only ones among members of the Court at this time.*

Davis wrote the Court's opinion in the famous case of *Ex Parte Milligan*, where the Court held that persons not in the military could not be tried before a military commission so long as the civil courts were open.

In the disputed election of 1876, in which Rutherford B. Hayes, the Republican, and Samuel Tilden, the Democrat, vied for the office, the Supreme Court was drawn into the controversy not as a body, but because five of its Justices were named to a 15-member commission which would in effect have the final say as to how votes from the disputed states were to be counted. Two known Republicans and two known Democrats on the Court were easily agreed upon, but the fifth member from the Court, whose vote would obviously be decisive, was harder to pick. One proposal that gathered considerable support in Congress was to pick the Justice by lot. Tilden, who was on the whole a rather cold and calculating individual, balked at this, and in one of his rare *bons mots* said that he might lose the presidency, but he would not raffle for it. Finally, Davis—who, although a Republican appointee, had shown considerable independence in his views—was chosen. He had received some votes for president at the Liberal Republican Convention in Cincinnati in 1872 and was hoping for a spot on one of the tickets in 1880. But just as the commission was about to begin its deliberations, the Illinois legislature elected Davis a Senator from that state, and he resigned from the Court to take his seat in the Senate. After much consternation, Bradley was chosen by the other four Justices as the most impartial, and was thereby put in an impossible position. If he were to vote with the Democrats in a way that would seat Tilden, he would of course be applauded for his impartiality and his independence. But if he were to vote in a way that would seat Hayes, he would be denounced as simply a partisan tool. He did vote to seat Hayes, and was accordingly denounced, with little, if any, justification.

In 1896, the Court, in an opinion by Justice Henry B. Brown of Michigan, ruled in *Plessy v. Ferguson* that the Equal Protection Clause of the Fourteenth Amendment was not offended if a state provided separate facilities for whites and blacks so long as they were equal. This decision ratified the Jim Crow regime in the South, and was overruled more than 50 years later in *Brown v. Board of Education*.

Miller died in 1890, Bradley in 1892. Field lived until 1899, and his last years at the Court were not happy ones.

In 1901, Theodore Roosevelt succeeded William McKinley when the latter was assassinated in Buffalo. His first appointment to the Supreme Court was caused by the retirement of Horace Gray of Massachusetts. Senator Henry Cabot Lodge of Massachusetts urged him to appoint Oliver Wendell Holmes, Jr., then Chief Justice of the Supreme Judicial Court of Massachusetts. Roosevelt demurred until Lodge could assure him that Holmes was sound on the "Insular Cases." This incident illustrates the transience of constitutional doctrine. Surely not one law student in 50 could say what the "Insular Cases" were, and I daresay the same is true of most readers. But they were very important to the President at the turn of the century. The United States had defeated Spain in the Spanish American War, had acquired Puerto Rico and the Philippine Islands as possessions, and had acquired a temporary mandate to govern in Cuba. The question was whether the Constitution followed the flag; could Philippine citizens familiar only with the civil law system demand a right to jury trial? These questions have long since either been solved or disappeared, just as many of the questions that now perplex this Court will meet a similar fate a century from now.

The Once and Future Supreme Court

By David J. Garrow
American History, February 2005

This past October the United States Supreme Court began its 2004–05 term with the same nine justices who have served together since 1994. Going 10 years without any change in Court membership has not previously occurred since the early 1820s. But now the increasing age of the justices alone—Chief Justice William H. Rehnquist has just turned 80, and senior Associate Justice John Paul Stevens is 84—virtually ensures that the next president will be able to nominate at least two new justices during the four-year term that commences on January 20, 2005.

Indeed, the next president may very well get to choose more than two. Justice David H. Souter, the Court's second-youngest member, just celebrated his 65th birthday, leaving only 56-year-old Justice Clarence Thomas as the Court's one nonsenior citizen. Justices Sandra Day O'Connor, now 74, and Ruth Bader Ginsburg, 71, are the other most likely retirees during this new presidential term. Justices Antonin Scalia and Anthony M. Kennedy are now both 68 years old, and Stephen G. Breyer, who has now served 10 full years as the court's "junior" justice, is 66.

News media speculation over which justices will be the first to retire, however, diverts attention from the far more notable and consequential change that the Court's composition quietly has undergone over the past four decades. From President Franklin D. Roosevelt in the late 1930s through his successor, Harry S. Truman, Republican Dwight D. Eisenhower in the 1950s, and Democrats John F. Kennedy and Lyndon B. Johnson in the 1960s, the predominant pattern in Supreme Court nominations was for presidents to select highly experienced national-level political figures. Since 1969, however, that practice has changed dramatically as another series of presidents—Republicans Richard M. Nixon, Gerald R. Ford, Ronald Reagan, and George H.W. Bush, plus Democrat Bill Clinton—have almost without exception named little-known appellate judges to the Court.

The resulting transformation of the Supreme Court has been dramatic indeed, even if the change is one that daily news accounts almost never highlight. Much critical commentary about the Court, for well over a decade now, from liberals and conservatives alike, has consistently highlighted the self-aggrandizing expansion of the

Court's own power, both in federalism cases that have significantly curtailed Congress' legislative authority and in abortion, gender discrimination, and gay rights rulings. Such conservative justices as Scalia, Thomas, and Chief Justice Rehnquist have been eager to assertively exercise the Court's power in federalism decisions that have insulated the states from the effects of congressional regulatory legislation, and liberal jurists such as Stevens, Souter, Ginsburg, and Breyer have done likewise in abortion and gay rights cases where the conservatives are in dissent.

But the Supreme Court's two dominant "swing" justices, O'Connor and Kennedy, have been quite comfortable in joining both liberal and conservative rulings that are undeniably assertive. This consistent pattern has given the lie to the outdated but commonplace notion that only liberals are "judicial activists" whereas self-described conservatives are "strict constructionists" who minimize the exercise of judicial power. On today's U.S. Supreme Court, judicial activists hold all nine seats, and only the substance of a particular case, rather than the justices' over-arching principles, determines whether the Court's assertiveness is pigeonholed

---

On today's U.S. Supreme Court, judicial activists hold all nine seats.

---

as "liberal" or "conservative" by media commentators.

Perhaps it should not be surprising that a Supreme Court composed almost exclusively of career jurists is so consistent in advancing the reach of judicial power. Of today's nine justices, all except Chief Justice Rehnquist were already serving on other appellate tribunals when they were nominated to the high court. (At the time of his 1971 nomination, Rehnquist headed the U.S. Justice Department's legal policy office.) Seven of the justices were promoted from the federal courts of appeal; O'Connor was serving on Arizona's appellate court when President Reagan named her as the first female justice in 1981.

Justice O'Connor is also the only current justice who has ever held (or run for) public elective office. She was twice elected to the Arizona Senate and then won election to a state trial court before being promoted to the appellate bench. Justice Thomas, who served as chairman of the U.S. Equal Employment Opportunity Commission (EEOC) from 1982 to 1990, probably ranks second in terms of "real world" political experience. Along with the chief justice, Justice Scalia, who for more than two years in the mid-1970s held the same important Justice Department post in which Rehnquist previously served, and Justice Breyer, who served two stints as a top staff member on the U.S. Senate's Judiciary Committee, round out the more politically experienced half of the current Court.

Mark Wilson/Getty Images

Associate Justice Ruth Bader Ginsburg

Justice Souter was New Hampshire's gubernatorially appointed attorney general for two years before becoming a state court judge, and Justice Stevens served in a politically sensitive Illinois state appointive post before becoming a federal appellate judge in 1970. Justice Ginsburg litigated a series of important gender discrimination cases on behalf of the American Civil Liberties Union in the 1970s, and Justice Kennedy's Sacramento law practice included many California political contacts before he became a federal judge in 1975.

Three current justices—Scalia, Ginsburg, and Breyer—spent much of their pre-judicial careers as law professors, and both Stevens and Kennedy taught law part time. Breyer spent 14 years and Ginsburg 13 as federal appellate judges before being named to the Supreme Court by President Clinton in 1994 and 1993 respectively, and Kennedy served more than 12 years on the U.S. Court of Appeals for the Ninth Circuit before being nominated to the high court in 1987. Justice Souter's pre–Supreme Court judicial experience also totaled a dozen years, and Justices O'Connor, Stevens, and Scalia served between four and six years as lower court judges before joining the high bench. Only Chief Justice Rehnquist, with no judicial experience, and Justice Thomas, with hardly a year on the U.S. Court of Appeals for the District of Columbia Circuit, were relative "rookies" when they first became justices.

This Court, with its strong predominance of heavily experienced and academically oriented appellate jurists, differs sharply and dramatically from the Supreme Court of the 1940s, '50s, and '60s. In those decades, president after president named experienced politicians to the high bench, giving the Court a decidedly different composition than what has marked the post-1968 era. When President Franklin Roosevelt, after waiting more than four years without any Supreme Court vacancies to fill, finally had the opportunity to remake the Court's membership with eight new nominees between 1937 and 1943, his selections tended heavily toward justices with practical political experience rather than prior judicial service. Roosevelt's first choice, U.S. Senator Hugo L. Black, was a prominent Alabama Democrat whose only judicial experience had come on a Birmingham city police court. Roosevelt's second nominee, Stanley F. Reed, was the administration's politically appointed solicitor general, and his third, Felix Frankfurter, was a Harvard Law School professor whose political activism overshadowed his well-known academic work.

Roosevelt's second trio of selections was similar. William O. Douglas, also a law professor, had achieved political renown as the hard-charging chairman of the U.S. Securities and Exchange Commission. Frank Murphy, Roosevelt's attorney general, had previously been elected governor of Michigan and, before that, mayor of Detroit. Like Black, Murphy's judicial experience consisted only of premayoral service as a police court judge. James F. Byrnes of South Carolina was a 10-year veteran of the U.S. Senate and, before that, a seven-term member of the U.S. House of Representatives.

FDR's next-to-last nominee, Robert H. Jackson, was a longtime Roosevelt political supporter from the president's home state of New York, whom Roosevelt had named to succeed Murphy as U.S. attorney general. Only Roosevelt's final nominee, Wiley B. Rutledge, a five-year veteran of the federal appellate court for the District of Columbia and, before that, dean of the University of Iowa Law School, was a relatively little-known jurist rather than a highly visible Roosevelt administration official or partisan.

Roosevelt's practice of naming experienced political veterans to the high court was likewise followed by his successor, Truman.

Roosevelt's practice of naming experienced political veterans to the high court was likewise followed by his successor, Truman. President Truman's first nominee, as chief justice, was Frederick M. Vinson, his secretary of the Treasury and, before that, a 12-year veteran of the House of Representatives. Truman's three subsequent high court choices were, like Vinson, political as well as personal buddies of the president: Ohio Republican Senator Harold H. Burton, a former legislative colleague; Attorney General Tom C. Clark, a Texas political veteran; and Indiana Democratic Senator Sherman Minton. At the time, and in subsequent decades, many Court historians have strongly criticized Truman for naming friends with less-than-impressive legal skills.

Roosevelt's nominees may have had no more judicial experience than Truman's, but with the exception of only Murphy, Roosevelt's choices, unlike Truman's, generally have received high marks from commentators and historians.

The quintessential example of a crucial Supreme Court appointment going to a politician with no prior judicial experience was President Eisenhower's choice of California Republican Governor Earl Warren to replace Vinson as chief justice in 1953. Warren had played a crucial role in helping Eisenhower capture the 1952 Republican presidential nomination over Ohio Senator Robert Taft, and the Supreme Court nomination was an agreed-upon reward for his earlier political support.

Had Warren's career as chief justice turned out differently than it did, the explicit quid pro quo of his selection might be regarded as a scandalous act of using a Supreme Court seat as simple political barter. Warren never became one of the Court's more legally knowledgeable or analytically astute justices, but his leadership qualities within the group of nine, plus the simple and direct common sense that often was visible in his opinions, more than sufficed to make him, along with John Marshall a century earlier, one of the two greatest chief justices in American history.

Warren's remarkable success, notwithstanding his complete lack of any prior judicial experience, was due in part to the justices who followed him to the high court. President Eisenhower's next two appointees, John M. Harlan and William J. Brennan Jr., eventually emerged as the two most highly rated members of the "Warren Court." Harlan had served only briefly on the U.S. Court of Appeals based in New York before his nomination, and Brennan was promoted from the New Jersey Supreme Court, but both men, unlike Warren, were selected based upon their legal and judicial track records, and not their political experience or connections.

Harlan and Brennan turned out to be arguably the two finest Supreme Court jurists of their era. Harlan, though often pigeonholed as a conservative, was a thoughtful and sometimes unpredictable justice, someone who quickly emerged as the Court's top judicial craftsman. Brennan, sometimes stereotyped as a glad-handing strategist, became Warren's closest friend and counselor and soon was authoring some of the Court's most pathbreaking opinions.

President Eisenhower's two final appointees, federal appeals court judges Charles E. Whittaker and Potter Stewart, fell short of Harlan and Brennan's stature. Whittaker, a Kansas friend of Eisenhower's family, had served as a lower court federal judge for three years before his elevation, and Stewart had spent four years on the U.S. Court of Appeals prior to his promotion. Stewart became an influential voice within the Court during the 1960s and 1970s, but Whittaker retired after only five personally stressful and unproductive years of service.

Eisenhower's four final Supreme Court appointees were all little-known appellate judges at the time of their selection, not governors, senators, or cabinet secretaries. Those selections marked a significant change from the earlier Black-through-Warren roster of nominees, but during the ensuing Kennedy-Johnson years, presidential practice returned to the Roosevelt-Truman norm.

President Kennedy's first appointee, Deputy Attorney General Byron R. White, had been an active participant in the president's 1960 election campaign and before that had won national fame as a college and professional football player. Kennedy's second nominee, Arthur J. Goldberg, was serving as secretary of labor and later, after leaving the Court to become U.S. ambassador to the United

Nations, ran unsuccessfully for governor of New York. As the successor to Justice Frankfurter, Goldberg also represented a political commitment to keeping at least one Jewish justice on the Court.

When President Johnson persuaded Goldberg to take the U.N. post, Johnson replaced him with presidential buddy and counselor Abe Fortas, a Washington wheeler-dealer with no prior judicial experience. Johnson's second and final Supreme Court nomination made his solicitor general, Thurgood Marshall, who previously had sat on the U.S. Court of Appeals in New York following an illustrious two decades as the top lawyer for the National Association for the Advancement of Colored People, the first black justice ever. Both men were accomplished litigators, but their selections fell squarely in the Roosevelt-Truman-Kennedy political tradition. Late in Johnson's presidency, an attempt to promote Fortas to chief justice, and then name another presidential buddy, former Texas Congressman Homer Thornberry, to Fortas' seat, failed in the face of widespread Senate opposition.

Johnson's successor, President Nixon, was able to name four new justices to the Court between 1969 and 1972. Warren E. Burger, who took Earl Warren's place as chief justice, was a little-known judge on the U.S. Court of Appeals in Washington, D.C., who previously had worked in the Eisenhower Justice Department. Nixon's second successful appointee, Harry A. Blackmun, was a childhood friend of Burger's who had served for more than a decade as a federal appellate judge. Prior to Blackmun's nomination, however, Nixon's two previous choices, Southern federal judges Clement Haynsworth and Harrold Carswell, had each been rejected by the U.S. Senate, the first such Supreme Court confirmation defeats in 40 years.

Neither of Nixon's two final appointees, Rehnquist and Lewis F. Powell Jr., had any prior judicial experience, yet both men were experienced lawyers notwithstanding their relative public obscurity. Powell was a former president of the American Bar Association, and Rehnquist was a top Justice Department attorney.

Chief Justice Rehnquist has now served on the U.S. Supreme Court for more than 32 years, one of the longest periods of service in American history, but those 32 years represent more than just a personal milestone. Rehnquist also was the last Supreme Court nominee who was not an appellate judge to be put forward for the high bench. All eight of Rehnquist's present colleagues, from Stevens through Breyer, were appellate jurists at the time of their nomination, as were both of the unsuccessful nominees, Robert H. Bork and Douglas Ginsburg, whom President Reagan sent to the U.S. Senate prior to the subsequent successful confirmation of Kennedy.

All the nominees of the entire post-1968 era, from Nixon through Clinton, thus differ measurably from those of the 1937 to 1968 period, excepting only Eisenhower's four final choices. From Presidents Ford, who selected Stevens; through Reagan, who named

O'Connor, Scalia, and Kennedy; then George H. W. Bush, who nominated Souter and Thomas; and finally Clinton, who chose Ginsburg and Breyer; all eight new justices were experienced appellate court judges before they joined the U.S. Supreme Court. (No vacancies occurred during either Jimmy Carter's 1977–81 term or George W. Bush's 2001–05 term.)

How different a Supreme Court would we have today if, for example, either Ronald Reagan or George H.W. Bush had selected Utah Republican Senator Orrin Hatch as a justice, or if Bill Clinton had named former New York Governor Mario Cuomo? If both Hatch and another experienced Republican politico, plus Cuomo and a second national Democrat, had joined the Court between 1986 and 1994, in place of, say, Justices Kennedy, Souter, Ginsburg, and Breyer, today's Court would look—and almost certainly act—radically different than it does.

Those hypothetical nominations would have represented a return to the old Hugo Black–Earl Warren pattern but, ironically, it may be that the jurists on today's Supreme Court are actually far more

---

Both highly conservative and relatively liberal justices have repeatedly embraced judicial activism.

---

comfortable with exercising far-reaching judicial power than would be electorally experienced national politicians who for more than a half-century now have been passed over for every vacancy since Warren's selection in 1953.

There can be little argument that the last dozen years of the Rehnquist Court have witnessed a consistent pattern of muscular judicial assertiveness. There likewise is no doubt that both highly conservative and relatively liberal justices have repeatedly embraced judicial activism. To argue that a Court with more politically experienced justices would be far more inclined than the current bench to practice true judicial restraint at both ends of the ideological spectrum is, of course, inherently speculative, but that analysis is one that bears serious consideration as a new generation of Supreme Court vacancies looms on the horizon.

The highly political nominees that Roosevelt and Truman placed on the Court often exhibited considerably more deference toward executive branch actions and congressional legislation than do our present-day justices. That may at first glance seem surprising, but opposition to the reactionary judicial activism that characterized the pre-1937 Supreme Court was a defining element in New Deal politics. In addition, the extremely close personal and political ties that most of the Roosevelt and Truman nominees had to either the White House and/or the Congress also created a situation in which most, if not all, justices had a firsthand understanding of, and perhaps even sympathy for, the policies and practices of the Court's two coordinate federal branches.

Naming experienced national political figures to the Supreme Court may, counterintuitively, produce a bench that is more reluctant and measured in exercising judicial power than is a bench composed primarily of career jurists who largely lack any significant personal political experience. For more than a decade now, the Rehnquist Court has cut back on the legislative powers of the U.S. Congress in a series of sometimes abstruse rulings based upon the Constitution's Commerce Clause or the highly obscure Eleventh Amendment. These decisions do not generate large headlines in daily newspapers, but cumulatively they have represented a remarkable reallocation of power between a previously unconstrained Congress and a Supreme Court that now has repeatedly asserted its own authority as the ultimate arbiter of federal legislative decision-making. A Court with one or more justices who were themselves congressional veterans might well take a dramatically different, and far more deferential, attitude toward congressional power than have the judicially self-confident jurists of the Rehnquist era.

During the Supreme Court's 2003–04 term, the presidential election may have caused the justices to draw back from any of the widely visible acts of judicial assertiveness that had marked prior terms. In 2000, of course, the Court was squarely in the middle of the disputed presidential election that its 5-to-4 ruling in *Bush v. Gore* decisively resolved. In 2003, in *Lawrence v. Texas*, Justice Kennedy's majority opinion not only voided all remaining state sodomy statutes punishing consensual and private adult sexual relations but also delivered a ringing moral declaration of the fundamental equality of gay and lesbian Americans.

When it so chooses, as in *Lawrence*, as in *Brown v. Board of Education* in 1954, which initiated the slow desegregation of racially segregated Southern public schools, or as in *Planned Parenthood v. Casey* in 1992, when it forcefully reaffirmed *Roe v. Wade*, the 1973 ruling that had given constitutional protection to a woman's right to choose abortion, the Supreme Court can "pull out all the stops" in telling the American people that a historic change must indeed be made.

Such moments of moral invocation occur only rarely, and none took place during the Court's 2003–04 term, notwithstanding three hotly contested cases challenging the George W. Bush administration's executive detention of two U.S. citizens, and some 600 foreigners, whom it alleged were active supporters of the Al Qaeda terror network. The cases offered the Court an opportunity to either roundly condemn or expressly endorse President Bush's pursuit of the war on terror. The Court responded almost delicately, however, requiring that judicial recourse be made available to all the detainees but declining to spell out whether such opportunities for appeal would actually allow any of the captives to contest their status and obtain their freedom.

Those rulings effectively postponed any decisive action concerning the detainees until after the 2004 presidential election. A similar desire to avoid controversies that might have thrust the Court into the midst of the 2004 contest also seemed apparent in the two other most highly visible legal cases of the 2003–04 term.

In *Cheney v. U.S. District Court,* Bush administration critics sought access to confidential documents generated by a politically controversial energy policy task force headed by U.S. Vice President Dick Cheney. Much as in the terror detainee cases, the Court handed down a less-than-decisive ruling that effectively delayed any clear resolution of the dispute for many months.

The Court's best-known and most closely watched case was *Elk Grove Unified School District v. Newdow,* in which an atheist parent objected to his daughter being confronted each morning in her public school classroom with the words "under God" that are part of the Pledge of Allegiance to the U.S. flag. A lower court had agreed with

---

A majority of the justices chose to duck the merits of the controversial religious issue.

Michael Newdow that the U.S. Constitution's prohibition of any government "establishment" of religion made the invocation of "God" unconstitutional, but when the California school district appealed that decision to the U.S. Supreme Court, a majority of the justices chose to duck the merits of the controversial religious issue. Finding that a child custody dispute between Newdow and his daughter's mother made the case unfit for decision, the high court simply vacated the lower court ruling. Had the justices instead affirmed the lower court's decision, they almost certainly would have made themselves a major presidential election issue.

The 2003–04 term's unusual outbreak of judicial meekness may well represent a strategic calculation by the justices to keep themselves as far distant from a presidential election year's partisan debates as possible, particularly in light of how the Court itself ended up deciding the 2000 contest. With the detention cases, Vice President Cheney's dispute, and the Pledge of Allegiance controversy all sidelined until sometime in 2005 or later, campaign arguments about the Court, and about the kinds of nominees George W. Bush or John F. Kerry would add to the bench when the inevitable vacancies occur over these next four years, remained far down the list of presidential election issues.

That relative absence of the Court, its justices, and its potential future justices from the 2004 election may point toward a continuation of the low-visibility appellate jurist selections that have occurred without interruption for more than a third of a century now. In a more politicized climate, a new president might well opt to revert to the Roosevelt-Truman-Kennedy-Johnson model and look toward a top political ally, or a close personal acquaintance, to fill a crucial high court vacancy. But where the Court instead has kept itself as far distant as possible from partisan firefights, the new president may feel wholly comfortable in continuing the new tradition of promoting little-known but well-experienced appellate judges to the nation's highest court. If so, it's a safe bet that those new justices, irrespective of whether they are named by a Democratic president or a Republican, will be just as at home with the resolutely aggressive exercise of judicial power as are the current justices. Should that indeed come to pass, the Supreme Court's unchallenged stature as the ultimate and final arbiter of U.S. governmental power will be ratified once more.

The last four decades have witnessed a fundamental transformation in the types of men, and now women, who exercise the broad and untrammeled judicial power of the U.S. Supreme Court. Not so long ago it was common practice for judicially inexperienced national politicians to be placed at the pinnacle of judicial power.

However, for more than a generation now, a new pattern, embraced by presidents as different as Richard Nixon, Ronald Reagan, and Bill Clinton, has instead filled the U.S. Supreme Court with jurists whose career experiences have occurred predominantly in the quiet chambers of appeals courts rather than in the halls of Congress or the White House cabinet room. This change has drawn little public comment or debate, even as its consequences have indisputably accumulated.

A United States in which the Supreme Court only rarely defers to the president or Congress may be a country in which individual rights and freedom from unfair government conduct are indeed well protected, but it may also represent a redistribution of political power that has occurred by quiet accretion rather than robust debate or explicit decision. Most Americans, if they understand and ponder the changes the U.S. Supreme Court has undergone in their lifetimes, may choose to endorse rather than object to those changes, but the transformation is one that should be appreciated rather than ignored.

II. Landmark Decisions: Cases That Made the Court

Editors' Introduction

The ultimate expression of the Supreme Court's constitutionally prescribed powers is found in the rulings it hands down. These verdicts, unlike acts of Congress, cannot be vetoed by the president or repealed by any other federal body. Indeed, they can be reversed ony by a constitutional amendment, which is exceedingly rare given the stiff legal requirements; or through a subsequent Supreme Court decision, which is likewise unlikely since precedent, in the form of prior rulings, is one of the determining factors in any judgment, and the Supreme Court is loathe to overrule itself. Consequently, a Supreme Court verdict is all but final, becoming, at the moment of its issuance, for better or worse, the settled law of the land.

The articles in this chapter examine some of the more significant rulings rendered by the Court since its inception. The first selection, "The Trial of a Young Nation," by Charles F. Hobson, recounts perhaps the most important case in U.S. history—*Marbury v. Madison*. Hobson discusses *Marbury*'s origins in an obscure patronage dispute that emerged in the aftermath of the election of 1800 and examines how it evolved into a bold and definitive affirmation of the Supreme Court's authority over judicial review.

Few Supreme Court rulings have been as widely celebrated as *Brown v. Board of Education*, the unanimous 1954 verdict that struck down the system of legalized racial segregation in public education that existed in much of the United States. Recalling the case in the pages of *The Nation*, Michael J. Klarman argues that though it was decided 9–0, the *Brown* ruling could have come down in favor of the opposite side. He also considers the aftermath of the verdict—particularly the white backlash that led to the rise of segregationist politicians such as George Wallace—and its implications for the country as a whole.

The next two selections focus on Supreme Court cases that established basic protections for accused criminals, cases that have become deeply ingrained in our national culture. The first article, by Marshall J. Hartman, "40 Years and Waiting," recounts the Supreme Court's decision in *Gideon v. Wainwright*, which found that an indigent defendant has the right to a court-appointed attorney. The 1966 *Miranda v. Arizona* verdict is addressed in the subsequent piece, "Police Tactic to Sidestep *Miranda* Rights Rejected," by Jerry Markon. This decision decreed that an arresting officer must inform the accused of what has come to be termed his *Miranda* rights—the right to remain silent and the right to an attorney—prior to conducting an interrogation.

While reversing a Supreme Court ruling is exceedingly rare, it is not unheard of. If one heeds the rhetoric of both pro-choice and pro-life partisans, the 1973 *Roe v. Wade* verdict guaranteeing a women's right to an abortion is one or two Supreme Court appointments away from being overturned. In

"Both Sides on Abortion Wary of Supreme Court," Jan Crawford Greenburg describes the case and the potential for its reversal, taking into account the strong feelings on both sides of the issue. Accompanying the article are two timelines, the first of which charts various legislation and other factors that have had a bearing on the abortion debate, while the second lists important abortion-related court decisions.

The landmark ruling in *Bush v. Gore* effectively decided the election of George W. Bush to the presidency in 2000 by calling off a recount ordered by the Florida Supreme Court. Debra Rosenberg, for *Newsweek*, attempts to put the controversial decision into perspective.

Closing out the chapter is an article by Klarman entitled "Are Landmark Court Decisions All That Important?" By considering rulings within their historical circumstances, Klarman argues "that Supreme Court decisions generally reflect the social and political context of the times." In other words, he claims, Court verdicts do not so much shape society as reflect it. By this reasoning, the Constitution is not an immutable document but one whose meaning is influenced by the historical milieu in which it is read.

The Trial of a Young Nation

By Charles F. Hobson
Humanities, January/February 2003

Marbury v. Madison enjoys the status of a landmark, perhaps the most prominent, of American constitutional law. In deciding this case, the Supreme Court for the first time declared an act of Congress void as contrary to the Constitution. Chief Justice John Marshall's decision became the leading precedent for "judicial review," the Court's power to pass upon the constitutionality of legislative acts.

Marbury can scarcely be understood without anchoring it in the political context of Thomas Jefferson's first administration. Jefferson's landslide victory in 1800—his "bloodless revolution"—was the new nation's first transfer of power from a dominant regime to an opposition party. When the Federalists were ousted, neither they nor the Jeffersonian Democrats could anticipate what would occur. Party conflict had yet to be considered legitimate; during the volatile presidential campaign, the Federalist press had called Jefferson a pagan, an atheist, and a traitor to George Washington and John Adams. There was speculation about whether or not Adams would step down. It was in this uncertain climate that the judicial branch would attempt to establish its authority to judge other branches of government.

Marshall's opinion, delivered just two years into the new administration, was interpreted by contemporaries in partisan terms. Even today, critics find fault with Marshall for using the case to lecture the president, while admirers praise him for striking a blow for judicial independence in the face of an assault by the Jeffersonian political majority. Yet to read the opinion solely in the light of the raging party battles of the day, or to read it only as a landmark that established the doctrine of judicial review, is to miss its full significance.

Marshall considered this case to be among the most important decided during his tenure as chief justice. The part of his opinion that is most read and remembered today is the concluding and comparatively brief section setting forth the doctrine of judicial review, which reads, "It is also not entirely unworthy of observation, that in declaring what shall be the *Supreme* law of the land,

---

the *constitution* itself is first mentioned; and not the laws of the United States generally, but those only which shall be made in *pursuance* of the constitution, have that rank.

"Thus the particular phraseology of the constitution of the United States confirms & strengthens the principle, supposed to be essential to all written constitutions, that a law repugnant to the constitution is void; and that *courts*, as well as other departments, are bound by that instrument."

In December 1801 the Court had received an application from a man named William Marbury for a writ of mandamus that would command the secretary of state to deliver Marbury's commission as justice of the peace for the District of Columbia.

Charles Lee, Marbury's attorney, moved to require Secretary of State James Madison to commission Marbury and two others, Robert T. Hooe and Dennis Ramsay.

Marbury and his fellow plaintiffs were among 42 persons who had been nominated justices of the peace by President Adams on 2 March 1801, his last day in office. The Senate confirmed these appointments the same day, signed the commissions, and transmitted them to Secretary of State Marshall, whom Jefferson had asked to stay on.*

The commissions languished for two days as the new president took power. Assuming that he had discretion to revoke the judicial appointments because the commissions had not been delivered, Jefferson made appointments of his own, reducing the number of justices to 30. Although Jefferson reappointed many nominated by his predecessor, Marbury, Hooe, and Ramsay were not among them.

After a series of delays, *Marbury v. Madison* began in February 1803. Marshall, now chief justice, and three of his associate justices were in attendance. Lee tried to show that his clients had been nominated and confirmed as justices of the peace and that their commissions had been signed, sealed, and recorded. Rebuffed in his efforts to obtain from the Senate a certified record of the confirmation of the appointments, he summoned several State Department clerks to give their testimony. Ordered by the Court to be sworn, the reluctant witnesses accordingly testified.

A singular circumstance of this case is that the chief justice himself, as President Adams's secretary of state, was the official responsible for sending out the commissions of Marbury and the other appointees. Had the case arisen from Marshall's inattention to duty? Writing to his brother two weeks after Jefferson's inauguration, Marshall had defended his conduct: "I did not send out the commissions because I apprehended such as were for a fixd time to be completed when signd & sealed & such as depended on the will of the President might at any time be revokd. To withhold the commission of the Marshal is equal to displacing him which the President I

---

* Editor's note: Marshall served as Jefferson's secretary of state for one day—March 4, 1801, Jefferson's inaugaration day.

presume has the power to do, but to withhold the commission of the Justices is an act of which I entertaind no suspicion." At the time, then, Marshall believed the process of commissioning justices of the peace was complete without actual delivery, a position he was to maintain two years later in the opinion. Whatever the merits of his position on this technical point, Marshall's failure to deliver the commissions provided President Jefferson the opportunity to withhold them.

Marbury's application to the Supreme Court for a mandamus was more than a private legal dispute. It arose from resentment at the outgoing administration's 11th-hour appointments to a host of new judicial offices created by the Judiciary Act of 1801 and an act concerning the District of Columbia. The lame-duck Federalist Congress had enacted both laws during the waning days of Adams's presidency. The very bringing of the action, which coincided with the meeting of the first session of the new Congress under a Republican majority, hastened the repeal of the recent judiciary act.

The Marbury *opinion has been acclaimed as a brilliant political coup.*

Given the unavoidable connection between Marbury's claim to his commission and the political defeat of the Federalists, the Court faced the task of writing an opinion that breathed disinterested judicial statesmanship.

The first part of the opinion affirmed that Marbury had a legal right and remedy—but the entire opinion centered on the issue of jurisdiction. Before deciding whether a mandamus could issue in this particular case, the Court had to consider the more general question of whether there were any cases in which a high officer of the executive department could be made answerable in court for his conduct.

The denial of the mandamus turned on a fine point regarding section 13 of the Judiciary Act of 1789. The act empowered the Supreme Court to issue that writ, and Marshall determined that it was an unconstitutional enlargement of the Court's original jurisdiction. No part of the opinion has provoked more commentary by legal scholars than this holding. Why did the Court resort to judicial review, seemingly going out of its way to contrive a constitutional conflict?

The chief justice wanted to declare the authority of the Court to bring certain acts of the executive under judicial cognizance and to draw a line that would separate political from legal questions. Given the vulnerable situation of the federal judiciary, he avoided direct confrontation with the administration. Instead, he broadened the Court's jurisdiction to include the legislative as well as the executive branch.

Seen in this light, the *Marbury* opinion has been acclaimed as a brilliant political coup, at once bold and cautious, a masterpiece of judicial statesmanship in which the Court yielded the immediate point—whether or not Marbury should receive his commission—while achieving its more important long-range aim of establishing its authority. The seeming willful disregard of past practice and precedents pale into insignificance when viewed against the larger purposes accomplished by the chief justice.

In retrospect, *Marbury* has the appearance of an ingenious act of judicial politics, the handiwork largely of John Marshall. Yet hindsight may obscure what to the chief justice and his associates was a tentative, makeshift, and unsatisfactory resolution of the case. Was the author of the opinion as calculating as has been assumed? Did he have it in mind, as part of his agenda, to establish a precedent for judicial review? The almost matter-of-fact exposition of judicial review was perhaps a clever tactic to win acceptance of a highly controversial view. On the other hand, this language may have been nothing more than a straight-forward expression of Marshall's belief that judicial review was a settled question, that the Court was not boldly asserting a claim to a new power but merely restating a power it already possessed.

It Could Have Gone the Other Way

By Michael J. Klarman
The Nation, May 3, 2004

In the 50 years since it was decided, *Brown v. Board of Education* has become a legal icon. The rightness of this famous decision invalidating racial segregation in public schools is no longer open to debate. Conservative legal commentators and prospective judicial nominees still criticize many landmark decisions of the Warren Court, but not *Brown*. No constitutional theory or theorist failing to support the result in *Brown* will be taken seriously today.

Such was not always the case. A Gallup poll taken the summer after *Brown* revealed that nearly half of all Americans opposed the decision. In the 1950s, eminent judges and law professors—including the great jurist Learned Hand—questioned whether it was rightly decided. Perhaps most surprisingly, the Justices who decided the case had grave doubts themselves whether invalidating school segregation was legally justified.

In a memorandum dictated the day *Brown* was decided, Justice William O. Douglas observed that a vote taken after the case was first argued in 1952 would have been "five to four in favor of the constitutionality of segregation in the public schools." Justice Felix Frankfurter's head count was only slightly different: He reported that a vote taken at that time would have been five to four to overturn segregation, with the majority writing several opinions.

Brown was hard for many of the Justices because it posed a conflict between their legal views and their personal values. The sources of constitutional interpretation to which they ordinarily looked for guidance—text, original understanding, precedent, and custom—indicated that school segregation was permissible. By contrast, most of the Justices privately condemned segregation, which Justice Hugo Black called "Hitler's creed." Their quandary was how to reconcile their legal and moral views.

Frankfurter preached that judges must decide cases based on "the compulsions of governing legal principles," not "the idiosyncrasies of a merely personal judgment." In a 1940 memorandum, he noted that "no duty of judges is more important nor more difficult to discharge than that of guarding against reading their personal and debatable opinions into the case."

"It Could Have Gone the Other Way" by Michael J. Klarman. Reprinted with permission from the May 3, 2004, issue of *The Nation*. For subscription information, call 1-800-333-8536. Portions of each week's *Nation* magazine can be accessed at *http://www.thenation.com*.

Yet Frankfurter abhorred racial segregation. In the 1930s he served on the legal committee of the NAACP, and in 1948 he hired the Court's first black law clerk, William Coleman. Nonetheless, he insisted that the Court could invalidate segregation only if it was found legally as well as morally objectionable.

Frankfurter had difficulty finding a compelling legal argument for striking down segregation. His law clerk, Alexander Bickel, spent a summer reading the legislative history of the Fourteenth Amendment, and he reported to Frankfurter that it was "impossible" to conclude that its supporters had intended or even foreseen the abolition of school segregation.

To be sure, Frankfurter believed that the meaning of constitutional concepts can change over time, but as he and his colleagues deliberated, public schools in 21 states and the District of Columbia were still segregated. He could thus hardly maintain that evolving social standards condemned the practice. Furthermore, judicial precedent, which Frankfurter called "the most influential factor in giving a society coherence and continuity," strongly supported it. Of 44 challenges to school segregation adjudicated by state appellate and federal courts between 1865 and 1935, not one had succeeded. On the basis of legislative history and precedent, Frankfurter conceded that "*Plessy* is right." (*Plessy v. Ferguson* was the 1896 "separate but equal" decision upholding the constitutionality of state-mandated segregation on railroads.)

Brown presented a similar dilemma for Robert Jackson. In a 1950 letter Jackson, who had left the Court during the 1945–46 term to prosecute Nazi war criminals at Nuremberg, wrote to a friend: "You and I have seen the terrible consequences of racial hatred in Germany. We can have no sympathy with racial conceits which underlie segregation policies." Yet, Jackson thought judges were obliged to separate their personal views from the law, and he was loath to overrule precedent.

Jackson revealed his internal struggles in a draft concurring opinion that began: "Decision of these cases would be simple if our personal opinion that school segregation is morally, economically, or politically indefensible made it legally so." But because Jackson believed that judges must subordinate their personal preferences to the law, this consideration was irrelevant. When he turned to the question of whether existing law condemned segregation, he had difficulty saying that it did: "Layman as well as lawyer must query how it is that the Constitution this morning forbids what for three-quarters of a century it has tolerated or approved. . . . Convenient as it would be to reach an opposite conclusion, I simply cannot find in the conventional material of constitutional interpretation any justification for saying that in maintaining segregated schools any state or the District of Columbia can be judicially decreed, up to the date of this decision, to have violated the Fourteenth Amendment."

That the nine Justices who initially considered *Brown* would be uneasy about invalidating segregation is unsurprising. All of them had been appointed by Presidents Roosevelt and Truman on the assumption that they supported, as Jackson put it, "the doctrine on which the Roosevelt fight against the old court was based—in part, that it had expanded the Fourteenth Amendment to take an unjustified judicial control over social and economic affairs." For most of their professional lives, these men had criticized judicial activism as the thwarting of the popular will by unelected judges who were inscribing their social and economic biases onto the Constitution. Jackson's law clerk, William Rehnquist, wondered, if school segregation were found unconstitutional, whether any distinction would remain between this Court and its predecessor, except in "the kinds of litigants it favors and the kinds of special claims it protects."

> *In the end, even the most conflicted Justices voted to invalidate segregation.*

Several Justices doubted that the Court was the right institution to forbid segregation. Chief Justice Fred Vinson insisted, "It would be better if [Congress] would act." Jackson lamented that if the Court had to decide the question, "then representative government has failed."

In the end, even the most conflicted Justices voted to invalidate segregation. How were they able to overcome their initial doubts? In 1954 the law—as understood by most of the Justices—was reasonably clear: Segregation was constitutional. For the Justices to reject a result so clearly indicated by the conventional legal sources suggests that they had very strong personal preferences to the contrary.

And they did. Although the Court had unanimously and casually endorsed public school segregation as recently as 1927, by the early 1950s the views of most of the Justices reflected the dramatic popular changes in racial attitudes and practices that had resulted from World War II. The ideology of the war was antifascist and prodemocratic, and the contribution of African-American soldiers was undeniable. Upon their return to the South, thousands of black veterans tried to vote, many expressing the view of one such veteran that "after having been overseas fighting for democracy, I thought that when we got back here we should enjoy a little of it." Thousands more joined the NAACP, and many became civil rights litigants. Others helped launch a postwar social movement for racial justice.

Other developments in the 1940s fueled African-American progress. Over the course of the decade more than one and a half million Southern blacks, pushed by changes in Southern agriculture and pulled by wartime industrial demand, migrated to Northern cities. This mass relocation—from a region in which blacks were almost universally disenfranchised to one in which they could vote nearly without restriction—greatly enhanced their political power; indeed, they became a key swing constituency in the North. Other blacks migrated from farms to cities within the South, facilitating the creation of a black middle class that had the inclination, capacity, and opportunity to engage in organized social protest.

The onset of the cold war in the late 1940s created another impetus for racial reform. In the ideological contest with Communism, American democracy was on trial, and Southern white supremacy was its greatest vulnerability. The Justice Department's brief in *Brown*, which urged the Court to invalidate school segregation, emphasized that "racial discrimination furnishes grist for the Communist propaganda mills." After *Brown*, a supporter of the decision boasted that America's leadership of the free world "now rests on a firmer basis" and that American democracy had been "vindicat[ed] . . . in the eyes of the world."

By the early 1950s such forces had produced concrete racial reforms. In 1947 Jackie Robinson desegregated major league baseball. In 1948 Harry Truman issued executive orders desegregating the federal military and civil service. Dramatic changes in racial practices were occurring even in the South. Black voter registration there increased from 3 percent in 1940 to 20 percent in 1950. Dozens of urban police forces in the South, including some in Mississippi, hired their first black officers. Minor league baseball teams, even in such places as Montgomery and Birmingham, Alabama, signed their first black players. Most Southern states peacefully desegregated their graduate and professional schools under court order. Blacks began serving again on Southern juries. In many Southern states, the first blacks since Reconstruction were elected to urban political offices, and the walls of segregation were occasionally breached in public facilities and accommodations.

As they deliberated over *Brown*, the Justices expressed astonishment at the extent of the recent changes. Sherman Minton detected "a different world today" with regard to race. Frankfurter noted "the great changes in the relations between white and colored people since the first World War" and remarked that "the pace of progress has surprised even those most eager in its promotion." Jackson may have gone furthest, citing black advancement as a constitutional justification for eliminating segregation. In his draft opinion he wrote that segregation "has outlived whatever justification it may have had. . . . Negro progress under segregation has been spectacular and, tested by the pace of history, his rise is one of the swiftest and most dramatic advances in the annals of man." Blacks had thus overcome the presumption of inferiority on which segregation was based.

It was these sorts of changes—political, social, demographic, and ideological—that made *Brown* possible. Frankfurter later conceded that he would have voted to uphold public school segregation in the 1940s because "public opinion had not then crystallized against it."

The Justices in *Brown* did not think they were creating a movement for racial reform; they understood that they were working
with, not against, historical forces.

If *Brown* was more a product than a cause of the civil rights
movement, what precisely were the decision's effects? *Brown*
played a role both in generating direct action and in shaping the
response it received from white Southerners. Any social protest
movement must overcome a formidable hurdle in convincing potential participants that change is feasible, and the *Brown* ruling
made Jim Crow seem more vulnerable. It raised the hopes and
expectations of black Americans, which were then largely dashed
by the massive resistance to desegregation engineered by Southern
whites; this demonstrated that litigation alone could not produce
meaningful social change. *Brown* also inspired Southern whites to try to destroy the NAACP, with some
temporary success in the Deep South. This effort unin-
tentionally forced blacks to support alternative protest
organizations, which embraced philosophies more sympathetic to direct action.

> *If* **Brown**
> *was more a*
> *product than*
> *a cause of*
> *the civil*
> *rights*
> *movement,*
> *what*
> *precisely*
> *were the*
> *decision's*
> *effects?*

Finally, and perhaps most important, *Brown* produced a political backlash among Southern whites,
which increased the chances that once civil rights demonstrators appeared on the streets, they would be
greeted with violence rather than with gradualist concessions. As Southern blacks, inspired by the Court's
ruling, filed school desegregation petitions and lawsuits, Southern whites mobilized extraordinary resistance in response. Politics moved dramatically to the
right, moderates lost power, and extremists prospered.
In the mid-1950s racial retrogression characterized the
South, as progress that had been made in black voting,
university desegregation, and the integration of ath-
letic competitions was halted and then reversed. Politicians used
extremist rhetoric that encouraged violence, and some of them,
such as Bull Cannor and George Wallace, correctly calculated that
the violent suppression of civil rights protests would win votes.
Court-ordered desegregation also created concrete occasions for
violence, usually in settings that insured that white supremacists
would look bad.

That landmark Supreme Court decisions sometimes produce
such backlashes is unsurprising. When the Justices resolve controversies that rend the nation, their rulings naturally arouse opposition among those who lost in the Court. Perhaps more important,
Court decisions can disrupt the order in which social change might
otherwise have occurred by dictating reform in areas where public
opinion is not yet ready to accept it. In the early 1950s most Southern blacks were more intent on securing voting rights, curbing
police brutality, improving black schools, and winning access to
decent jobs than they were on integrating grade schools. Most

Southern whites were far more resistant to desegregating schools than they were to making concessions on black voting, school equalization, and so forth. Given these contrasting preferences, political negotiation between blacks and whites, assuming that blacks had sufficient clout to compel negotiation, would certainly not have focused immediately on school desegregation. Yet courts respond to agendas set by litigants, not by political negotiation. By demanding change first on an issue where whites were most opposed to it, the *Brown* decision encouraged massive resistance.

Backlashes themselves may have unpredictable consequences. The violence that *Brown* fomented in the South, especially when it was directed at peaceful protesters and broadcast on national television, produced a counterbacklash. In 1954 most Northerners agreed with *Brown* in the abstract, but their preferences were not strong enough to make them willing to face down the resistance of Southern whites. It was violence against civil rights demonstrators that transformed national opinion on race. By the early 1960s, Northerners were no longer prepared to tolerate brutal beatings of peaceful black demonstrators, and they responded to such scenes by demanding civil rights legislation that attacked Jim Crow at its core.

Brown mattered, but it did not fundamentally transform the nation; Supreme Court decisions never do. The Justices are too much a product of their time and place to launch social revolutions. And, even if they had the inclination to do so, their capacity to coerce change is too heavily constrained. The Justices were not tempted to invalidate school segregation until a time when half the nation supported such a ruling. They declined to enforce the *Brown* decision aggressively until a civil rights movement had made Northern whites as keen to eliminate Jim Crow as Southern whites were to preserve it. And while *Brown* did play a role in shaping both the civil rights movement and the violent response it received from Southern whites, deep historical forces insured the development of a racial reform movement in America regardless of what the Supreme Court did or did not do.

40 Years and Waiting

By Marshall J. Hartman
Chicago Daily Law Bulletin, April 26, 2003

One of the most pervasive problems of American law has been the indigent client caught in the web of the criminal justice system. The Sixth Amendment to the U.S. Constitution provides that, "In all criminal prosecutions, the accused shall enjoy the right . . . to the assistance of counsel for his defense." However, up until the landmark decision by the Supreme Court 40 years ago in *Gideon v. Wainwright*, 372 U.S. 355 (1963), this right was largely enjoyed by those who could afford to pay for counsel—and largely unavailable for the poor.

In the early part of the 20th century, there were attempts to alleviate the problem of the indigent defendant by establishing assigned counsel programs, voluntary defender programs, and rudimentary public defender offices. But these bureaus lacked the constitutional backing of the Sixth Amendment. Therefore, the kind of defense they provided was generally lacking.

For example, this early type of public defender was typically characterized as follows, "The assigned counsel, whose retained clients are his chief concern, easily convinces himself that he has done his duty to his pauper client if the prosecutor will accept a plea of guilty to a lesser form of crime or . . . recommend a moderate sentence." (Goldman, 1974).

The services themselves were no better. The Portland public defender, whose office opened before 1917, described his goals as follows: "As the work was new here there were some questions as to how far the public defender should go, or how energetic he should be. . . . The public defender should limit his defense to assisting the court in bringing out the prisoner's side of the case, rather than making a vigorous fight . . . to secure an acquittal." (Barak, 1980).

Similarly, the stated purpose of the Cook County public defender's office, which opened in 1930, was simply to assist the court and to expedite guilty pleas.

However, as deficient as the representation of the poor might have been, the overarching problem was that public defender systems or organized assigned counsel programs operated in fewer than 3 percent of the counties before 1963.

Typical of what occurred in the other counties prior to the *Gideon* decision is illustrated by what happened to Gideon himself.

Clarence Earl Gideon had been accused of breaking into a Florida pool hall. When he appeared before the trial court he said, "Your Honor . . . I request this court to appoint counsel to represent me in this trial."

"Mr. Gideon," the judge responded, "I am sorry, but I cannot appoint counsel to represent you in this case. Under the laws of the State of Florida, the only time the court can appoint counsel to represent a defendant is when that person is charged with a capital offense."

Gideon shot back: "The United States Supreme Court says I am entitled to be represented by counsel." (Anthony Lewis, *Gideon's Trumpet*, 1964)

The trial judge refused to appoint an attorney, and so Gideon acted as his own lawyer—and lost. He appealed all the way to the nation's highest court, which accepted his case and reversed. The Supreme Court held for the first time that the Sixth Amendment right to counsel was applicable to the states through the due process clause of the 14th Amendment and was therefore enforceable in state criminal courts. Moreover, where a defendant charged with a felony had insufficient funds to hire his own lawyer, the defendant was entitled to counsel provided by the court.

> *"Your Honor . . . I request this court to appoint counsel to represent me in this trial."*
> —Clarence Earl Gideon

On retrial—represented by a lawyer—Gideon was acquitted.

The impact of *Gideon* was twofold. First, the question of how vigorous a defense to provide a defendant became a matter of constitutional dimension. The defense counsel, whether court-appointed or a public defender, was no longer beholden to charitable contributions from merchants or funds from counties that merely wanted an office to expedite guilty pleas. Under the Constitution, the public defender or appointed counsel worked for the defendant, not for the court nor the county board, and the defendant was entitled to the most vigorous defense mandated by law.

Recently, the American Bar Association passed the "Ten Principles of a Public Defense Delivery System." These principles call for the independence of public defenders from the courts or from politics, reasonable caseloads for lawyers, early representation of the client after arrest, continuous representation of the defendant by the same lawyer throughout the court process, training and supervision for assistant public defenders, and parity with the prosecution in the same jurisdiction.

The second impact of *Gideon* was the institutional response of the nation's states and counties in the wake of the decision. Whereas under prior decisions counsel was required only in capital cases, suddenly courts and county and state governments were required to provide for the appointment of counsel in approximately 500,000 felony cases. The response, aided by a grant in 1964 from the Ford Foundation to the National Legal Aid and Defender Association which was prepared to assist the counties, resulted in the immediate establishment of 74 public defender or coordinated assigned-counsel programs throughout the United States to accept appointments in felony cases.

In contrast to the 3 percent of the counties that had programs before 1963, by 1996, 82 percent of state felony defendants in the 75 largest counties in America were represented by public defender or assigned-counsel programs. By 1999 an estimated $1.2 billion was spent by indigent criminal defense programs that handled felony cases at the trial level in the 100 most populous counties. These programs dealt with approximately 4.2 million cases. (Bureau of Justice Statistics Report, November 2000)

However, the mere fact that the Supreme Court and the bar associations mandated effective assistance of counsel for the indigent accused, does not mean that the problem was solved. Realistically, public defender caseloads which now included misdemeanors, juvenile, appellate, and probation cases with suspended sentences, are still too high all over the country, and resources for public defender and assigned counsel cases are limited.

"As currently funded," the ABA's Special Committee on Criminal Justice in a Free Society reported, "the criminal justice system cannot provide the quality of justice that the public legitimately expects. . . . Compromise will . . . necessarily limit the quality of services that can be delivered as long as the criminal justice system must operate without adequate resources." (*Criminal Justice in Crisis*, ABA 1988)

Specifically, with respect to public defense the committee found that today, "In the case of the indigent defendant, the problem is not that the defense representation is too aggressive but that it is too often inadequate because of underfunded and overburdened public defender offices."

In response to this report, the National Legal Aid and Defender Association in 1996 appointed a blue-ribbon advisory committee that encouraged the evaluation of public defender offices, the provision of technical assistance to meet the nationally recognized standards for indigent defense programs, and, ultimately, the establishment of a national accreditation commission for public defender and assigned-counsel programs to ensure that these standards are maintained.

Our society has come a long way in the 40 years since *Gideon* to meet the mandate of effective counsel for all Americans, rich and poor alike. But the battle is not yet won, and we must redouble our efforts to guarantee that the dream of *Gideon* becomes a reality.

Police Tactic to Sidestep *Miranda* Rights Rejected

By Jerry Markon
The Washington Post, June 29, 2004

The Supreme Court ruled yesterday that police officers may not deliberately avoid warning suspects of their right to remain silent before beginning questioning, asserting that a law enforcement tactic of interrogating suspects twice—before reading them their rights and then after—undermines the familiar *Miranda* right.

The 5 to 4 decision affirms the rights of suspects not to speak to investigators and is intended to end what the Court said was an increasing police practice of twice questioning suspects in the hope of eliciting a confession. The decision rejects what the Court called "a police strategy adapted to undermine the *Miranda* warnings."

Writing for the majority, Justice David H. Souter said that a Missouri woman's statements about her involvement in a murder plot were inadmissible because police had arrested her at 3 A.M., elicited her confession, and only then advised her of her rights. She subsequently incriminated herself again.

"The reason that question-first is catching on is as obvious as its manifest purpose, which is to get a confession the suspect would not make if he understood his rights at the outset," Souter wrote in his opinion, which was joined by Justices John Paul Stevens, Ruth Bader Ginsburg, and Stephen G. Breyer. Justice Anthony M. Kennedy filed a separate concurring opinion.

"The sensible underlying assumption is that with one confession in hand before the warnings, the interrogator can count on getting its duplicate, with trifling additional trouble," Souter wrote.

The ruling came in one of two closely watched cases decided yesterday that clarify the court's landmark 1966 ruling in *Miranda v. Arizona*, which first established "the right to remain silent." The justices upheld *Miranda* in 2000, declaring that the Constitution requires police to inform suspects of their right not to answer questions and have attorneys present before interrogations can proceed. But the 2000 decision was broad and did not address interrogation techniques or other specific components of *Miranda*.

In the other case yesterday, the justices ruled that prosecutors may use physical evidence against a suspect even if it was obtained by officers who had not given the suspect a *Miranda* warning.

Supporters of *Miranda* had been especially tracking the case about the questioning of suspects, *Missouri v. Seibert*, No. 02-1371. In the case, Patrice Seibert was convicted and sentenced to life in prison after her second confession was admitted into evidence.

Seibert had been concerned that she would be charged with neglect in the death of her severely disabled son, Jonathan, at the family's mobile home, because of bedsores on his body. Two of her teenage sons and two of their friends hatched a plan in Seibert's presence to burn the trailer. To make it seem that Jonathan, 12, had not been left alone, they left a mentally disabled youth, Donald Rector, 17, in the trailer before setting it afire. Rector died of smoke inhalation.

Richard Hanrahan, a police detective in Rolla, Mo., elicited Seibert's confession, took a 20-minute break, then read her rights to her before she confessed again. The Missouri Supreme Court threw out the confession and the state, joined by the Bush administration, appealed.

Hanrahan said that he had been trained to question before and after giving a *Miranda* warning by a "national institute." The International Association of Chiefs of Police said yesterday that it does not endorse the tactic and does not teach it.

In an interview, Steven D. Benjamin, a Richmond lawyer who is on the board of the National Association of Criminal Defense Lawyers, said the two-step process has become so common that it has a name in the criminal justice community: "interrogating outside *Miranda*."

"It is an institutional practice among police. It happens every day," Benjamin said.

Souter wrote that the Court has no statistics on the practice. But he said that although it is not used "en masse" by police, it is taught in some police training programs and is clearly a tactic "of some popularity" among law enforcement.

Justice Sandra Day O'Connor wrote a dissent, joined by Chief Justice William H. Rehnquist, and Justices Antonin Scalia and Clarence Thomas.

In the second case, *U.S. v. Patane*, No. 02-1183, the court ruled 5 to 4 that physical evidence gathered because of a suspect's statement made without a *Miranda* warning does not have to be excluded from a case.

In the case, a detective began advising Samuel Francis Patane of his rights when Patane, a convicted felon, was arrested. Patane interrupted the agent, saying that he already knew his rights, and then directed the agent where to find a .40-caliber pistol. Patane sought to have that evidence excluded from his trial for illegal possession of a firearm.

The Denver-based U.S. Court of Appeals for the 10th Circuit agreed that the gun should be excluded.

But the high court overturned that ruling. Writing for the Court, Thomas said that excluding physical evidence derived from an unwarned statement would be an unlawful extension of *Miranda*. His decision was joined by Rehnquist and Scalia.

Kennedy wrote a concurring opinion, joined by O'Connor. Souter, Stevens, and Ginsburg dissented; Breyer dissented separately.

"There is, of course, a price for excluding evidence, but the Fifth Amendment is worth a price," Souter, Stevens, and Ginsburg said. "There is no way to read this case except as an unjustifiable invitation to law enforcement officers to flout *Miranda* when there may be physical evidence to be gained."

Civil liberties advocates said the decision ending the double questioning of suspects was extraordinarily important. But they said they are worried that the *Patane* ruling could help erode its impact by encouraging police to avoid *Miranda* if they need to find crucial evidence—a position endorsed by the four dissenting members of the Court.

"It's a very mixed message," said Christopher Dunn, associate legal director of the New York Civil Liberties Union and an expert on *Miranda* rights. "On one hand, the Court has wisely closed the door on police strategies designed to induce improper confessions. On the other hand, the Court may be encouraging similar strategies in cases where they care less about a confession and more about the evidence they can obtain through a coerced confession."

Both Sides on Abortion Wary of Supreme Court

Roe v. Wade: 30 Years Later

By Jan Crawford Greenburg
Chicago Tribune, January 21, 2003

When the Supreme Court struck down state laws three years ago banning late-term abortions, the pro-choice groups that had worked so hard for the victory nonetheless struck a worried tone.

While praising the ruling, the groups quickly focused on the closeness of the 5–4 decision. They concluded that *Roe v. Wade*, the landmark ruling 30 years ago establishing a woman's right to abortion, hung by a thread.

That conclusion has been a mantra for abortion-rights groups ever since, and it will be a way to galvanize the troops as they fight efforts to scale back the scope of *Roe* in statehouses, courtrooms, and Congress. With the possibility of a Supreme Court vacancy as early as this summer, they argue that fears of *Roe* being overturned could become reality.

"*Roe* does hang by one vote," said Nancy Northup, president of the Center for Reproductive Rights. "There is a danger if one of the five members on the Supreme Court were replaced by someone who was hostile to *Roe*, that *Roe* could be overturned."

To opponents of abortion, however, the decision in the late-term abortion case—the Court's most recent abortion ruling—does not look hopeful either. They see the case as, far from eroding *Roe*, a disappointing defeat in which a majority of the justices declined to outlaw what they believe is one of the most horrific of all abortion procedures. They note that, the late-term case aside, six justices on the Court probably would uphold the basic right found in *Roe*.

"It's become almost another amendment to the Constitution," Jay Sekulow, chief counsel for the American Center for Law and Justice, said of the Court's decision in *Roe*. "To overturn *Roe* would be a huge shift, a very significant shift on the Court."

In the 30 years since the Court announced one of the most contentious opinions in American life, the battle lines remain firmly entrenched, to the point that opponents and supporters of *Roe* find virtually no room for agreement, even on interpreting decisions like the late-term abortion case. The two factions' anxiety indicates the deep importance and high emotion they attach to the historic 1973 decision.

With Wednesday marking the 30th anniversary of *Roe v. Wade*, the controversy shows no signs of abating. Anti-abortion forces seek any chance to cut back or overturn a decision they believe has led to the deaths of millions, while abortion-rights groups defend a decision they say affirmed a critical right for women.

New legal issues are on the horizon, including the prospect of a late-term abortion ban at the federal level, which will draw immediate court challenges. Also on the front burner is the prospect of a more conservative tilt on the Supreme Court, which could make it easier for the federal and state governments to impose additional restrictions on abortion.

Moreover, abortion-rights groups are focusing on the federal appeals courts, fighting Bush nominees they believe are hostile to their viewpoint. A Democrat-controlled Senate Judiciary Committee last fall, for example, defeated Bush nominee Priscilla Owen after women's groups and others raised questions about her commitment to abortion rights.

With Republicans gaining a majority in the Senate in the fall elections, President Bush has renominated Owen to a seat on a New Orleans–based federal appeals court.

Abortion-rights groups believe that appeals court nominees should get close scrutiny on abortion because they can have the last word on state abortion laws if the Supreme Court declines to hear the case.

Evolution Since 1973

Since the Supreme Court decided *Roe*, it has taken up 30 cases involving the issue of reproductive rights. It has gradually allowed some restrictions on abortion, such as waiting periods and parental-consent requirements for minors. In deciding the constitutionality of state and federal abortion laws, the Court asks whether they unduly burden a woman's right to an abortion.

"A lot of legislatures are trying to restrict abortion as much as they can, by way of parental-notification requirements and requirements that you be counseled before you get abortions. They're really pushing and pulling to restrict the right," said University of Chicago Law School professor David Strauss. "And the standard that the Supreme Court has given us is very vague: 'Does this unduly burden the right to an abortion?' That's a big judgment call."

The Supreme Court articulated that standard in 1992 when it decided *Planned Parenthood v. Casey*, which presented the biggest threat to date to *Roe*. Abortion-rights supporters feared the Court would use the case to overturn *Roe*, but the Court instead reaffirmed it 5–4.

"Undue Burden" Standard

Three Republican appointees—Justices Sandra Day O'Connor, Anthony Kennedy, and David Souter—joined forces to articulate a new standard that states could impose restrictions on abortion, before the fetus could live outside the womb, to protect a woman's health or the life of the fetus. But those restrictions, the justices said, could not amount to an "undue burden" on a woman's right to choose.

"The *Casey* opinion set *Roe* in more concrete—or it at least raises the bar of what you'd have to get over," Sekulow said. "I'm not losing hope that it will be overturned, but I don't think abortion as we know it is going to be outlawed."

Instead, abortion opponents have shifted their focus to new legal frontiers. Sekulow said he is optimistic that Congress will pass a federal ban on late-term abortions, and Bush has indicated he will sign it.

Northup, anticipating that law, said her group is prepared to sue to block it. She said she believes it will be similar to the Nebraska ban on late-term abortions that the Court invalidated in 2000. Nebraska Dr. Leroy Carhart challenged that law as unconstitutional.

The Court struck it down as an undue burden on a woman's right to choose because the law was so broadly and vaguely written that it would ban other types of abortion. Moreover, it did not allow doctors to perform the procedure to protect the mother's heath.

The decision sharply split the three justices who joined forces in the 1992 case, with Kennedy in sharp dissent on whether the Nebraska law was, in fact, an undue burden. He accused the Court of misapplying the 1992 case and was particularly critical of O'Connor, generally viewed as a fellow moderate.

Kennedy's position in the case has convinced Northup and others that *Roe* is in danger and that four justices would like to overturn it.

But others note that Kennedy's dissent did not call into question his position in 1992, when he refused to overturn *Roe*. What's more, even if Kennedy had a change of heart, the Court still would be one vote short of overturning *Roe*. To get that vote, a justice who supported *Roe* would have to retire and be replaced by one with opposing views.

As Republican presidents well know, it is not so easy to predict how justices will rule: Souter, O'Connor, and Kennedy all were nominated by Republicans, as was the court's most liberal member, Justice John Paul Stevens.

"Our side is starting to understand, it's not that the president makes an appointment and we're there," Sekulow said.

30 Years Since *Roe v. Wade*

Key Legislation, Other Actions

In **1970**, Norma McCorvey (a.k.a. Jane Roe), an unmarried pregnant woman in Texas, challenged a state law forbidding doctors to perform an abortion unless a woman's life was at risk. In a landmark 1973 ruling, the U.S. Supreme Court legalized abortion under the right to privacy. Since then, however, the Court's ruling has been narrowed by other Court decisions and federal legislation.

1974: Federally funded research using fetal tissue is prohibited through the National Science Foundation Authorization Act.

1976: Congress passes the Hyde Amendment, banning the use of Medicaid and other federal funds for abortions. The legislation is upheld by the Supreme Court in 1980.

1993: President Bill Clinton lifts the so-called gag rule that forbade doctors in federally funded clinics from mentioning abortion as an option.

2000: The FDA approves the abortion pill, mifepristone (RU-486).

2001: President George W. Bush restricts federal funding to overseas groups that provide or advocate abortions.

Key Court Decisions

1976: The Supreme Court strikes down a Missouri law requiring a woman to obtain her husband's consent before having an abortion.

1979: A Missouri requirement that abortions after the first trimester be performed in hospitals is found unconstitutional. Another law mandating parental consent is upheld.

1980: In *Harris v. McRae*, the Court upholds a federal law banning the use of Medicaid funds for abortions, except when necessary to save a woman's life.

1983: The Court strikes down an Akron ordinance that requires doctors to give abortion patients anti-abortion literature, imposes a 24-hour waiting period, requires abortions after the first trimester to be performed in a hospital, requires parental consent, and requires the aborted fetus to be disposed of in a "humane" manner.

1989: In *Webster v. Reproductive Health Services*, a law in Missouri declaring that "life begins at conception" and barring the use of public facilities for abortions is found constitutional. It marks the first time the Supreme Court does not explicitly reaffirm *Roe v. Wade*.

1992: In *Planned Parenthood v. Casey*, the Court reaffirms *Roe*'s core holding that states may not ban abortions or interfere with a woman's decision to have an abortion. The Court does uphold mandatory 24-hour waiting periods and parental-consent laws.

1997: The Supreme Court upholds a buffer zone prohibiting all protests within 15 feet of an abortion clinic.

2000: The Supreme Court strikes down a Nebraska ban on late-term abortions, rendering similar bans in more than 30 states void.

Sources: Planned Parenthood Federation of America, National Abortion and Reproductive Rights Action League, Center for Reproductive Law and Policy.

A Long Shadow

By Debra Rosenberg
Newsweek, November 8, 2004

At a reunion with his former law clerks in May, Supreme Court Justice John Paul Stevens was in a reflective mood. As more than 100 clerks and other guests dined in an elegant room at the Court, the oldest justice rose to make a speech. Stevens quickly invoked one of the most painful moments in the Court's recent history— *Bush v. Gore*, the controversial 5–4 decision that handed George W. Bush the presidency in 2000. He paid tribute to the hardworking clerks who had weathered the electoral storm, inviting them to stand while the crowd applauded enthusiastically. Stevens has never backed away from his stinging dissent in the case. And his homage to the clerks is just one signal that, even four years later, *Bush v. Gore* is still on the justices' minds.

At the time it seemed like the perfect storm of a case—a razor-thin margin of victory in a decisive state thrown into question after orders from the state's highest court. The justices were eager to put the contentious decision behind them, even trying to dismiss it as an anomaly they hoped never to revisit. Public bitterness over the outcome seemed to fade in the aftermath of 9/11. But now, with polls suggesting this week's election is tight, a swarm of lawsuits is already working its way through the lower courts— some of which attempt to build on *Bush v. Gore* as a precedent. That not only raises the specter of the election once again landing in the justices' laps, but also brings back some of the old rancor. "All of the pent-up feelings on both sides have suddenly come to the surface again," says Harvard law professor Laurence Tribe, who argued part of the Democrats' case in *Bush v. Gore*.

Last week the political tension heightened with the news that Chief Justice William Rehnquist was being treated for thyroid cancer. Though Rehnquist was released from the hospital on Friday and is expected back on the bench this week, the Court released few medical details. Even White House officials urgently called around Washington, searching for clues about his condition, sources tell *Newsweek*. But the diagnosis alone was a reminder that the next president will likely fill at least one Court vacancy.

That's a task made tougher by the animosity still lingering after *Bush v. Gore*.

Mark Wilson/Getty Images

Associate Justice John Paul Stevens wrote the dissenting opinion in the controversial case of Bush v. Gore.

Initially, the justices had been reluctant to intervene in the 2000 election. When the Bush campaign first asked the Supremes to overturn the Florida Supreme Court's decision extending the time period for certifying recounted ballots, the justices punted. The Court agreed 9–0 to send the case back to Florida. But within a week, they agreed to take up the matter again. This time the Bushies appealed the Florida court's ruling ordering a statewide recount. The justices split over what to do. Three conservatives—Rehnquist, Antonin Scalia, and Clarence Thomas—believed the Florida court could not overrule the State Legislature by changing election rules mid-course. Those three plus two swing justices—Sandra Day O'Connor and Anthony Kennedy—also held that the recount violated voters' "equal protection" right to have each ballot counted in the same way. All five wanted to end the recount. Two of the four liberal justices—David Souter and Stephen Breyer—agreed on the equal-protection violations, but wanted the counting to continue. The others—Ruth Bader Ginsburg and Stevens—found no constitutional problems. In withering dissents, they voted to let the Florida judges make the call.

The 5–4 split touched off a nationwide furor. Liberals fumed that the conservative justices had installed their favorite candidate in the White House. Republicans claimed the ruling prevented the Florida court from stealing the election for Al Gore. Justices on both sides rushed to reassure the public the decision was legit. And four years later none of the justices has backed down. Last month Breyer reflected on whether politics had played a role. "I had to ask myself, would I vote the same way if the names were reversed," he told students at Stanford. "I said, 'yes.' But I'll never know for sure—because people are great self-kidders—if I reached the truthful answer." In a September appearance at Harvard, Scalia noted that seven of the justices had agreed on the equal-protection violations. "Would you rather have the president of the United States decided by the Supreme Court of Florida?" he challenged.

Many legal scholars still fault the decision for unsound legal reasoning. "If you dissect it a little bit, it's a fraud," Tribe says of the equal-protection rationale. Some of the partisan outrage over the case has ebbed. "All of the nine actually think what they [each] did was best for the country," says Tribe. But conservatives believe bitterness over the case has fueled

> ## *The 5–4 split touched off a nationwide furor.*

Democratic efforts to stymie Bush's judicial nominations to lower courts. "The decision cast a long shadow forward," says former White House counsel C. Boyden Gray.

Now the case could come back to haunt the justices. Last year, speaking to San Diego law students, Justice Ginsburg called *Bush v. Gore* a "one-of-a-kind case" and said "I doubt it will ever be cited as precedent by the Court on anything." But it has already cropped up in lower-court cases, says Loyola law professor Richard Hasen. Before the California recall vote, Democrats argued that using punch-card voting machines in some parts of the state but not others violated *Bush v. Gore*'s equal-protection rationale. And Republicans claimed that the New Jersey Supreme Court could not allow Democrats to switch Senate candidates late in the race without violating *Bush v. Gore*'s prohibition against courts' tinkering with election rules. But both efforts to use *Bush v. Gore* reasoning ultimately failed.

That won't stop lawyers from citing the case in any legal challenges to this week's election. The Democratic National Committee is already using it in Florida and Missouri to raise equal-protection concerns about provisional ballots counted differently across a state. Republicans accuse the Democrats of instigating most of the litigation—at Bush-Cheney headquarters, aides are tracking Democratic lawsuits with more than 40 red pushpins on a map—but say they could use the decision to argue against courts' changing election rules midstream. "Everyone's going to rely on *Bush v. Gore*," says one GOP official. "It's the law."

No one believes the Supreme Court is eager to wade into the election morass again. And chances are they won't have to. But, ironically, *Bush v. Gore* may have paved the way for legal fights that end on their doorstep. "This is now an acceptable electoral tool," says Washington lawyer Thomas Goldstein. Besides, some of the justices may not feel comfortable leaving the election's outcome in the hands of a lower court. That means the nation could be in for a long postelection overtime—an outcome only the legions of lawyers might relish. "My guess would be that there are nine justices whose last prayer on Monday night will be for someone to win in a landslide," says former Clinton solicitor general Walter Dellinger. A lot of voters may be whispering those prayers, too.

Are Landmark Court Decisions All That Important?

By Michael Klarman
The Chronicle of Higher Education, August 8, 2003

Since June, when the Supreme Court upheld the use of racial preferences in university admissions in *Grutter v. Bollinger*, people on both sides of the affirmative-action issue have been scrutinizing the ruling and planning how to respond. What has been largely overlooked, however, is the broader context in which important Supreme Court decisions are made and what history might tell us about the ultimate impact of those decisions. What, if anything, will be the lasting consequences of *Grutter*?

A review of earlier rulings provides needed perspective, demonstrating that Supreme Court decisions generally reflect the social and political context of the times. The justices did not extend the Equal Protection Clause of the Fourteenth Amendment to cover sex discrimination until 1971, after the rise of the women's movement. The Court interpreted the Establishment Clause of the First Amendment to constrain public displays of religiosity only after the influence of America's unofficial Protestant establishment had significantly waned, around the middle of the 20th century. During the Red scares after the First and Second World Wars, the justices interpreted free-speech guarantees to permit the persecution of political leftists. The Court shrank the Fourth Amendment's ban on "unreasonable searches and seizures" during the War on Drugs of the 1980s and 1990s. Today's campaign against terrorism has led lower courts to limit traditional civil rights and civil liberties.

This pattern does not mean that social and political context necessarily dictates the outcome of particular constitutional controversies. On many such issues, public opinion is split down the middle, and the justices could plausibly reach more than one outcome. That the Court could not have realistically created an abortion right before the women's movement does not mean that *Roe v. Wade* (1973) had to be decided as it was. That the Warren Court's criminal-procedure revolution depended on shifting social attitudes toward race and poverty does not mean that rulings such as *Miranda v. Arizona* (1966) had to come out as they did.

The Court's racial jurisprudence confirms the importance of historical context to constitutional interpretation. American race relations reached a post–Civil War nadir in the late 19th century. On average, 100 African-Americans a year were lynched in the 1890s. The Republican Party abandoned its traditional commitment to blacks' civil and political rights. Northern whites largely acquiesced to Southern whites' reasserting control over their own race relations. Most white Americans concluded that enfranchising blacks in the Fifteenth Amendment had been a mistake. Reflecting that context, the Court upheld racial segregation, black disfranchisement, and the exclusion of blacks from juries.

World War II proved to be a watershed in American race relations. African-American soldiers returned from fighting for democracy overseas to demand their own democratic rights, and they became the vanguard of the modern civil-rights movement. The war afforded blacks unparalleled opportunities for economic and political advancement. Millions of white Americans, repulsed by the Nazi Holocaust, re-evaluated their own racial (and religious) biases. The ensuing cold war inspired Americans to reform racial practices to rebut Soviet propaganda aimed at convincing third-world nations that democratic capitalism was tantamount to white supremacy. *Brown v. Board of Education* (1954), which invalidated racial segregation in public schools, was decided in this setting.

Northern whites largely acquiesced to Southern whites' reasserting control over their own race relations.

On affirmative action, the Court's jurisprudence is consistent with this paradigm of constitutional interpretation. Public opinion has always been divided on affirmative action, and so have the justices been. In *Regents of the University of California v. Bakke* (1978), Justice Lewis F. Powell imposed a compromise solution, sustaining the use of race in university admissions while repudiating quotas. In subsequent decisions the Court gradually circumscribed affirmative action by imposing stringent conditions on its use. Personnel changes made the Court more conservative through the Reagan and Bush administrations, and its stance toward affirmative action grew more skeptical. In light of that trend, the recent decision in *Grutter v. Bollinger* was somewhat surprising.

Justices' votes in affirmative-action cases have followed fairly predictable political lines. The three most conservative justices— William H. Rehnquist (the chief justice), Antonin Scalia, and Clarence Thomas—have never voted to sustain an affirmative-action plan but rather have insisted on a nearly absolute ban on government race-consciousness. The four most liberal justices—John Paul Stevens, David H. Souter, Ruth Bader Ginsburg, and Stephen G. Breyer—have rarely (or never) voted to invalidate an affirmative-action plan. Most Court watchers accurately predicted that the result in the University of Michigan cases would turn on the votes of Justice Sandra Day O'Connor and, to a lesser extent, Justice Anthony M. Kennedy.

Grutter reveals that O'Connor probably changed her mind about affirmative action over the past two decades. Before *Grutter*, she had never voted to sustain a race-based affirmative-action plan, though she had explicitly noted that such policies might be acceptable under certain stringent conditions. Based on her earlier opinions and votes, one might easily have predicted that O'Connor would invalidate the admissions policies of the University of Michigan on the grounds that they relied on the impermissible stereotype that race correlates with diversity of perspective and that they failed to adequately consider nonracial alternatives for securing a diverse student body.

> *Court rulings probably matter less than most lawyers believe they do.*

But O'Connor is a classic conservative, who values preservation of the status quo. In the early 21st century, multiculturalism and multiracialism have become entrenched features of American life. Predicting such a development even 20 years ago would have been difficult. Yet probably in response to the growing racial and ethnic diversity of the nation, and possibly in response to globalization forces as well, most Americans have come to accept that all important social, political, and economic institutions should "look like America." Friend-of-the-court briefs filed in the University of Michigan cases symbolized the extent to which even relatively conservative American institutions such as Fortune 500 companies and the U.S. military have embraced this multiracial vision. Those briefs warned the justices that America's economic success and military security depended on the continued use of affirmative action.

In *Grutter*, O'Connor declined to put the nation's elite universities at risk of becoming lily white. If most Americans assume that African-Americans should be on the Supreme Court and in the cabinet, why should they not be at the University of Michigan Law School? As O'Connor put it in *Grutter*: "In order to cultivate a set of leaders with legitimacy in the eyes of the citizenry, it is necessary that the path to leadership be visibly open to talented and qualified individuals of every race and ethnicity."

So how important are Supreme Court decisions generally, and how important is *Grutter* in particular? Court rulings probably matter less than most lawyers believe they do. For one thing, Court decisions are not self-enforcing. They can be evaded or sometimes even defied, especially when resistance is intense, when most individuals responsible for enforcing them are strongly opposed, and when political actors are unenthusiastic about carrying them out. Many of the Court's early civil-rights decisions were utterly inconsequential. Rulings that invalidated residential segregation ordinances and the judicial enforcement of racially exclusionary land covenants had almost no effect on segregated housing patterns. A full decade after *Brown*, just one black child in every hundred in the South attended a desegregated school.

To be sure, Court decisions can have other intangible effects, such as increasing an issue's salience, educating opinion, inspiring supporters, or mobilizing opponents. However, even those intangible consequences are easily exaggerated. Conventional wisdom notwithstanding, *Brown* neither educated many whites to abandon white supremacy, nor inspired many blacks to commence direct-action street protest.

Grutter's direct effects are likely to be limited. The ruling permits universities to continue existing affirmative-action plans, perhaps with slight alteration to accommodate the invalidation of point systems in *Grutter*'s companion case, *Gratz v. Bollinger*. Evaluating the impact of *Grutter* requires speculating on how efficacious a contrary ruling would have been. Proponents of affirmative action have insisted that terminating race-based preferences would dramatically decrease racial diversity on college campuses. But their incentive to exaggerate the impact of such a ruling is clear.

That a contrary decision in *Grutter* would have been very consequential seems unlikely. As Southern whites convincingly demonstrated after *Brown*, Court rulings can be evaded in myriad ways. Much as the primary enforcers of *Brown*—Southern school boards—were passionately opposed to the Court's ruling, so would the primary enforcers of a contrary decision in *Grutter*—university admissions officers—have been passionately opposed to its enforcement. Southern school boards used pupil-placement policies that employed multiple factors to keep segregation largely intact while purporting to comply with *Brown*; so could university admissions officers have used multifactored admissions policies to disguise the continued use of racial preferences had *Grutter* been decided differently. After *Brown*, Southern school boards capitalized on residential segregation to preserve racial separation in schools while dismantling *de jure* segregation; after a contrary decision in *Grutter*, university administrators could have capitalized on residential segregation to preserve racial diversity—as under the Texas plan that guarantees university admission to students in the top 10 percent of each high-school graduating class.

This is not to say that a contrary ruling in *Grutter* would have made no difference, only that it would probably have mattered less than affirmative-action proponents predicted. As Justice Thomas pointed out in his *Grutter* dissent, Boalt Law School has a higher percentage of minority students today than it did before California's Proposition 209 barred race-conscious admissions policies. University admissions officers will naturally be relieved that the Court has permitted them to do openly what they would otherwise have been inclined to do clandestinely. But it is hard to believe that the racial diversity of university student bodies would differ greatly under the two scenarios.

What intangible consequences might *Grutter* have? That the decision will persuade many skeptics of affirmative action to change their minds seems unlikely. Court rulings rarely have such an educational effect. *Roe v. Wade* (1973) apparently did not influence many Americans to change their abortion views, as the country remains divided on abortion, much as it was three decades ago. *Bowers v. Hardwick* (1986), which sustained the criminalization of homosexual sodomy even among consenting adults in private, has not persuaded many Americans to agree with the Court; rather, public opinion has gradually repudiated *Bowers*, which probably explains the Court's decision to overrule it in *Lawrence v. Texas* (2003). Recent opinion polls that reveal public support for capital punishment at 70 percent or higher suggest that *Furman v. Georgia* (1972), which invalidated arbitrary enforcement of the death penalty and hinted at its abolition, has not persuaded many Americans.

Even *Brown* did not impel many Americans to abandon their belief in white supremacy. Most white Southerners denounced the decision as "shocking, outrageous, and reprehensible." Most white Northerners endorsed it, but more because they already agreed with

---

Roe *mobilized right-to-life opposition that had not previously played a significant role in American politics.*

---

its principles than because they were educated by the decision. It was the civil-rights movement and the street confrontations of the 1960s, not *Brown*, that profoundly influenced the racial attitudes of many white Americans. Citizens have generally felt free to disagree with the Supreme Court and to make up their own minds about moral controversies. *Grutter* seems as unlikely to exert significant educational influence as other landmark Court rulings have been.

Might *Grutter* instead generate a backlash, mobilizing opposition to affirmative action? Some other prominent Court decisions have had such an effect. *Furman* apparently mobilized support for the death penalty by threatening to abolish it; within four years, 35 states had amended their death-penalty statutes in the hope of satisfying the justices' constitutional qualms. *Roe* mobilized right-to-life opposition that had not previously played a significant role in American politics. *Brown* crystallized Southern whites' resistance to racial change, propelling Southern politics sharply to the right, silencing racial moderates, and rewarding extremist politicians who encouraged violence.

Court decisions have generated backlashes when they mandated change faster than public opinion was prepared to tolerate. In the 1950s, many Southern whites were willing to accept increases in black voter registration and the equalization of black schools, but they drew the line at the race-mixing of young schoolchildren.

Unlike such backlash-inducing decisions, *Grutter* reaffirms the status quo, rather than commanding change. Thus it is no more likely to incite a backlash than were the affirmative-action policies that the ruling vindicated.

That a justice as conservative as Sandra Day O'Connor would validate an affirmative-action plan that weighed race as heavily as did that of the University of Michigan Law School is striking. *Grutter* reveals how deeply entrenched the notion that all of our social, political, and economic institutions should "look like America" has become. Justice O'Connor's conservative commitment to preserving the status quo trumped her ideological aversion to race-conscious government remedies. That *Grutter* is a striking result, however, is not to say that it is likely to be very consequential. University admissions officers are now free to do somewhat openly—not too openly, given *Gratz*—what they would have likely done anyway. That a contrary ruling in *Grutter* would have significantly eroded racial diversity on college campuses is far from clear. Nor is *Grutter* likely to educate opinion in favor of affirmative action or to mobilize opposition to it.

Race-based affirmative action in university admissions is likely to be with us for many years to come. O'Connor's opinion in *Grutter* ends by voicing an expectation that affirmative action will no longer be necessary in 25 years. Whether the Court will follow through on this delayed threat to terminate affirmative action, and whether such policies survive long enough to make execution of that threat necessary, will depend on changes in social attitudes and Court composition that are difficult to predict.

III. Current Issues: What's on the Docket?

The members of the Rehnquist Court circa 2004: back row, Associate Justices Ruth Bader Ginsburg, David H. Souter, Clarence Thomas, and Stephen G. Breyer; front row, Associate Justices Antonin Scalia and John Paul Stevens, the late Chief Justice William H. Rehnquist, and Associate Justices Sandra Day O'Connor and Anthony Kennedy.

Editors' Introduction

Understanding where a case fits within the larger framework of constitutional jurisprudence is often essential to grasping its underlying significance. Frequently, a verdict is not simply an end in itself, but rather one in a series of decisions that, taken together, seek to resolve a conflict between competing constitutional imperatives—by either striking a balance or tilting the scales in a particular direction. While some of these juridical tugs of war have been going on since the dawn of the Republic, others have a more modern genesis.

The selections in this chapter focus on particular cases that illuminate the larger conflicts that have perplexed the Court in recent years and are likely to trouble it in the decades ahead. Since the nation's earliest days, legal minds have grappled with the degree to which church and state should be kept separate. In "Controversy Continues over the Pledge of Allegiance," the first entry in this chapter, Martha M. McCarthy discusses a recent case that evokes this struggle—*Elk Grove Unified School District v. Newdow*. Michael Newdow, an avowed atheist and the father of an Oak Grove student, objected to the use of the phrase "under God" in the Pledge of Allegiance, arguing that it violates the Constitution's Establishment Clause, which bars the government from establishing a state church, by explicitly endorsing a monotheistic worldview. As McCarthy explains, the Supreme Court's ruling in the case failed to provide much resolution.

One of the more perceptible shifts in American society over the last generation has been the increasing tolerance and acceptance of homosexuals; this phenomena has in turn offended the sensibilities of many conservative and traditional religious groups. This evolving conflict has been taken up by the Supreme Court, which recently overturned a prohibitive Texas sodomy law in *Lawrence v. Texas*. The *Lawrence* case is the subject of "Gay Rights Groups Hail Landmark Decision in Texas Case," by Chuck Lindell. As Lindell notes, adherents on both sides of the debate see the *Lawrence* decision as a prelude to a greater battle in the years to come over same-sex marriage.

In the subsequent entry, James M. O'Neill details a recent affirmative action ruling that upheld a University of Michigan policy that considered minority status favorably in making admissions decisions. Affirmative action remains a contentious subject in American society today: Some perceive it as building on the promise of *Brown*, while others regard it as reverse discrimination. The Court has thus far developed a fairly nuanced stance on the matter, stating that it is acceptable to use race as a factor—though not as a determining factor—in admissions while expressing profound reservations about the use of quotas.

The war on terror has raised a number of legal dilemmas, chief among them are questions about how to achieve security without sacrificing on individual liberties, and the extent of the president's powers in waging this new conflict. In "Taking It to the Trenches," Phillip Carter discusses three recent verdicts—*Hamdi v. Rumsfeld*, *Rasul v. Bush*, and *Padilla v. Rumsfeld*—that address these and other issues relating to the war.

Few debates in American society and jurisprudence are as bitter and intractable as that over abortion. Robin Toner and Adam Liptak examine the Court's current take on the subject and anticipate how it may change in the years ahead. They note that though pro-life groups remain intent on overturning *Roe*, the prospects for its reversal are somewhat cloudy; consequently, *Roe* opponents have, for the time being, taken a more incremental approach, working to restrict rather than abolish abortion rights.

Not surprisingly, the technology boom of recent years has brought with it its own unique set of problematic legal issues. Chief among them is the controversy over Internet file sharing, whereby consumers download music through particular Web sites at little or no cost; the practice has angered record companies and recording artists who see it as a violation of their intellectual property rights. The Supreme Court concurred, as Linda Greenhouse and Lorne Manly note in "Justices Reinstate Suits on Internet File Sharing."

Controversy Continues over the Pledge of Allegiance

By Martha M. McCarthy
EDUCATIONAL HORIZONS, Winter 2005

> If there is any fixed star in our constitutional constellation, it is that no official . . . can prescribe what shall be orthodox in politics, nationalism, religion, or other matters of opinion or force citizens to confess by word or act their faith therein.
> —*West Virginia State Board of Education v. Barnette*[1]

Saying the Pledge of Allegiance in public schools has generated controversy for more than 60 years. On Flag Day, June 14, 2004, the U.S. Supreme Court sidestepped an opportunity to clarify the constitutionality of public school students reciting "under God" in the Pledge of Allegiance.[2] But this issue is not going away. Following the Supreme Court's decision, several families voiced interest in mounting new challenges to the religious reference in the Pledge. This article analyzes the 2004 decision and explores how the Supreme Court might rule in a subsequent case regarding the constitutionality of saying the current Pledge in public schools.

Context

The initial version of the "Pledge to the Flag" was written by Francis Bellamy for schoolchildren to say during activities celebrating the 400th anniversary of the discovery of America. It read: "I pledge allegiance to my Flag and to the republic for which it stands, one Nation, indivisible, with Liberty and Justice for all."[3] Subsequently, the wording was altered to clarify *which* flag by adding "of the United States" and later "of America" after "flag." In 1942, the Pledge became part of the United States Code, along with a detailed set of regulations pertaining to displaying the flag, and its official title became "The Pledge of Allegiance" in 1945.[4]

The final change in the Pledge occurred on Flag Day 1954, when the phrase "under God" was added after "one nation." The amendment's sponsors indicated that the purpose of the addition to the Pledge was to affirm the United States as a religious nation, distinguished from countries practicing atheistic communism.[5] In signing the law, President Eisenhower said: "In this way we shall constantly strengthen those spiritual weapons which forever will be our country's most powerful resource in peace and war."[6]

Even though it was established more than six decades ago that public school students cannot be required to recite the Pledge of Allegiance if such an observance conflicts with their religious or

> *Thirty-five states have laws or policies requiring the Pledge to be said in public schools.*

philosophical beliefs,[7] there have been some recent claims that students have been coerced to participate in the Pledge. For example, a Pennsylvania law was challenged because it required parental notification if public or private school students opted out of recitation of either the Pledge or the National Anthem at the beginning of the school day. The Third Circuit Court of Appeals held that the parental notification requirement had a coercive effect on student expression in violation of the First Amendment.[8] The court also found that application of the law to nonreligious private schools interfered with the schools' rights to promote particular values and philosophies. In another recent case, the Eleventh Circuit ruled that neither a principal nor a teacher was entitled to summary judgment on qualified-immunity grounds for disciplining a student who refused to participate in the Pledge, absent disruptive behavior.[9] Of course, students can be disciplined if they create a classroom disturbance during the Pledge.

The most volatile current controversy focuses on requiring recitation of the Pledge *at all* in public schools. In 1992, the Seventh Circuit rejected an Establishment Clause challenge to an Illinois law requiring daily recitation of the Pledge in public schools, concluding that addition of the words "under God" did not change this patriotic observance into a religious exercise that advances religion.[10] The court held that as long as students can decline to participate in the Pledge, the state law presents no infringement on individuals' constitutional right to refrain from such an observance. Regarding the Establishment Clause claim, the appeals court reasoned that the "ceremonial deism" in the Pledge "has lost through rote repetition any significant religious content," so the contested phrase does not represent religious coercion.[11]

Thirty-five states have laws or policies requiring the Pledge to be said in public schools.[12] In 2003 a Virginia federal district court reached the same conclusion as the Seventh Circuit in rejecting a constitutional challenge to a Virginia law requiring the recitation of the Pledge in public schools. Even though the school district at issue in that case considered recitation of the Pledge in a citizenship reward program, the court was not persuaded that students were psychologically coerced into accepting religious views sponsored by the school or that they were being punished by having to listen to classmates recite the Pledge.[13]

Elk Grove Unified School District v. Newdow

The Ninth Circuit attracted national attention in 2002 when it rejected the "ceremonial deism" justification and declared that saying the Pledge in public schools abridges the Establishment Clause by endorsing a belief in monotheism.[14] The Pledge recitation was challenged by Michael Newdow, an atheist, whose daughter was subjected to the daily exercise. The appellate panel emphasized that the words "under God" had been inserted in the Pledge to promote religion rather than to advance the legitimate secular goal of encouraging patriotism. The court reasoned that the Pledge in its current form "sends a message to nonbelievers that they are outsiders," which is "more acute" for schoolchildren because of the "indirect social pressure which permeates the classroom."[15] In an amended, narrower ruling, the Ninth Circuit did not invalidate the federal law adding "under God" to the Pledge, but reiterated that the school district's policy requiring recitation of the Pledge in public schools violates the Establishment Clause because of the coercive effect on students.[16]

On appeal to the U.S. Supreme Court, there were two issues: did Newdow have standing to challenge recitation of the Pledge in public schools since he was not the custodial parent, and if so, did such recitation abridge the Establishment Clause because of its religious reference? The Supreme Court's reversal of the Ninth Circuit's decision without addressing the constitutional claim was a great disappointment to both sides. The Court was unanimous in reversing the Ninth Circuit,[17] but only five justices based their conclusion on the standing issue. Writing for the majority, Justice Stevens reasoned that Newdow lacked standing to challenge his daughter's participation in the Pledge because California law deprived him of the right to bring suit as "next friend" on behalf of his daughter. Recognizing that Newdow retained the right to instruct his daughter regarding his religious views, the Court held that this right did not extend to curtailing his daughter's exposure to religious beliefs endorsed by her mother. The majority reasoned that the California family court had deprived Newdow of such "next friend" status, noting that Newdow's interests and those of his daughter "are not parallel and, indeed, are potentially in conflict."[18]

Three justices concurred with the result of reversing the Ninth Circuit's decision, but wrote separately to voice their disagreement with the majority's handling of the standing issue. These justices would have recognized Newdow's standing and reversed the Ninth Circuit's ruling based on their conclusion that the phrase "under God" does not implicate the Establishment Clause of the First Amendment.[19]

Future Challenges

If the Supreme Court does agree to address the constitutionality of the religious reference in the Pledge, it probably will agree with the *Newdow* concurring justices who asserted that the brief mention of God does not endorse any religion or turn a patriotic observance like the Pledge into a prayer or an endorsement of any religion.[20] The Court likely will rely heavily on the conclusion that the Pledge represents ceremonial deism, which does not make religious demands or call for individuals to do anything. Even Justice Souter, who has been at the separationist end of the continuum compared to the other sitting justices, has commented that the controversial phrase is "beneath the constitutional radar because the words had become so diluted and tepid and far removed from a compulsory prayer."[21]

However, there is some sentiment that the constitutionally correct response would be to prohibit saying the Pledge in public schools until the religious reference is removed. Indeed, Justice Thomas, although supporting the current wording in the Pledge, actually built a case that the Court should strike down saying "under God" in the Pledge to remain consistent with constitutional precedents. Thomas found greater potential for religious coercion in reciting the Pledge than in having clergy lead graduation prayers, which the Supreme Court invalidated in 1992.[22] To be consistent with long-standing precedent that individuals cannot be required to declare a belief, Thomas noted that it is "difficult to see how this [saying the Pledge] does not entail an affirmation that God exists."[23]

> *A constitutional violation accepted for years does not eliminate the impairment.*

The legislative history is clear that the amendment to insert "under God" in the Pledge was religiously motivated, and other religiously motivated legislative acts have been invalidated. For example, in 1985 the Supreme Court struck down an amended silent prayer law in Alabama because the amendment had the religious purpose of encouraging students to pray.[24] Also, the massive protests mounted by religious groups against the Ninth Circuit's decision belie the assertion that "under God" has no current religious significance. Indeed, shortly after the initial Ninth Circuit ruling, more than 100 Republican members of Congress gathered on the steps of the Capitol to recite the Pledge and to display their disdain for the appellate ruling. Both houses of Congress subsequently adopted resolutions denouncing the ruling, so it is difficult to argue that the contested phrase has no current religious meaning.[25]

Critics of the religious reference in the Pledge contend that simply because a sectarian term is frequently used over time does not make it less religious. In essence, a constitutional violation accepted for years does not eliminate the impairment. If it did, the recitation of various religious messages could be justified in public schools as long as they were regularly repeated over time. One commentator has noted that the ceremonial-deism justification can insulate from Establishment Clause scrutiny "long-standing public practices that invoke a nonspecific deity for secular purposes."[26] Newdow argued, and the Ninth Circuit agreed, that for schoolchildren who are saying "under God" *every day*, such recitation can influence their religious beliefs or at least their perception of what our government is telling them is the *correct* belief.[27]

Although the Bill of Rights was designed to remove certain subjects from the political process, the status of the Pledge is likely to remain engulfed in political controversy. Given the strong emotions involved, the Supreme Court may try to avoid this issue as long as possible. In the unlikely event that the Supreme Court should conclude that the Pledge cannot be said in public schools without eliminating "under God," the political response would be volatile and quite divisive. Instead of Congress simply returning the Pledge to its pre-1954 version, there would be political pressure to amend the Constitution to authorize saying the Pledge with "under God."[28] And given the widespread negative reaction to the Ninth Circuit's decision striking down recitation of this phrase in public schools, such a proposed amendment might very well be adopted.

Even if there is no constitutional amendment to authorize the Pledge's religious reference, widespread defiance to a change in its current wording would be assured, perhaps even greater than the noncompliance that arose when court rulings barred daily prayer and Bible reading from public education in the early 1960s.[29] In short, regardless of what the Supreme Court says about the constitutionality of schoolchildren reciting the Pledge with "under God," the current version is likely to be said in public schools across our nation for a long, long time.

Notes

1. *West Virginia State Bd. of Educ. v. Barnette*, 319 U.S. 624, 642 (1943).
2. *Elk Grove Unified Sch. Dist. v. Newdow*, 124 S.Ct. 2301 (2004).
3. This version first appeared in a Boston-based magazine for children, *The Youth's Companion*. See "Pledge of Allegiance & God," available at *About Agnosticism/Atheism*, <http://atheism.about.com/libraryFAQs/cs/blsm_gov_pledge.htm>.
4. 4 U.S.C. § 4 (2004).
5. See *H.R. Rep. No. 83-1693*, at 1–2 (1954), reprinted in 1954 U.S.C.C.A.N. 2339; Steven Epstein, "Rethinking the Constitutionality of Ceremonial Deism," *Columbia Law Review* 96 (1996): 2118–21.
6. See "Pledge of Allegiance & God."
7. See *West Virginia State Bd. of Educ. v. Barnette*, 319 U.S. 624 (1943).
8. *Circle Sch. v. Phillips*, 270 F.Supp. 2d 616 (E.D. Penn. 2003), *aff'd*, 381 F.3d 172 (3d Cir. 2004).
9. *Holloman v. Allred*, 370 F.3d 1252 (11th Cir. 2004). The student also alleged that the teacher encouraged students to pray during the moment of silence in

violation of the Establishment Clause, and this claim was allowed to proceed against the teacher and the school board.

10. *Sherman v. Cmty. Consol. Sch. Dist. 21 of Wheeling Township*, 980 F.2d 437, 447–48 (7th Cir. 1992).

11. Id. at 447 (citing *Lynch v. Donnelly*, 465 U.S. 668, 716 [1984]).

12. Jennifer Piscatelli, "Pledge of Allegiance," *StateNotes: Character/Citizenship Education*. Denver: Education Commission of the States (August 2003).

13. *Myers v. Loudoun County Sch. Bd.*, 251 F.Supp. 2d 1262, 1268–72 (E.D. Va. 2003).

14. *Newdow v. U.S. Congress*, 292 F.3d 597, 607–11 (9th Cir. 2002), *judgment stayed*, No. 00-16423, 2002 U.S. App. LEXIS 12826 (9th Cir. June 27, 2002), *opinion amended and superseded by* 328 F.3d 466 (2003), *rev'd sub nom. Elk Grove Unified Sch. Dist. v. Newdow*, 124 S.Ct. 2301 (2004).

15. *Newdow*, 292 F.3d at 608–09 (citing *Lee v. Weisman*, 505 U.S. 577, 592–93 [1992]).

16. *Newdow*, 328 F.3d 466, 468 (9th Cir. 2003). The panel voted unanimously to deny petitions for rehearing, and the request for reconsideration by the full court did not receive a majority of votes from the 24 active Ninth Circuit judges.

17. *Elk Grove Unified Sch. Dist. v. Newdow*, 124 S.Ct. 2301 (2004). Justice Scalia excused himself from the deliberations and decision because he had criticized the Ninth Circuit's decision.

18. Id., 124 S.Ct. at 2311.

19. Id. at 2312 (Rehnquist, C.J., concurring in judgment); id. at 2321 (O'Connor, J., concurring in judgment); id. at 2327 (Thomas, J., concurring in judgment).

20. Id.

21. Oral arguments before the U.S. Supreme Court in *Elk Grove Unified Sch. Dist. v. Newdow*, No. 02-1624 (March 24, 2004).

22. *Elk Grove*, 124 S.Ct. at 2328 (Thomas, J., concurring in judgment). See *Lee v. Weisman*, 505 U.S. 577 (1992).

23. Id., 124 S.Ct. at 2329.

24. *Wallace v. Jaffree*, 472 U.S. 38 (1985).

25. S. Res. 292, 107th Cong., 148 *Cong. Rec.* S6105 (daily ed. June 27, 2002); H. Res. 459, 107th Cong., 148 *Cong. Rec.* H4125 (daily ed. June 28, 2002).

26. Charles G. Warren, "No Need to Stand on Ceremony: The Corruptive Influence of Ceremonial Deism and the Need for a Separationist Reconfiguration of the Supreme Court's Establishment Clause Jurisprudence," *Mercer Law Review* 54 (2003): 1686.

27. See Michael Newdow, "Pledging Allegiance to My Daughter," *New York Times*, op-ed contributor (June 21, 2004).

28. Such proposals to amend the Constitution to authorize prayers in public schools have been offered on a regular basis since the Supreme Court barred daily prayer and Bible reading from public schools in the early 1960s.

29. See *Abington Township v. Schempp*, 374 U.S. 203 (1963).

Gay Rights Groups Hail Landmark Decision in Texas Case

By Chuck Lindell
Austin American-Statesman, June 27, 2003

Handing gay Americans a watershed legal victory, the U.S. Supreme Court struck down Texas' "deviant sexual intercourse" law on Thursday in a broad ruling that bans all states from regulating private sexual expression between consenting adults.

The 6–3 decision also scrapped anti-sodomy laws in 12 other states regardless of whether the laws applied only to homosexuals or to homosexuals and heterosexuals.

"The Texas statute furthers no legitimate state interest which can justify its intrusion into the personal and private life of the individual," said Justice Anthony Kennedy, who wrote the majority opinion. "(Gay Americans) are entitled to respect for their private lives. The state cannot demean their existence or control their destiny by making their private sexual conduct a crime."

The decision gave gay rights groups all they had hoped for, including a reversal of *Bowers v. Hardwick*, a 1986 Supreme Court decision that upheld Georgia's anti-sodomy law based on the belief that "homosexual sodomy is immoral and unacceptable."

"This is a giant leap forward to a day where we are no longer branded as criminals," said Ruth Harlow, lead attorney in the case and legal director for Lambda Legal, a civil rights group for gays and lesbians. "This is a wonderful day for gay Americans because the Court has gone from what it referred to as a demeaning attitude to a very respectful one.

"The ruling is magnificent. It's clear. It's very powerful," she said.

Religious and politically conservative groups, which supplied the bulk of the Supreme Court briefs in favor of sodomy laws, reacted with disappointment and disgust.

"Shame on them," said Cathie Adams, president of Texas Eagle Forum. "What has made America strong has been our traditions—the traditional family included. When the Supreme Court recognizes an entity that is unnatural, and certainly an unhealthy lifestyle, then they are undermining the cornerstone of our culture."

Mark Wilson/Getty Images

Associate Justice Antonin Scalia wrote a scathing dissent in the Lawrence v. Texas *case.*

Justice Antonin Scalia, writing a dissent that included Chief Justice William Rehnquist and Justice Clarence Thomas, feared the Texas decision would have far-reaching impact on laws banning same-sex marriages, as well as other morality-based statutes on bigamy, adultery, prostitution, bestiality, and obscenity.

"Every single one of these laws is called into question by today's decision," Scalia wrote.

The case, *Lawrence v. Texas*, began in September 1998 with a false report to the Harris County sheriff's department. Officers, told an armed man was "going crazy" inside an apartment, walked through an unlocked door to find John Lawrence and Tyron Garner having sex. The men were arrested for violating the Texas sodomy law, spent the night in jail, and eventually pleaded no contest, each paying $341 in fines and court costs.

Lawrence and Garner appealed their convictions, saying Texas' sodomy law singled out homosexuals and violated their privacy rights. A Texas court of appeals disagreed, setting up this year's eagerly awaited Supreme Court ruling.

The case was argued March 26. During arguments, it became apparent that state sodomy laws—Texas, Oklahoma, Kansas, and Missouri outlawed only same-sex contact, while nine states banned all oral and anal sex—were in trouble.

Harris County District Attorney Charles Rosenthal, arguing his first Supreme Court case, was challenged repeatedly by Justices Ruth Bader Ginsburg and Stephen Breyer to justify the Texas law. After Rosenthal appeared ill-prepared and surprised by several questions, the justices resorted to sparring with one another as he stood watching.

Thursday's ruling adds private sexual expression to the list of constitutional protections under the Fourteenth Amendment's liberty, or privacy, provisions—which to date had applied to decisions involving marriage, having children, raising children, education, and contraception.

"This Court's obligation is to define the liberty of all, not to mandate its own moral code," Kennedy's opinion stated.

Gay rights groups have long complained that sodomy laws, though rarely enforced, have been used to justify discrimination against gays and lesbians in employment and in child-custody and adoption decisions.

Kennedy agreed. "The stigma the Texas criminal statute imposes, moreover, is not trivial," said the majority decision, which was joined by Justices John Paul Stevens, David Souter, Ginsburg, and Breyer.

Mark Wilson/Getty Images

"We never chose to be public figures or to take on this fight, but we also never thought we could be arrested this way," Lawrence told reporters via conference call from Houston. "We share this victory with gay people in all 50 states who are better off today than they were yesterday, thanks to this ruling."

Associate Justice Anthony Kennedy wrote the majority opinion in Lawrence v. Texas.

Justice Sandra Day O'Connor, who voted to uphold the Georgia law in 1986, concurred with the majority, but her narrower opinion focused on the Texas law's unequal treatment of homosexuals, who were subject to prosecution for acts that were legal for heterosexuals.

"A law branding one class of persons as criminal based solely on the state's moral disapproval . . . runs contrary to the values of the Constitution," she wrote.

Only two other justices who ruled on the Georgia case remain on the Court. Rehnquist voted in 1986 to uphold that law; Stevens dissented.

Scalia's dissent Thursday was sharply critical of the majority opinion, declaring that countless laws and judicial decisions have relied on "a governing majority's belief that certain sexual behavior is immoral and unacceptable."

Scalia criticized a law-profession culture that he said has endorsed the gay rights agenda and influenced the Court. "It is clear from this that the Court has taken sides in the culture war, departing from its role of . . . neutral observer," he wrote.

Thomas, who filed a one-page note expanding on Scalia's dissent, derided the Texas sodomy law as silly.

"If I were a member of the Texas Legislature, I would vote to repeal it," Thomas wrote. "Punishing someone for expressing his sexual preference . . . does not appear to be a worthy way to expend valuable law enforcement resources."

However, Thomas noted, his duty is to the Constitution, and the Constitution contains no general right of privacy, he said.

Gay rights groups hope Thursday's decision opens the door to additional advances, such as same-sex marriages.

"It certainly puts us on much stronger footing to attack other forms of discrimination," Harlow said. "They certainly gave a very powerful statement that gay people are entitled to equal liberty, but it will be a future day that decides the question of discrimination in marriage."

Excerpts from Majority and Minority Opinions

Justice Anthony Kennedy's opinion for the majority:

Liberty protects the person from unwarranted government intrusions into a dwelling or other private places. In our tradition the State is not omnipresent in the home. And there are other spheres of our lives and existence, outside the home, where the State should not be a dominant presence. Freedom extends beyond spatial bounds. Liberty presumes an autonomy of self that includes freedom of thought, belief, expression, and certain intimate conduct. The instant case involves liberty of the person both in its spatial and more transcendent dimensions.

The question before the Court is the validity of a Texas statute making it a crime for two persons of the same sex to engage in certain intimate sexual conduct. . . .

The case does involve two adults who, with full and mutual consent from each other, engaged in sexual practices common to a homosexual lifestyle. The petitioners are entitled to respect for their private lives. The State cannot demean their existence or control their destiny by making their private sexual conduct a crime.

In his dissent, Justice Antonin Scalia wrote:

Today's opinion is the product of a Court, which is the product of a law-profession culture, that has largely signed on to the so-called homosexual agenda, by which I mean the agenda promoted by some homosexual activists directed at eliminating the moral opprobrium that has traditionally attached to homosexual conduct.

One of the most revealing statements in today's opinion is the Court's grim warning that the criminalization of homosexual conduct is "an invitation to subject homosexual persons to discrimination both in the public and in the private spheres." It is clear from this that the Court has taken sides in the culture war, departing from its role of assuring, as neutral observer, that the democratic rules of engagement are observed. Many Americans do not want persons who openly engage in homosexual conduct as partners in their business, as scoutmasters for their children, as teachers in their children's schools, or as boarders in their home. They view this as protecting themselves and their families from a lifestyle that they believe to be immoral and destructive.

Court Upholds Use of Race in Admissions

By James M. O'Neill
The Philadelphia Inquirer, June 24, 2003

A split Supreme Court yesterday gave America's colleges a green light to continue considering race in admissions. But it narrowed the scope of how affirmative action may be carried out, knocking down a numerical system at the University of Michigan that gives minority applicants 20 extra points.

That new restriction will not matter to most colleges, since few use a point system the way Michigan has.

The landmark decisions in a closely watched pair of cases give colleges greater legal foundation for practicing affirmative action, expanding on a fractured 1978 Supreme Court opinion. But law experts said the action was not likely to have influence beyond higher education.

The rulings, in which justices cited the social benefits of student diversity, had academics rejoicing. "This is a resounding affirmation that will be heard across the land," University of Michigan president Mary Sue Coleman said.

University of Pennsylvania president Judith Rodin said she was "delighted the Supreme Court recognized the importance of diversity on campus."

The rulings centered on two challenges to Michigan admissions practices. *Grutter v. Bollinger* looked at whether the university's law school acted constitutionally when considering race as one among many factors in its admissions decisions. *Gratz v. Bollinger* involved Michigan's undergraduate admissions process, which uses a 150-point system to weigh candidates and gives 20 points to students who are minorities.

In a 6–3 decision written by Chief Justice William H. Rehnquist, the Court determined that the undergraduate point system did not pass legal muster, because the consideration of race was not narrowly tailored and therefore race could end up being decisive in admissions decisions.

But in a 5–4 decision written by Justice Sandra Day O'Connor, the Court upheld the law school's practice of considering race in a more general way.

The Court had to determine whether there was a compelling state interest in allowing an exception to the 14th Amendment, which requires equal treatment under the law, as well as Title VI of the 1964 Civil Rights Act, which prohibits institutions that receive federal money from discriminating based on race.

> *[The] decisions struck an ideological blow to the Bush administration.*

In 1978, Justice Lewis Powell, in the fractured decision in *Regents of the University of California v. Bakke*, found there was a compelling state interest in practicing affirmative action in college admissions, because of the diversity that results in the student body and the educational benefits that accrue.

For 25 years, colleges across the country took Powell's decision as the established thinking of the Court, but opponents of affirmative action did not.

Yesterday's action gave colleges a broader legal foundation, because five justices agreed with Powell's lonely premise that a diverse student body is in the state's interest.

And while Powell argued the educational benefit to diversity, O'Connor went further yesterday, arguing broader benefits to society.

It was clear that two legal briefs, filed by retired military generals and by some corporations, played a significant role in O'Connor's majority opinion.

"Numerous studies show that student-body diversity promotes learning outcomes, and 'better prepares students for an increasingly diverse workforce and society, and better prepares them as professionals,'" she wrote.

"These benefits are not theoretical but real, as major American businesses have made clear that the skills needed in today's increasingly global marketplace can only be developed through exposure to widely diverse people, cultures, ideas and viewpoints," O'Connor said.

She quoted the brief filed by the generals, who said they needed affirmative action at their service academies to ensure a qualified, racially diverse officer corps, which was essential "to the military's ability to fulfill its principal mission to provide national security."

Some legal experts said that the military brief was a masterful stroke by Michigan's lawyers, and that its impact was heightened because of post–Sept. 11 concern over terrorism and the increased importance of the military in addressing it.

Yesterday's decisions struck an ideological blow to the Bush administration, which had argued that, while diversity was a laudable goal, a college needed to exhaust every other avenue to achieve that goal before resorting to race-conscious admissions.

President Bush, in a statement, said the Court "has made clear that colleges and universities must engage in a serious, good-faith consideration of workable race-neutral alternatives."

"We're very disappointed the Court missed an opportunity to answer a question that has been unresolved for 25 years," said David Gersten, executive director of the Center for Equal Opportunity, a conservative think tank and one of several groups opposed to affirmative action. "I expect it to remain very cloudy about how race can be used. The Court really dropped the ball."

And while many hoped the new opinions would clarify the Court's thinking, Justice Antonin Scalia argued that the split in the cases seemed "perversely designed to prolong the controversy and the litigation."

While most competitive colleges already practice affirmative action in the broad manner upheld in *Grutter*, the ruling could have a larger impact in Texas and other Southern states, where the U.S. Court of Appeals for the Fifth Circuit ruled in 1996 that student diversity did not pose a compelling enough state interest to allow affirmative action.

That decision, in *Hopwood v. Texas*—a case the Supreme Court declined to take up—forced the University of Texas and other schools to drop affirmative action. With the new Supreme Court decision undermining the lower court's argument, Texas and other schools in the South that had been bound by *Hopwood* may pursue affirmative action again if they wish.

The *Grutter* ruling, however, would not affect affirmative-action bans that California and Washington voters approved in the 1990s. That is because the ruling allows, but does not require, affirmative action in admissions.

And legal experts said O'Connor chose her words carefully enough to make clear she does not want lower courts to draw implications for the legality of affirmative action beyond higher education.

Legal and academic experts were unsure yesterday what effect the decisions would have on other programs that have come under legal attack recently, such as minority-only scholarships, internships, and summer orientation programs.

Some suggest that dissenting opinions, specifically Scalia's, plant the seeds for a new kind of attack on affirmative action—one that challenges the sincerity of institutions that use it.

"Tempting targets," he suggested, "will be those universities that talk the talk of multiculturalism and racial diversity in the courts but walk the walk of tribalism and racial segregation on their campuses—through minority-only student organizations, separate minority housing opportunities, separate minority student centers, even separate minority-only graduation ceremonies."

Associate Justice Clarence Thomas wrote the dissenting opinion in Grutter v. Bollinger.

Justice Clarence Thomas, the Court's only black member, quoted in his dissent in *Grutter* an 1865 speech that Frederick Douglass gave to abolitionists, saying Douglass' message was "lost on today's [Court] majority." He quoted Douglass as saying, "What I ask for the negro is not benevolence, not pity, not sympathy, but simply justice. The American people have always been anxious to know what they shall do with us. . . . I have had but one answer from the beginning. Do nothing with us! Your doing with us has already played the mischief."

Thomas wrote, "Like Douglass, I believe blacks can achieve in every avenue of American life without the meddling of university administrators." He called the law school admissions policy "elitist."

"He flat out makes the argument that affirmative action is bad for black people," said Robert Reinstein, a constitutional law expert and dean of Temple University's law school. "Not just that it stigmatizes them, which he has argued before, but that it's holding them back, that it's a bad idea."

In recent years, the Supreme Court has approved only affirmative-action programs that are designed to address specific past discrimination and that had a clear time limit.

During April oral arguments in the Michigan cases, O'Connor expressed serious concern about the open-ended nature of affirmative action. She addressed that concern in her decision.

In the 25 years since Powell approved the use of race to further an interest in student-body diversity, she wrote, "the number of minority applicants with high grades and test scores has indeed increased. We expect that 25 years from now, the use of racial preferences will no longer be necessary to further the interests approved today."

Taking It to the Trenches

BY PHILLIP CARTER
SLATE, JUNE 29, 2004

Lawyers and scholars will likely wrangle for some time over the implications of Monday's Supreme Court decisions in *Hamdi v. Rumsfeld*, *Rasul v. Bush*, and *Padilla v. Rumsfeld*. The three terrorism cases decided this week have profound implications for America's separation of constitutional powers, balance between liberty and security, and commitment to the rule of law.

But for the U.S. military and intelligence personnel now fighting the war on terrorism, these decisions also have important and more immediate repercussions. The Court's omissions are almost as vital as what it did. The decisions did not substantially impinge on the president's actual powers to wage war or on the military's right to take prisoners during war. But the Court did speak to the kinds of procedures necessary to lawfully hold combatants. By levying procedural due-process requirements on the government in *Hamdi*, the Court likely created new requirements for soldiers in the field when they detain prisoners. It also may have fundamentally changed the way our nation gathers intelligence in the war on terrorism. And by opening the federal courts to the Guantanamo detainees, the high court may have altered the nature of U.S. detention operations—and created a new means of resistance for detainees in U.S. captivity.

The Constitution divides war powers between the executive and legislative branches—Congress has the power to declare war, raise armies, regulate the military, and levy taxes to pay for these purposes; the president serves as "Commander in Chief of the Army and Navy of the United States." For most of the nation's history, courts have been reluctant to step in between those bodies on questions of national security. Only in rare circumstances has the Supreme Court overruled an act of the president in wartime—such as President Truman's unconstitutional steel-mill seizures during the Korean War—in cases where the president has acted against the law or without congressional authorization. The war powers rest with the two "political branches" because they're elected and theoretically accountable to the people. A recent example of this doctrine in action is the 1st Circuit Court of Appeals' decision to not enjoin President Bush from invading Iraq in March 2003.

The president's power to wage war was not itself at issue in any of this week's Supreme Court decisions. But the power to detain prisoners is a subset of those powers—and ultimately of the larger power to kill in wartime—so it was something the Court could have touched upon if it chose to. In its *Hamdi* decision (the most important of the three), the Supreme Court all but affirmed the use of force by the president since Sept. 11, saying that Congress' resolution from Sept. 18, 2001, provided both the explicit power to wage war and the "explicit congressional authorization for the detention of individuals in the narrow category we describe." At the end of the day, the White House emerged with its broad war powers intact, including the power to take prisoners on the battlefield, so long as it acts with the authorization of Congress.

> *Only in rare circumstances has the Supreme Court overruled an act of the president in wartime.*

Within that broad scope of war power, however, the Court did carve out a few important exceptions that will impact the way America fights terrorism. The most significant of these comes from the case of Yaser Hamdi, a young U.S. citizen captured on the Afghanistan battlefield in late 2001. The Court held that "a citizen-detainee seeking to challenge his classification as an enemy combatant must receive notice of the factual basis for his classification, and a fair opportunity to rebut the Government's factual assertions before a neutral decisionmaker," importing a body of law known as "procedural due process" to settle cases where a U.S. citizen charges he's wrongfully detained as an enemy combatant. The Court declined to concretely define this process but said it might look something like the Army's procedures to sort combatants on the battlefield pursuant to Article 5 of the 3rd Geneva Conventions governing prisoners of war. In other words, the government must offer more due process than what Hamdi has received so far, but substantially less than he would get as a criminal defendant in a civilian court.

One operational implication from this ruling is that soldiers in the field will need to become substantially more diligent about their actions at the "point of capture" than they have been. When military personnel capture someone now, they are supposed to fill out a short form with tiny boxes for "date and time of capture" and "description of weapons, special equipment, documents." Additionally, prisoners are generally interrogated when captured, in the hopes that they will provide valuable battlefield intelligence. It's not clear whether these measures will create enough of an evidentiary record to satisfy the kind of process envisioned by Justice Sandra Day O'Connor in the *Hamdi* decision. If they don't, the military will need to develop some new mechanism for gathering evidence, such as the creation of special Judge Advocate General teams whose sole job is to interview soldiers after they capture detainees, in order to create an evidentiary record for future detention hearings.

Justice O'Connor's opinion in *Hamdi* also may have imposed a substantial limit on the reasons a detainee can be held, in addition to the requirements for due process. The Bush administration vociferously argued that it needed the power to detain combatants to gather intelligence about future terrorist operations—indeed, that detainee interrogations were one of its best tools in this shadowy war on terrorism. The Court tackled that argument obliquely: "The purpose of detention is to prevent captured individuals from returning to the field of battle and taking up arms once again," O'Connor wrote, adding later that "Hamdi contends that the [Congressional authorization of force] does not authorize indefinite or perpetual detention. Certainly, we agree that indefinite detention for the purpose of interrogation is not authorized." The operational implication from this language isn't altogether clear, because the Court didn't specify just how much detention it would allow for the purpose of interrogation. One indicator of how the Court might see this issue comes from Justice Anthony Kennedy's concurrence in *Rasul*, where he wrote that "as the period of detention stretches from months to years, the case for continued detention to meet military exigencies becomes weaker." Still, it's not clear whether the courts will find that all protections afforded in *Hamdi* will automatically be offered to the Guantanamo detainees.

This point matters a great deal because the Bush administration has used the interrogation rationale to justify a litany of other measures, including the denial of access to counsel. In a declaration filed early in the *Hamdi* case, Navy Cmdr. Donald Woolfolk made the following assertion regarding lawyers and their effect on the intelligence process:

> [T]he need to maintain the tightly controlled environment, which has been established to create dependency and trust by the detainee with his interrogator, is of paramount importance. Disruption of the interrogation environment, such as through access to a detainee by counsel, undermines this interrogation dynamic. . . . Most importantly, the disruption occasioned by the insertion of outside counsel will sever the intelligence gathering value of this detainee.

The Court's *Hamdi* decision implies that it will not accept this rationale as a reason for indefinite detention. It stands to reason that the Court will also not accept the interrogation justification as a reason for denial of the 6th Amendment right to counsel for any U.S. citizen held as a combatant. If the Pentagon's predictions are true, this will substantially impede efforts to gather intelligence from detainees captured in the war on terrorism. Interrogation operations form the cornerstone of the U.S. "human intelligence" collection strategy because it's so hard to penetrate terrorist cells in order to gather actionable human intelligence the cloak-and-dagger way. If the Pentagon is right, this may cause substantial and irreparable harm to the war effort. But similar arguments have been made before, most notably by police agencies before and after the Supreme Court's decision in *Miranda v. Arizona.* The sky did not fall after the Court required police agencies to warn suspects of their rights; indeed, many police today see the *Miranda* warning as a procedural formality that barely affects interrogation in practice.

The *Rasul* decision will impact the war on terrorism insofar as it grants detainees the right of access to U.S. courts to challenge their detention. The Court did not define the exact parameters of this right, so it's impossible to tell how much of an effect it will have. But if the Guantanamo detainees receive the full right to petition for a writ of habeas corpus in federal court, and that right includes access to counsel to assist with the filing of the petition, then the Court may have unwittingly opened a new front in the war on terrorism. First, this will affect interrogations, as discussed above—detainees who talk to their lawyers will be less likely to spill their guts during interrogations. Second, detainees may come see filing a habeas petition as part of their duty to resist American captivity, just as U.S. soldiers are duty-bound to resist their captors under the Code of Conduct "by all means available." In a worst-case scenario, every single Guantanamo detainee will now seek the writ of habeas corpus, along with every detainee now held by the United States in Iraq or Afghanistan. Whether this happens or not depends on the way lower courts construe the fractured opinion in *Rasul*, specifically the way it distinguishes past precedent that barred "enemy aliens" from U.S. courts.

Most significant, the *Rasul* decision pushed the Pentagon to announce today that it was moving forward with its plans for military tribunals. The language in Justice Kennedy's concurrence— "Indefinite detention without trial or other proceeding presents altogether different considerations. . . . It suggests a weaker case of military necessity and much greater alignment with the traditional function of habeas corpus"—clearly encouraged this decision. Faced with the choice between arguing against habeas corpus petitions in federal district court and prosecuting detainees in a highly deferential military setting, the Pentagon took the most obvious choice.

Over time, these operational implications may change, particularly as the Pentagon changes its policies in response to these decisions. But in the long run, the symbolic effect of these terrorism opinions may be what's most important. On Monday, the Supreme Court drew a line in the sand demarcating the outer boundaries of executive power, in what is perhaps the most quintessential of all executive powers—the power to defend the nation. Where the constitutional imperative to provide for the common defense clashes with the individual rights and liberties of persons, the Court decided that it alone shall have the final say as to how far the president may go. In doing so, the Court reaffirmed America's commitment to the rule of law at a critical time in our nation's history.

The images of shackled prisoners at Guantanamo Bay and naked prisoners at Abu Ghraib have not helped America win many friends in the world, nor have the memoranda from Bush administration lawyers arguing that such tactics are justifiable means to a worthy end. But in limiting the president's power to detain combatants, the Supreme Court may have taken the most significant step yet toward rehabilitating the commitment of the United States to the rule of law.

In New Court, *Roe* May Stand, So Foes Look to Limit Its Scope

By Robin Toner and Adam Liptak
The New York Times, July 10, 2005

In 2003, abortion opponents took a calculated gamble and pushed through the Partial Birth Abortion Ban Act, a federal law very similar to a state law ruled unconstitutional just three years before. Critics asserted they were defying the Court and doomed to fail in any legal challenge.

Strategists for the anti-abortion movement were betting that the Supreme Court would soon be different: more conservative, and more open to an array of new abortion restrictions. With the retirement of Justice Sandra Day O'Connor, part of the Court's majority for abortion rights, that gamble may soon begin to pay off.

The basic right to abortion, declared in *Roe v. Wade* in 1973, will survive regardless of who replaces Justice O'Connor, given that the current majority for *Roe* is 6 to 3, many experts agree. Chief Justice William H. Rehnquist was one of the two original dissenters from the *Roe* decision; if he retires, as has been widely speculated, President Bush would presumably replace him with a similar conservative, so that would not change the balance on *Roe*.

But a number of cases that are likely to reach the Court in the next few years, including the latest versions of the ban on the procedure that critics call partial-birth abortion, may give a new set of justices the opportunity to restrict abortion in significant ways.

In short, even without overturning *Roe*, the new Court could seriously limit the decision's reach and change the way abortions are regulated around the country, experts say. This means that Mr.Bush's nominees will be intensely scrutinized, by all sides, on their records, past rulings, and general philosophy on abortion.

In the term beginning this fall, the Court will review its first major abortion case in five years, involving a parental notification law from New Hampshire. Not far behind, perhaps, will be the 2003 "partial birth" law. On Friday, the United States Court of Appeals for the Eighth Circuit, in St. Louis, upheld a lower court's decision to strike down the law as unconstitutional, a case that could also end up before the Supreme Court. Those cases could give the Court a chance to revisit one of the most bitterly disputed areas of abortion law: whether an abortion statute must include an explicit exception to allow the procedure, if necessary, to preserve the woman's health.

Abortion opponents assert that such health exceptions give doctors who perform abortions too much discretion to circumvent restrictions by invoking the woman's health, even if it involves emotional and nonphysical issues. Essentially, they say, "health" is so broadly interpreted that it renders many laws meaningless.

The anti-abortion movement has been waiting for a new Court for a long time. For years, abortion opponents have focused on passing step-by-step abortion restrictions in state legislatures and the Congress, only to have them challenged in federal court and sometimes thrown out. Justice O'Connor, in their view, was an obstacle in the way of restrictions that had broad political and popular support, notably the "partial birth" ban. "She was an extremist on abortion," asserted James Bopp Jr., general counsel for the National Right to Life Committee.

For abortion rights advocates, it is a moment of growing peril. In their view, Justice O'Connor was perhaps the last protection against a Congress, a president, and a sizable number of state leg-

---

The anti-abortion movement has been waiting for a new Court for a long time.

---

islatures intent on chipping away at the rights established in *Roe*. "There's enormous concern," said Nancy Northup, head of the Center for Reproductive Rights.

While *Roe* may stand, some advocates and analysts assert, the right to obtain an abortion could become so restricted in parts of the country that it becomes largely meaningless. "One prospect is that *Roe* gets progressively eviscerated without being formally overruled," said Reva Siegel, a law professor at Yale.

Justice O'Connor was crucial in developing the Court's consensus on abortion over the past 15 years, including the basic legal standard used to evaluate the constitutionality of state and federal abortion laws. In *Planned Parenthood v. Casey*, the 1992 decision co-written by Justice O'Connor, the Court said states could enact restrictions on abortion, as long as those restrictions did not impose "an undue burden" on women.

The Court said that term was "shorthand for the conclusion that a state regulation has the purpose or effect of placing a substantial obstacle in the path of a woman seeking an abortion of a nonviable fetus."

For example, the Court ruled that 24-hour waiting periods and many parental notification provisions were constitutional, but a requirement that a married woman tell her husband of her intent to have an abortion was not.

But the contours of the undue burden standard are not well defined. Kathleen M. Sullivan, a law professor at Stanford, said the standard was typical of Justice O'Connor's pragmatic approach to the law. "Undue burden is 'permit, but discourage,'" said Professor Sullivan, alluding to the author Roger Rosenblatt's description for the American public's attitude toward abortion. "It tracks the polls as of 1992 and probably today." But she added that the standard was amorphous, and that short of an outright ban, it was not clear what a majority of a new Court would consider an undue burden.

Douglas W. Kmiec, a law professor at Pepperdine University, said a more conservative post-O'Connor Court could mean "a greater receptivity to regulatory choices made by the state in terms of spousal notice, in terms of clinical practice in clinics and hospitals, and in terms of outlawing the partial birth-type procedure."

The so-called partial birth ban has been, for many years, at the center of the struggle over what is, and is not, a constitutionally permissible abortion restriction. The law involves a relatively rare procedure used to terminate pregnancies in the second and third trimesters, a procedure known medically as intact dilation and extraction. Abortion opponents contend the procedure typically involves delivering the lower part of the fetus's body, collapsing the skull while it is still inside the woman's body, and then delivering a dead but largely intact fetus.

Abortion opponents have cited this practice for years as an example of how unbridled, in their view, the right to abortion has become. (Indeed, regardless of the legal outcome, this legislation has become a powerful organizing tool for the anti-abortion movement.) Surely, abortion opponents argued, the states and the federal government could outlaw the procedure. They succeeded in passing bans in dozens of states, but in 2000, in *Stenberg v. Carhart*, a 5-to-4 decision with Justice O'Connor in the majority, the Court invalidated those laws when they struck down a Nebraska ban on two grounds.

The Court held that the procedure, while rare, might be safer for some women in some circumstances; therefore, the Court said, the law must have an exception allowing its use to preserve the woman's health. The Court also held that the procedure being outlawed was so vaguely defined that it could be viewed as applying to other, more common abortion procedures—and thus amounted to an undue burden on women.

Abortion opponents were furious. In his dissent, Justice Clarence Thomas wrote, "A health exception requirement eviscerates Casey's undue burden standard and imposes unfettered abortion-on-demand. The exception entirely swallows the rule."

Within months of the ruling, after the 2000 and 2002 elections, abortion opponents found themselves with allies in control of the White House, the House, and the Senate; they decided to try again. In their new federal law, eventually passed in 2003, they tried to address the Court's objections on "vagueness" by defining the procedure in greater detail. But while they included an exception to allow the procedure if the woman's life is in danger, they did not include an exception to allow its use to preserve her health.

Abortion rights advocates in Congress said opponents were not even trying to pass constitutional muster but simply positioning themselves for a more sympathetic Court. "I understand what the other side wants to do," Senator Hillary Rodham Clinton, Democrat of New York, said at the time. "They are hoping to get somebody new on the Supreme Court and to turn the clock back completely, to overrule *Roe v. Wade*."

Douglas Johnson, legislative director for the National Right to Life Committee, acknowledged that abortion opponents were in part playing a waiting game. "We hope that by the time this ban reaches the Supreme Court, at least five justices will be willing to reject such extremism," Mr. Johnson said.

The new law was almost immediately challenged by abortion rights groups. In the past year, it has been held unconstitutional by federal district courts in California, New York, and Nebraska, and the Nebraska ruling was affirmed by the Eighth Circuit on Friday, meaning it is probably on the way to the Supreme Court soon.

The Eighth Circuit struck down the law on health exception grounds, ruling that "the constitutional requirement of a health exception applies to all abortion statutes, without regard to precisely how the statute regulates abortion." But, the appeals court went on, a single doctor's opinion does not suffice. "When 'substantial medical authority' supports the medical necessity of a procedure in some instances," the court ruled, "a health exception is constitutionally required."

A case involving a similar law passed by the State of Virginia was struck down by the United States Court of Appeals for the Fourth Circuit, in Richmond, Va., last month, also because it did not have a health exception.

If a case concerning this procedure does reach the Supreme Court, some analysts say, almost any justice appointed by Mr. Bush to replace Justice O'Connor can be expected to vote to reverse the 2000 decision. The only constraint, Professor Sullivan said, is the force of precedent.

"They usually wait a decent 10 years or so before overruling a case," she said.

Abortion rights advocates say such laws could have profoundly chilling effects on many doctors' willingness to perform second-trimester abortions. David J. Garrow, a scholar of abortion rights, agreed. "The real effect of anything like the partial-birth abortion act being upheld is the extent to which it intimidates doctors."

Abortion opponents say it is a reasonable line for a civilized society to draw.

More immediately, the Court will hear arguments in its next term on *Ayotte v. Planned Parenthood*, concerning the New Hampshire parental-notification law. The case presents two important legal questions: the first is whether such laws must also contain an exception for pregnant minors whose health is at risk.

The second issue is what standard courts must use in evaluating challenges to abortion laws that have not yet taken effect. In ordinary cases, plaintiffs pursuing such challenges must prove that there is "no set of circumstances" under which the law would be valid.

In at least some abortion settings, the Court has offered a different calculation: that a law may be struck down if even "a large fraction" of women directly affected would suffer an "undue burden" in obtaining an abortion. The state of New Hampshire is challenging that approach.

Abortion rights groups warn that, in the end, the combination of a more conservative Court and the anti-abortion movement's piecemeal approach to new abortion restrictions means that *Roe* could be overturned piece by piece. "They don't want Americans to see what they're up to," said Nancy Keenan, president of Naral Pro-Choice America. "They want this to be by stealth."

Anti-abortion leaders say they are simply trusting in democracy, noting that laws on parental notification and "partial-birth" abortion are quite popular. "Do we respect the judgment of the American people?" Mr. Bopp asked. "That's what is fundamentally at stake here."

Justices Reinstate Suits on Internet File Sharing

By Linda Greenhouse and Lorne Manly
The New York Times, June 28, 2005

The Supreme Court handed a major victory to the entertainment and recording industries on Monday by reinstating a copyright-infringement suit against two file-sharing services.

In a unanimous opinion, the Court strongly suggested that the services, Grokster and StreamCast Networks, should be found liable for the vast copyright infringement committed by those using their software to download music and movies.

Two lower federal courts in California had ruled in favor of the two companies, dismissing the lawsuit without a trial on the basis of a legal analysis that the Supreme Court found seriously flawed.

In his opinion for the Court on Monday, Justice David H. Souter suggested that when properly evaluated, the evidence against Grokster and StreamCast was, in fact, so strong that the entertainment-industry plaintiffs might be entitled to summary judgment.

At the least, he said, MGM Studios and the other plaintiffs—including the Recording Industry Association of America, the Motion Picture Association of America, and a class of 27,000 music publishers and songwriters—were entitled to a trial to prove their accusations that the file-sharing companies were in business primarily to enable and induce computer users to find and download copyrighted material.

In the Supreme Court's view, the plaintiffs have effectively made that case already. Justice Souter called the record "replete with evidence" that the companies "acted with a purpose to cause copyright violations by use of software suitable for illegal use." The opinion referred to "evidence of infringement on a gigantic scale" and said that "the probable scope of copyright infringement is staggering."

The movie and music industries, even armed with a decision affirming their legal recourse, have a long way to go to capitalize on it, and they plan new efforts to persuade or force those actually doing the downloading to desist.

Digital rights advocates, while somewhat relieved that the Court did not go further, were concerned that the ruling could invite a deluge of lawsuits and a risk that they would inhibit innovation.

There is no dispute that individual users violate copyright law when they share files of copyrighted material, and the industry has had some modest success in seeking fines from college students and others. But with millions of users downloading billions of files each month, retail prosecution proved inefficient, so the music and entertainment industries turned their attention several years ago to the commercial services that make the file sharing possible.

That effort led to the Supreme Court's most important copyright case since its ruling in 1984 that shielded the manufacturers of the videocassette recorder from copyright liability for possibly infringing use by home consumers.

The Court based its decision then, in *Sony v. Universal City Studios*, on a finding that the VCR was "capable of substantial noninfringing uses," like time-shifting, in which home users simply recorded programs for viewing later.

In ruling last year for Grokster and StreamCast, the United States Court of Appeals for the Ninth Circuit in San Francisco relied on the *Sony* decision, finding that the file-sharing software had possible noninfringing uses. Because the software operates in a decentralized way without using a central computer, the appeals court found, Grokster and StreamCast could not track users and had no direct knowledge of any specific instance of infringement.

Joyce Naltchayan/AFP/Getty Images

Associate Justice David H. Souter spoke for the entire Court in his opinion against Grokster and StreamCast.

The Supreme Court on Monday held that the appeals court had misapplied the *Sony* decision by focusing only on the technology, without regard to the business model that the technology served.

"One who distributes a device with the object of promoting its use to infringe copyright, as shown by clear expression or other affirmative steps taken to foster infringement, is liable for the resulting acts of infringement by third parties," Justice Souter wrote.

Movie and music industry executives hailed the decision. "If you build a business that aids and abets theft, you will be held accountable," said Dan Glickman, chief executive of the Motion Picture Association of America, the lobbying organization for the major Hollywood studios. BMI, representing more than 300,000 songwriters and composers, called the decision "good news indeed for the creative community whose work has been blatantly infringed."

The movie and music industries had warned that file sharing was hurting them financially, and could ultimately inhibit the creation of content. The music industry has blamed song-swapping over the Internet for its decade-long sales slump.

While movies and television shows are more difficult to trade online because of the size of their files, technological advances are making that easier and threatening the rich source of cash that DVD sales have become for the studios.

On the other hand, groups including the American Civil Liberties Union, Consumers Union, the Consumer Electronics Association, and other elements of the computer and technology industries warned the Court that too broad a rule of contributory copyright infringement would stifle innovation if there was a possibility that consumers might put a product to an infringing use.

> ### *The movie and music industries had warned that file sharing was hurting them financially, and could ultimately inhibit the creation of content.*

It was clear from the opinion, *Metro-Goldwyn-Mayer Studios Inv. v. Grokster Ltd.*, No. 04-480, that the justices had taken note of that argument and tried to draw a line that would protect both copyright holders and innovators. The Court identified the line as "inducement"—deliberately urging consumers to make illicit use of the product or showing them how it could be done.

"Mere knowledge of infringing potential or of actual infringing uses would not be enough here to subject a distributor to liability," Justice Souter said. He added: "Nor would ordinary acts incident to product distribution, such as offering customers technical support or product updates, support liability in themselves. The inducement rule, instead, premises liability on purposeful, culpable expression and conduct, and thus does nothing to compromise legitimate commerce or discourage innovation having a lawful promise."

James Gibson, a professor of intellectual property and computer law at the University of Richmond School of Law, applauded what he called a balancing act between artistic creators and technological innovators.

By putting so much weight on proving companies' bad behavior, he said, the decision could create more legal expenses and unpredictability for technology companies. At the same time, he added, it should provide peace of mind to creators of technology that could be used for both legitimate and infringing uses.

But several technology advocates expressed concern, saying innovators would now be saddled with the befuddling notion of "intent." Matthew Neco, StreamCast's general counsel, said the ruling turned Hollywood and the recording industry into "thought police."

Michael Petricone, vice president for technology policy at the Consumer Electronics Association, said that without clear guidelines from the Court on what a company must do to avoid being held liable for contributing to copyright infringement, "the legal clarity has decreased and the risk of litigation has increased."

Attorney General Alberto R. Gonzales said he was pleased the Court had "determined that those who intentionally induce or encourage the theft of copyrighted music, movies, software, or other protected works may be held liable for their actions." The Bush administration joined the argument in support of the studios.

While the Court's judgment was unanimous, the justices did not share the same view of how useful the *Sony* precedent remained after more than 20 years of changing technology. A concurring opinion by Justice Ruth Bader Ginsburg, which Chief Justice William H. Rehnquist and Justice Anthony M. Kennedy joined, suggested that the *Sony* case's reference to "substantial noninfringing use" was too easily misunderstood by lower courts and might have to be tailored for different types of technology.

The file-sharing software might be used to swap large numbers of noninfringing files, Justice Ginsburg said, but even a big number would be "dwarfed by the huge total volume of files shared."

Justice Stephen G. Breyer, in a concurring opinion also signed by Justices John Paul Stevens and Sandra Day O'Connor, said the *Sony* decision had basically achieved its "innovation-protecting objective" and struck the right balance between protecting copyrights and technology. It should be retained, he said.

IV. The Rehnquist Court

The late Chief Justice William H. Rehnquist

Editors' Introduction

With the death of Chief Justice William H. Rehnquist in September 2005, one of the most significant periods in American judicial history came to a close. Appointed to the Supreme Court as an associate justice in 1972 by President Richard Nixon and elevated to chief justice in 1986 by Ronald Reagan, succeeding the retiring Warren Burger, Rehnquist spearheaded a conservative judicial revolution that fundamentally reshaped the ideological make-up not only of the Court, but of American jurisprudence as a whole.

Nevertheless, Rehnquist did not win over everyone. His liberal and progressive detractors consider his legacy a shabby one, symbolized by his opposition to *Brown v. Board of Education* in the 1950s, allegations that he challenged the right of many African Americans to vote at the polls in the early 1960s, and his controversial role in the 2000 *Bush v. Gore* decision. His judicial opinions notwithstanding, Rehnquist's fellow justices view his stewardship of the Court quite positively, frequently praising his fairness and equanimity.

Now that the Rehnquist era has ended, the articles in this chapter focus on the late chief justice's place in Court history. In the first entry, "Rehnquist the Great?" Jeffrey Rosen takes an in-depth look at Rehnquist's tenure on the Court and explores his overall judicial philosophy. Ultimately, the piece casts Rehnquist as one of the more significant chief justices, thus concluding that the designation "Rehnquist the Great," is not entirely unwarranted. Cliff Sloan takes a different perspective in the subsequent piece, "A Limited Legacy," contending that Rehnquist was actually a rather ineffective chief justice whose "limted successes were far from the legacy of greatness that [his] champions claim."

In a more personal analysis, "The Rehnquist Difference" by Alan J. Borsuk traces the chief justice's journey from his Wisconsin roots up through his tenure on the Court. Included in the article are details about Rehnquist's large family and a timeline noting important dates in his life.

Richard Brust, for the *ABA Journal*, examines certain rulings authored by the late chief justice that further illuminate his particular ideological bent. According to Brust, one of the more impressive aspects of Rehnquist's tenure on the Court was his ideological consistency: "There have been few U.S. Supreme Court justices who espoused a philosophy and stuck with it as tenaciously as William H. Rehnquist," Brust notes.

An essential element of the Rehnquist era has been the role played by Justice Sandra Day O'Connor. On a Court closely divided along partisan lines, O'Connor, the first woman ever to serve on the bench, has often cast the deciding vote in 5–4 decisions. Thus some have suggested the Rehnquist Court really ought to be called the O'Connor Court. With O'Connor's retirement imminent, Michael McGough explores her impact on the Court in "O'Connor's Legacy More Than a Mere Swing Vote."

Rehnquist the Great?

By Jeffrey Rosen
The Atlantic Monthly, April 2005

In his 34 years on the Supreme Court, William Rehnquist participated enthusiastically in the annual Christmas party for the justices and their clerks. "He and I wrote the Christmas show the
year I clerked for him, in 1975," recalls Craig M. Bradley, who now
teaches law at Indiana University.

One carol that year was sung to the tune of "Angels From the
Realms of Glory." It went like this: "Liberals from the realm of theory should adorn our highest bench / Though to crooks they're
always chary / at police misdeeds they blench." ("The word 'blench'
came from Rehnquist," Bradley says. "I didn't know it meant
'blanch.'") The members of the chorus then fell to their knees and
sang, "Save *Miranda*, save *Miranda*, save it from the Nixon Four."
The so-called Nixon Four were Supreme Court Justices Warren
Burger, Harry Blackmun, Lewis Powell, and, of course, Rehnquist.

Twenty-five years later, after having repeatedly ridiculed the
constitutional soundness of the decision requiring police officers to
read suspects their *Miranda* rights, Rehnquist voted to uphold it.
"*Miranda* has become embedded in routine police practice to the
point where the warnings have become part of our national culture," he wrote in a 7–2 opinion for the Court in *Dickerson v. U.S.*,
in 2000. Rehnquist's apostasy provoked one of Justice Antonin Scalia's most vitriolic dissenting opinions. Joined by Justice Clarence
Thomas, Scalia declared, "Today's judgment converts *Miranda*
from a milestone of judicial overreaching into the very Cheops' Pyr-
amid (or perhaps the Sphinx would be a better analogue) of judicial
arrogance."

Rehnquist's evolution from *Miranda*'s leading critic to its improb-
able savior infuriated conservatives and confused liberals; but in
fact it was emblematic of his career. Throughout his long tenure,
liberals always simplistically lumped Rehnquist together with the
other conservatives on the Court, whereas conservatives never
fully embraced him as one of their own. Furthermore, liberals have
never understood how significantly and frequently Rehnquist
departed from doctrinaire conservative ideology, and conservatives
have failed to grasp that his tactical flexibility was more effective
than the rigid purity of Scalia and Thomas. In truth, Rehnquist
carefully staked out a limbo between the right and the left and
showed that it was a very good place to be. With exceptional effi-

ciency and amiability he led a Court that put the brakes on some of the excesses of the Earl Warren era while keeping pace with the sentiments of a majority of the country—generally siding with economic conservatives and against cultural conservatives. As for judicial temperament, he was far more devoted to preserving tradition and majority rule than the generation of fire-breathing conservatives who followed him. And his administration of the Court was brilliantly if quietly effective, making him one of the most impressive chief justices of the past hundred years.

> *One of Rehnquist's unique and abiding talents was for getting along with his ideological opponents.*

The chief justice, like each of his colleagues, has one vote; his greatest power lies in choosing who will write an opinion when he's in the majority—himself or another justice who he thinks will best reflect his views. On this score Rehnquist proved to be a master tactician, unlike his inept and pompous predecessor, Warren Burger, who infuriated his colleagues by changing his votes in order to seize the best opinions for himself and then losing his majorities. And Rehnquist's judicial philosophy also made it easier for him to reshape the Court in his own image. He was essentially a pragmatist who believed in certain core conservative values—primarily states' rights and convicting criminals—but didn't fuss too much about how he achieved his aims. In contrast, Scalia and Thomas are more concerned about ideological purity than about persuading a majority of their colleagues, which is why neither would make an effective chief.

One of Rehnquist's unique and abiding talents was for getting along with his ideological opponents. When he first joined the Court, at the age of 47, he was taken under the wing of the liberal activist William O. Douglas, a fellow westerner who saw in the irreverent young conservative an incarnation of his youthful self. Rehnquist's other liberal colleagues were similarly impressed by his fairness and good nature: Thurgood Marshall called Rehnquist "a great Chief Justice," and William Brennan described him as "the most all-around successful" chief he had known—including Earl Warren. On the current Court, Rehnquist has been praised frequently and effusively by Ruth Bader Ginsburg, who, despite her philosophical differences with the chief justice, admires his administrative skills so much that after the complicated campaign-finance case last term, she told clerks how happy she was that the rumors he was retiring weren't true. One former clerk remembers Rehnquist best for his sensitivity toward colleagues: "He was very concerned about hurt feelings among the justices, and he was very careful and observant of the way that certain memos or interactions would make other justices react or feel. He always avoided invective in his own memos, and smoothed over hurt feelings when other justices used it."

A hallmark of Rehnquist's rule was his unparalleled organizational skill: he got opinions out quickly and made the arguments run on time both in and out of court. When, in a rare interview last year, Charlie Rose asked him how he would most like to be remembered, Rehnquist said as a good administrator; he had tried, he said, to run "a relatively smoothly functioning Court." And he suggested that his ability to get along

> *A hallmark of Rehnquist's rule was his unparalleled organizational skill.*

with a group of strong personalities reflected "a relatively passive nature," a "very high boiling point," and the ability to compromise.

Certainly he was a creature of habit; his daily routine in his chambers remained the same for more than 30 years. He would arrive between 8:30 and 9:00, say hello to his two secretaries, go through his mail, and smoke a cigarette (for years he was a two-cigarettes-a-day man—no more, no less). At exactly 9:30 he would call in his clerks, gently reminding them, if they were even a minute late, that "the doctor doesn't wait for you." A trivia buff, he loved to test the mettle of his clerks at the morning meeting, asking them, for example, to name the five largest states in order of their area. He would often go to the University Club for a swim, to alleviate chronic back pain, and he usually left the office at 4:00. He was not known for taking work home with him. When he assigned the writing of an opinion to himself, he would set a deadline for the first draft 10 days away and then start asking his clerks about it after a week. He was insistent that his fellow justices meet his exacting standards for punctuality, and would punish those who fell behind on their opinions (including the notoriously slow Harry Blackmun) by not assigning them new ones. And he ran an especially tight ship during the justices' private conferences, the twice weekly meetings after oral arguments, at which the justices cast their preliminary votes. Briskly going around the table, in order of seniority, to allow each justice to give his or her views, he refused to let discussion wander. Some colleagues complained that this format discouraged active debate, but Rehnquist argued that because most of the justices had already made up their minds, a protracted colloquy would be a waste of time.

Rehnquist's courtroom style was similarly unvarying. He would cut lawyers off in mid-sentence when the red light on the bench began to flash, indicating that their allotted time had expired. (Each side gets precisely 30 minutes.) Some lawyers grumbled about this rigidity, but Rehnquist's clockwork discipline looked appealing in retrospect when Justice John Paul Stevens, who has presided in the chief justice's place during his battle with thyroid cancer, recently let one advocate have extra time and was then compelled to grant an extension to his opponent as well.

The two chief justices Rehnquist most admired, John Marshall and Charles Evans Hughes, were both politicians who had a knack for bringing together unlike-minded colleagues: Marshall, who served from 1801 to 1835, had been a Virginia congressman and secretary of state; Hughes, who served from 1930 to 1941, had been the governor of New York, a Republican candidate for president, and secretary of state. As Rehnquist told the C-SPAN interviewer Brian Lamb in a *Booknotes* appearance in 1993, Marshall had "an ability to get along with other people and persuade them that stood him in good stead when he was chief justice." And in a 1976 article in the *Hastings Constitutional Law Quarterly*, "Chief Justices I Never Knew," Rehnquist wrote that he especially admired Hughes's businesslike conduct of his private conferences, which lasted only six hours as opposed to the two or three days under Hughes's successor, Harlan Fiske Stone. Rehnquist concluded that "Hughes's superiority to Stone in presiding over the conference has a definite connection to their different amount of exposure to active political life."

Rehnquist is tied with Stephen Breyer for the role of second most restrained justice, after Ruth Bader Ginsburg.

Rehnquist's own political sensibility and experience were similarly central to his stewardship of the Court. By temperament and training he represented an older and what has come to be seen as milder strain of conservatism, rooted in the Goldwater wing of the Republican Party. Having cut his political teeth in Arizona in the heyday of Goldwaterism, he came to the Court with a far less angry and embattled attitude toward American democracy than younger conservatives like Scalia and Thomas. And unlike Scalia and Thomas, Rehnquist was never invested in fighting the culture wars from the bench, because of his overriding commitment to majority rule regardless of what the majority decides.

If judicial activism is defined by a judge's willingness to strike down federal or state laws, then Scalia and Thomas are among the most activist justices on the Court today, surpassed only by Anthony Kennedy and, perhaps surprisingly, Sandra Day O'Connor. In contrast, Rehnquist is tied with Stephen Breyer for the role of second most restrained justice, after Ruth Bader Ginsburg. And while all the conservatives on the Rehnquist Court say for public consumption that the judiciary should occupy a modest role in American politics and should defer to the judgment of elected legislators, Rehnquist has most consistently practiced what he preaches.

"I'm a strong believer in pluralism." Rehnquist told *The New York Times Magazine* in 1985, the year before he was appointed chief justice. "Don't concentrate all the power in one place. . . . You don't want all the power in the Government as opposed to the people. You don't want all the power in the Federal Government as opposed to the states." When pressed about the source of these views, he joked, "It may have something to do with my childhood."

Rehnquist's Robert Taft–style conservatism—his faith in local majorities and his suspicion of broad federal power—does indeed reflect his midwestern upbringing. Born in 1924, he was raised, along with his sister, Jean, in Shorewood, Wisconsin, an affluent Milwaukee suburb known during the Depression for its Republicanism. Rehnquist's father, the son of Swedish immigrants, was an enthusiastic Republican who had never attended college and made his living selling paper wholesale. His mother, who had majored in French at the University of Wisconsin, was fluent in five foreign languages and worked as a translator for local export businesses.

Rehnquist's early years were suffused with old-fashioned patriotism. He enthusiastically supported U.S. intervention in World War II, and in 1941 he participated in a reenactment of America's founding called United States of Young Americans. That strong strain of patriotism has been an essential part of his makeup throughout his judicial career. In 1989, when Justices Scalia and Kennedy, both First Amendment libertarians, reluctantly voted to strike down a ban on flag-burning, Rehnquist produced an emotional dissenting opinion quoting John Greenleaf Whittier's Civil War poem "Barbara Frietchie": "'Shoot, if you must, this old gray head, / But spare your country's flag,' she said." It was one of the most personally revealing dissents he ever wrote.

Rehnquist won a scholarship to Kenyon College, in Ohio, but dropped out after one quarter, having found the atmosphere intellectually frivolous. He enlisted in the Army Air Corps and spent three years as a weather observer, ending up in Morocco and Egypt (where he was photographed on horseback in front of the Sphinx). Reluctant to return to the cold Milwaukee winters ("I wanted to find someplace like North Africa to go to school"), he enrolled on the GI Bill at Stanford, where he majored in political science.

While he was in the Army Air Corps, Rehnquist encountered a book that would be crucial to the development of his judicial philosophy: Friedrich A. Hayek's *The Road to Serfdom*. "This book was an advocacy book trying to show that state planning and socialism and that sort of thing didn't work economically and were dangerous politically," Rehnquist told Brian Lamb in a later *Booknotes* interview. "It made quite an impression on me."

Rehnquist graduated Phi Beta Kappa from Stanford in 1948 with a bachelor's and a master's degree, and then got a second master's degree in political science from Harvard, in the hopes of becoming a professor of government. While at Harvard he started a thesis about the conservative British political philosopher Michael Oakeshott, whose insistence on the importance of continuity and tradition for social stability resonated strongly with Rehnquist. Oakeshott, like Hayek, called into question the centrally planned welfare state, as part of a larger warning against the concentration of power in the hands of government. But Oakeshott resisted Hayek's effort to construct a rigid libertarian ideology as the answer to collectivism; he argued that the best way to protect limited government was with a pragmatically conservative approach to politics, rather than with abstract theories about the true nature of the state.

"The chief's conservatism seems to reflect Oakeshott more than libertarians like Hayek," observes Richard Garnett, a former clerk who now teaches law at Notre Dame, and with whom Rehnquist discussed his admiration for Oakeshott. "It's not always about swashbuckling ideological adherence to first principles. It's also about temperament and disposition, about an attachment to traditions and institutions, and about stability and regularity."

After Harvard, Rehnquist attended Stanford Law School and graduated in 1952 at the top of an impressive class that included Sandra Day O'Connor. Based on his stellar academic record and genial personality, he won a clerkship with Supreme Court Justice Robert Jackson, who had been Franklin Roosevelt's attorney general and was committed to the principle of judicial deference to legislatures. During his clerkship, which began in 1952, Rehnquist wrote two highly controversial memos to Jackson that would provoke firestorms during his own confirmation hearings, in 1971 and 1986. In the memos Rehnquist seemed to urge Jackson to dissent in two historic civil-rights cases: *Brown v. Board of Education*, which would strike down school segregation, and *Terry v. Adams*, which would block efforts to exclude blacks from the pre-primary selection of Texas Democrats. Rehnquist claimed during the hearings that he was expressing these views at Jackson's request—an assertion disputed by Jackson's secretary. Several legal scholars believe that Rehnquist probably lied in denying that the views were his. He appears to have been the only Supreme Court clerk during the 1952 term who supported *Plessy v. Ferguson*—this at a time when the country as a whole was evenly split over desegregation. Whether he was speaking for himself or for Jackson, the central position that Rehnquist laid out in the memos—stressing the importance of judicial deference to the majority will—succinctly summarized what would become his judicial philosophy throughout his career.

> *Several legal scholars believe that Rehnquist probably lied in denying that the views [on Brown] were his.*

In the *Brown* memo Rehnquist wrote that the Supreme Court was ideally suited to mediate disputes between the states and the federal government or between branches of the federal government. In contrast, he said, "where a legislature [is] dealing with its own citizens, it [is] not part of the judicial function to thwart public opinion except in extreme cases." *Brown* was not one of those cases, Rehnquist argued, because "in the long run it is the majority who will determine what the constitutional rights of the minority are." Similarly, in *Terry v. Adams*, Rehnquist insisted that "the Constitution does not prevent the majority from banding together, nor does it attaint success in the effort. It is about time that the Court faced the fact that white people in the South don't like the colored people."

As jarring as these memos appear now, they are consistent with the views of many political scientists today, who argue that the Court, except in rare cases, neither can nor should thwart the will of a determined national majority, and that it invites political backlash when it attempts to do so. After Rehnquist joined the Court, he was asked whether justices are able to isolate themselves from the pressures of public opinion. "My answer was that we are not able to do so, and it would probably be unwise to try," he recalled. Rehnquist's highly evolved pragmatism convinced him that the courts cannot ignore broad cultural shifts. This, as much as anything, distinguished Rehnquist from the later generation of judicial conservatives.

After his Supreme Court clerkship ended, in 1953, Rehnquist moved to Phoenix, always in search of warm weather and conservative politics. He joined a small law firm and became active in local Republican circles, which had been revitalized under the newly elected Senator Barry Goldwater. A decade later Rehnquist would write speeches for Goldwater's ill-fated 1964 presidential campaign, which united disparate parts of the conservative movement while alienating the liberal Rockefeller wing of the Republican Party. His speeches for Goldwater singled out for attack the Warren Court's landmark decisions requiring school busing. But unlike the Dixiecrats, who fought to protect the power of local communities to enforce traditional values, Goldwater was no social conservative, as his later support for birth control and gay rights would attest; he was a populist who ardently opposed the excesses of federal, state, and local authority. Although Goldwater dutifully denounced the Warren Court's liberal obscenity and school-prayer decisions, he had little patience for his party's growing moralistic forces, which insisted that Christian virtue, rather than liberty, should be the Republicans' highest calling. The Republican Party of the 1960s, for all its associations with extremism at the time, seems in retrospect a less strident and more inclusive organization than the party of today.

In 1957, after the Warren Court issued a series of controversial decisions protecting the rights of suspected Communists, Rehnquist, then a young lawyer, wrote an article in *U.S. News & World Report* criticizing the law clerks he had known for their predominantly "'liberal' point of view," which he defined as "extreme solicitude for the claims of Communists and other criminal defendants, expansion of federal power at the expense of State power, great sympathy toward any government regulation of business—in short, the political philosophy now espoused by the Court under Chief Justice Earl Warren." Rehnquist also strongly disagreed with the Warren Court's prominent role in advancing the civil-rights movement. Testifying as a private citizen before the Phoenix City Council in 1964, he opposed a local public-accommodations law, charging later that it would summarily do away with "the historic right of the owner of a drug store, lunch counter, or theater to choose his own customers." That same year Rehnquist had urged Goldwater to vote against the Civil Rights Act. During his 1971 confirmation hearings Rehnquist said that he had changed his mind about public-accommodations laws, acknowledging that he hadn't understood how strongly minorities felt about protecting their rights.

Every political movement has its moral blind spots, and civil rights was certainly a moral blind spot for Goldwater Republicanism. Rehnquist's insistence on deferring to the will of the people is hard to reconcile with his indifference to the then emerging majority of Americans who supported upholding the rights of black people. Goldwater and Rehnquist were never white supremacists, like Strom Thurmond, of South Carolina, and James Eastland, of Mississippi, but they seemed unconcerned that their devotion to states' rights could lead to enshrining racism. (Justice Byron White, a Kennedy Democrat of the same generation who shared Rehnquist's devotion to majority rule, did not make the same mistake.)

Both Goldwater and Rehnquist came belatedly to recognize the error of their ways. Rehnquist ultimately embraced the Warren Court's *Brown* decision, and after he joined the Court he made no attempt to dismantle the civil-rights revolution, as political opponents feared he would. His change of position reflected not only his reverence for the Court as an institution but also his sense that once a majority has spoken, the decision has a legal force that must be obeyed. Compare Rehnquist's attitude on these points with that of Clarence Thomas, who refuses to accept decisions that he thinks are wrong. Even Scalia has been critical of Thomas for this; as he recently told Thomas's biographer, Ken Foskett, Thomas "does not believe in *stare decisis*, period." "If a constitutional line of authority is wrong, he would say let's get it right," Scalia continued. "I wouldn't do that."

When Richard Nixon was elected president in 1968, he appointed as deputy attorney general Richard Kleindeinst, a Phoenix lawyer who had worked on his campaign. Kleindeinst persuaded Attorney General John Mitchell to hire his friend Rehnquist. As head of the Justice Department's Office of Legal Counsel, which provides constitutional advice to the president, Rehnquist distinguished himself as a conservative intellectual and an enthusiastic defender of executive power in the face of widespread social unrest. The country, Rehnquist said in a Kiwanis Club speech in 1969, had to devote all its energies to countering "the danger posed by the new barbarians." Two years later he staunchly defended the mass arrest of Vietnam protesters. That year, with Justices Hugo Black and John Marshall Harlan retiring, Nixon considered some three dozen candidates to fill the two vacancies, including Vice President Spiro Agnew and

Senator Howard Baker, of Tennessee. In an entertaining memoir, *The Rehnquist Choice*, John Dean, who was the White House counsel at the time and was later instrumental in Nixon's downfall, claims the credit (and also the blame) for being first to float the name of Rehnquist, who then was in charge of screening the other Supreme Court candidates. When Nixon first met Rehnquist, who was given to the loud shirts and psychedelic ties of the era, he wondered aloud,

> *The only cases in which Rehnquist was consistently willing to question federal power involved states' rights.*

"Who's the guy dressed like a clown?" Upon hearing Rehnquist's name, Nixon said, "Is he Jewish? He looks it." But when the other candidacies fell by the wayside, the man Nixon was prone to call "Renchburg" won him over with his conservative credentials and unquestioned ability.

Rehnquist's first confirmation hearings focused on whether he had been truthful when he denied having challenged black and Hispanic voters as an Arizona poll watcher, and again in his account of one of his pro-segregation memos for Justice Jackson. Although Rehnquist was unanimously praised as an accomplished lawyer, he came under fire from a group of liberal Democrats on the Judiciary Committee, including Edward Kennedy, who charged that his record "reveals a dangerous hostility to the great principles of individual freedom under the Bill of Rights and equal justice for all people." Rehnquist was confirmed by a vote of 68 to 26.

As an associate justice, Rehnquist held fairly steadily to the views expressed in his *Brown v. Board of Education* memo of 1952. He almost invariably deferred to state legislatures on matters involving individual rights, and struck down federal laws only when he thought that Congress or the president had exceeded the bounds of constitutionally enumerated powers. The only cases in which Rehnquist was consistently willing to question federal power involved states' rights. During his first decade on the bench the most important states'-rights case for which Rehnquist wrote the majority opinion was *National League of Cities v. Usery*, in 1976; that case heralded the beginning of the so-called federalism revolution, which imposed meaningful limits on congressional power for the first time since the New Deal. In his opinion Rehnquist argued for limiting the federal government's ability to regulate the wages and hours of state and local government employees. The Tenth Amendment, he said, prevents Congress from acting in a way that "impairs the States' integrity or their ability to function effectively in a federal system." Although Rehnquist had mixed success maintaining majorities for this principle in the 1970s and 1980s, by the 1990s he had found at least four reliable allies—Scalia, Thomas, Kennedy, and O'Connor. But by not consistently deferring to Congress, Rehnquist failed to fulfill his oft-stated commitment to judicial restraint; under his leadership the Court indulged in an overconfident rhetoric of judicial supremacy and struck down 30 federal laws in one seven-year period—a higher rate than in any other Court in history.

In most cases, however, Rehnquist voted to uphold federal and state laws. When I re-read his youthful and often solitary dissents, which earned him the nickname "the Lone Ranger," it was hard not to be impressed by their energy, lack of pretense, and lack of anger. "The 1970s dissents were magnificent," says Jack Goldsmith, a constitutional scholar at Harvard Law School. "Rehnquist didn't have an overarching substantive theory of constitutional interpretation, but he was always respectful of the Court as an institution, even when he thought it was off the tracks."

Despite his conservative temperament, Rehnquist was never unduly preoccupied with following judicial precedents. In a biting critique published in *The New Republic* in 1982, Charles Krauthammer, the conservative essayist, and Owen Fiss, a liberal scholar at Yale Law School, charged that Rehnquist "repudiates precedents frequently and openly, and if that is impossible (because the precedent represents a tradition that neither the Court nor society is prepared to abandon), then he distorts them." Perhaps one answer to this criticism is that Rehnquist was always focused on moving the law in a fundamentally conservative direction while trying to circumvent any potential roadblocks along the way. His clerks, past and present, report that he would simply remove the reasoning from opinions if it got in the way of the result.

"He took each case as it came," recalls Michael K. Young, a former clerk who is now president of the University of Utah. "He thought that the Constitution was not designed to shape all of our behavior but to box in elected officials at the margins. . . . He didn't see the sky falling, the way Scalia sometimes does, and if you read his dissents, they're often pragmatic. I've never been able to figure out *Bush v. Gore*, but in general he just deferred to the political process."

But even Rehnquist's highly controversial vote to stop the manual recount in Florida in the 2000 presidential election may be an expression of his pragmatism, for better or worse. In a speech to a Catholic service organization soon after the election, Rehnquist defended the participation of Supreme Court justices in deciding the presidential election of 1876 and seemed to be justifying *Bush v. Gore* in similarly practical terms. "There is a national crisis, and only you can avert it," he said. "It may be very hard to say no."

Typical of Rehnquist's early opinions was his 1973 dissent from *Roe v. Wade*. Without huffing and puffing or personal invective, Rehnquist made a straightforward but powerful case for majority rule. "The fact that a majority of the States, reflecting, after all, the majority sentiment in those States, have had restrictions on abortion for at least a century is a strong indication, it seems to me, that the asserted right to an abortion is not [deeply rooted in tradition]," Rehnquist observed. It's striking to compare his even-tempered dissent with Scalia's wrathful and apocalyptic one nearly 20 years later. In *Planned Parenthood v. Casey*, the case that reaffirmed *Roe v. Wade*, Scalia equated abortion with slavery—both of them issues "involving life and death, freedom and subjugation"—and predicted that the Court would detonate a culture war in the same way that its *Dred Scott* decision, in 1857, precipitated the Civil War.

Rehnquist's moderate religious views (he is a Lutheran, although not a conspicuously observant one) may have contributed to his relative equanimity about abortion and prayer. "If I were a betting man, I would say personally Rehnquist thinks prayer in schools is pretty silly." Michael Young says. "You won't find him as hysterical about abortion and prayer as born-again Christians, who view these decisions as substantively essential to the moral fiber of the country. Rehnquist is willing to have it decided either way by the legislatures. Scalia couches it in a concern about democratic decisions, but that's not why Scalia cares."

> *Because of* Roe, *a conservative judicial movement arose in the 1980s that was determined to curtail judicial discretion at all costs.*

Rehnquist reads broadly and avidly but, unlike Scalia, never comes off as a know-it-all and has never tried to lord his intelligence over his colleagues. While Scalia rails against popular culture, Rehnquist loves to rent movies—both new and old—and also goes to movie theaters by himself to see them. (His wife, Natalie, died in 1991 after a long struggle with ovarian cancer.) It is impossible to imagine him denouncing the Court for taking sides in the culture wars, as Scalia routinely does. "The Court must be living in another world," Scalia wrote in 1996. "Day by day, case by case, it is busy designing a Constitution for a country I do not recognize."

Temperament and religious sensibility may go a long way toward explaining differences of approach—between Rehnquist, on the one hand, and Scalia and Thomas, on the other. (It's worth noting that over the past 10 years Rehnquist has voted more frequently with Kennedy and O'Connor than with Scalia and Thomas.) But another part of the explanation has to do with the reaction to *Roe* within the legal community itself. Because of *Roe*, a conservative judicial movement arose in the 1980s that was determined to curtail judicial discretion at all costs. *Roe* galvanized the religious right and unleashed far more conservative outrage against the

Court than Earl Warren ever did. After he became, president. Ronald Reagan, declaring that he wanted to avoid what he saw as Nixon's mistakes in picking moderate justices like Harry Blackmun, Warren Burger, and Lewis Powell, directed his Justice Department to find more-reliable ways of identifying doctrinaire strict constructionists. A turning point for this conservative judicial movement came in 1985, when Reagan's attorney general, Edwin Meese, delivered a speech to

> *The gulf between Rehnquist and the Scalia-Thomas axis only widened this term and last.*

the American Bar Association denouncing the Burger Court for its "jurisprudence of idiosyncrasy." Meese asserted, "It has been and will continue to be the policy of this administration to press for a jurisprudence of Original Intention," which he defined as an "endeavor to resurrect the original meaning of constitutional provisions and statutes as the only reliable guide for judgment."

Although Rehnquist's opinions referred intermittently to this doctrine of "originalism" (most notably in cases involving the separation of church and state), he invoked constitutional history when it was convenient and otherwise ignored it. From the moment that Scalia and Thomas joined the Court, in 1986 and 1991, respectively, they took a very different approach. Embracing the new orthodoxy with almost catechistic devotion, they insisted on the importance of construing each constitutional provision according to the presumed intentions of the Framers, no matter how disruptive or radical the consequences might be. For example, in 2003 Rehnquist wrote a majority opinion holding that Congress could allow state-government employees to sue their states for violating the Family and Medical Leave Act: Scalia and Thomas argued that this violated states' rights. "Scalia and Thomas embrace top-down theories of originalism and textualism as a principled way to control judicial discretion," Jack Goldsmith, of Harvard Law School, says. "Rehnquist is in a different, older, more pragmatic conservative tradition. He is less theoretical, often looks beyond text and history in discovering the relevant legal intentions, is more deferential to the political branches, and doesn't attempt to impose a general methodology across the board."

The gulf between Rehnquist and the Scalia-Thomas axis only widened this term and last. In *U.S. v. Booker*, decided in January, and *Blakeley v. Washington*, decided last spring, Scalia and Thomas joined three liberals on the Court in voting to strike down federal and state sentencing guidelines and in attempting to impose a sweeping new requirement that would have compelled juries to vote on each fact used to increase a sentence. Rehnquist, in contrast, sided with the more pragmatically minded justices—Breyer, O'Connor, and Kennedy—in upholding the sentencing guidelines, and avoided chaos by making the federal guidelines advisory rather than mandatory. Along the same lines, in an important terrorism case Rehnquist joined O'Connor in voting to allow the president to detain enemy combatants, but with a modest degree of judicial oversight. Meanwhile, Scalia and Thomas, in dissent, took rigid (and, as it happened, diametrically opposed) positions: Scalia argued that the president had no power to detain with-

> *Rehnquist's successes as chief justice provide an object lesson for future holders of the office.*

out congressional authorization, whereas Thomas contended that the president could do whatever he liked, without judicial or congressional oversight. Rehnquist will always take half a loaf over no loaf at all, and as chief justice he has proved far more willing than most of his colleagues to support, for the good of the Court, opinions with which he disagrees.

Rehnquist's successes as chief justice provide an object lesson for future holders of the office: having a judicious temperament is far more important than having a consistent judicial methodology. Rehnquist has always understood the political demands of whatever role he is asked to play, and was careful not to transgress its boundaries. His performance in presiding over the impeachment trial of President Clinton was masterly because he refused to pontificate, confining his interventions to rulings on procedural motions, which he handed down with confidence and skill. Had he played his part in a more intrusive or polarizing way, the trial might have turned into a political circus. (As a gesture of thanks, the majority and minority leaders of the Senate gave him a ceremonial cup.) By refusing as chief justice to give interviews except about his books on Supreme Court history, and by devoutly guarding his privacy, he has helped maintain and enhance the Court's carefully cultivated aura of mystery and authority.

The younger generation of justices, both conservative and liberal, have a dramatically different attitude toward questions of personal exposure. Clarence Thomas, for example, is far more accessible and emotionally revealing; he frequently gives speeches to groups of African-American students, in which he talks, in raw and intimate detail, about his childhood, his sense of inadequacy, and his abiding anger toward the civil-rights establishment. It is impossible to imagine the intensely private Rehnquist selling a memoir for $1.5 million, as Thomas recently did. But we are living in an age of celebrity that is ravenous for personal disclosure, and pressures on the justices to accede to these demands will only grow more insistent. It may not be long before we see them turning up on the morning talk shows, as O'Connor has done, to promote themselves and discuss their feelings.

"I've always admired Robert E. Lee for his refusal to write his memoirs," Rehnquist told Brian Lamb. "If memoirs are going to be interesting, if they're not going to be saccharine, you have to say some people didn't measure up and others did. . . . I think of a memoir as saying, 'When I came on the Court there were eight other justices and three or four were quite smart, but a couple of the others were creepy.' I don't want to get into that."

If the next chief justice turns out to be, as many Court watchers fear, less of a pragmatist and more of a rigid ideologue than Rehnquist, he or she may well end up dividing the Court that Rehnquist unified, and squandering its carefully constructed reserves of public trust. In that case Rehnquist's faith in majority rule, and his ability to resist the public's insistence that officeholders bare themselves in the spotlight, may seem like the scruples of a forgotten era. He may be the last of the old-fashioned judicial conservatives, who already look far more judicious than the conservatives who have arisen in their wake. And liberals may find themselves missing Rehnquist more than they could ever have imagined.

A Limited Legacy

By Cliff Sloan
The Washington Post, September 5, 2005

Many commentators are rushing to proclaim William Rehnquist one of the "great" chief justices because of his impact on the Supreme Court. Not so fast. With all due respect to his memory, it is clear that on many important issues, Rehnquist lost the Court that bore his name. And during some of the most heated battles, rather than an influential chief rallying the Court, Rehnquist was the Court's missing man, seeming to watch from the sidelines.

Since Rehnquist became chief in 1986, the Court's record often has moved exactly opposite of the direction that Rehnquist wanted to go. On issue after issue, Rehnquist lost key fights. The Court rejected his call to overrule *Roe v. Wade* (from which he had dissented in 1973). It refused to outlaw public support for affirmative action. And on it went—with Rehnquist dissenting, the Court rejected Ten Commandments displays in Kentucky courthouses, upheld campaign finance restrictions, struck down a criminal ban on gay sex, allowed local governments to take private property for economic development, and embraced many other positions he opposed.

Rehnquist's Court took some steps in directions that he favored, but the limits of those opinions highlight the limits of his legacy. It upheld some abortion restrictions, but *Roe v. Wade* remains firmly ensconced. A Rehnquist opinion rejected a college affirmative action program, but his Court's approval of a law school program prevented a wholesale repudiation of affirmative action. Rehnquist permitted school voucher programs with parochial schools, but the Court's much-attacked precedents on separation of church and state are stronger than ever after the Ten Commandments decision. The Rehnquist Court restricted habeas corpus, but the Warren Court's major criminal law precedents remain solidly in place.

Although Rehnquist saw his Court make some movements in his direction, they were incremental steps around the edges. The ramparts that Rehnquist assaulted did not fall. His limited successes were far from the legacy of greatness that Rehnquist champions claim.

To give him his due, Rehnquist had a major impact in two important areas—restrictions on Congress's power and the immunity of state governments from federal law. For the first time since the early New Deal, the Supreme Court rejected laws as beyond Congress's power under the commerce clause, which gives Congress authority to regulate interstate commerce. For 5 to 4 majorities, Rehnquist ruled that Congress had not proved an adequate interstate basis for laws about guns near schools and violence against women. And, in a series of 5 to 4 opinions, Rehnquist's Court shielded state governments from imposition of federal law. Even in these areas, though, Rehnquist lost momentum. Over his dissents, the Court upheld federal power to ban California's medical marijuana law and to subject states to federal lawsuits about disability access in local courthouses.

As striking as Rehnquist's failures in other areas was his occasional invisibility. The most prominent example is the historic decision giving detainees in Guantanamo Bay access to federal courts. If ever there was a decision tailor-made for an important chief justice role, this was it, with the fundamental charting of the president's

---

Rehnquist will be remembered as a chief whose court took steps in directions he favored but fell far short of where he wanted to take it.

---

war powers and the courts' role. But Rehnquist not only was on the losing side—he was also a mute losing vote, silently joining Justice Antonin Scalia's dissent. Even when he was on the winning side, Rehnquist frequently failed to achieve the hallmark of a great chief: an opinion that speaks with clarity and finality on deeply disputed issues. In its best-known opinion, *Bush v. Gore*, the Rehnquist Court issued a brief unsigned opinion for five justices and a separate, additional opinion by Rehnquist for three of those five justices—hardly the kind of clear and ringing statement that one would expect in so momentous a case.

Of course, the chief justice has only one vote, and it will be pointed out that it was the votes of other justices that led to the contrary results. But such a defense proves the case of Rehnquist's middling legacy. It cannot be claimed, in the same breath, that he was a giant in his impact on the Court and that he cannot be held responsible for his lack of results.

In the end, Rehnquist will be remembered as a chief whose Court took steps in directions he favored but fell far short of where he wanted to take it. The interesting question will be whether the new Supreme Court, with a new chief and a new associate justice, will produce the sweeping changes that Rehnquist sought but failed to achieve.

The Rehnquist Difference

By Alan J. Borsuk
Milwaukee Journal Sentinel, June 27, 2004

He likes to make small bets on the Packers and play bridge and poker with friends. He likes Gilbert and Sullivan operettas and astronomy. He has given up tennis since slipping on some stairs and injuring a leg a couple of years ago.

History is a big interest. He's written four books on it.

Far more important, he's made a lot of it. He'll make more of it this week, and most likely for a while to come.

It's more than "Shorewood boy succeeds." It's "Shorewood boy leaves huge impact on American life."

Who is president today? What's the balance of power between Congress and the states? How easy is it to get an abortion? What's allowed when police stop someone? He's been at the heart of answering those and a long list of other hefty questions.

When the nine justices of the U.S. Supreme Court take the bench Monday morning, most likely to issue a landmark decision on the legal rights of suspected terrorists, William Hubbs Rehnquist will be sitting in the middle, voting from the right and the only one left from the presidency of Richard Nixon.

At 79—he'll be 80 on Oct. 1—Rehnquist will be ending the annual cycle of Supreme Court life for the 33rd time. He has been chief justice for 18 of those cycles.

"One of the three most important chief justices in history"—that's what Walter Dellinger, acting solicitor general in the Clinton administration, called Rehnquist in 2002.

Erwin Chemerinsky, a law professor at the University of Southern California and a noted authority on the Court, said in an interview, "I really think that he's somebody who will be regarded in hindsight as having had a tremendous influence on the course of constitutional law."

Rehnquist came to the Court with a strongly conservative vision, and "over time much of that vision has become constitutional law," Chemerinsky said. "He's left a mark, and the Court's functioning very differently than it used to, and I think he's responsible for that."

Quiet Branch of Government

You see the president on television all the time, and almost everyone knows a lot about him. Congress is largely an open book, and its members generally seek attention as a way to get votes.

The Supreme Court is the quiet, almost inscrutable branch of government—never on television, its decision-making done in private, its members generally inaccessible to the media, its proceedings long on intellect and ritual and short on pizzazz.

In many ways, the low-profile Rehnquist—would you recognize him if he passed you in the grocery store?—is a good match for the Court.

Described by many as friendly, low key, and unpretentious, he would never make it if image building were essential. Even the writing style he uses in opinions is straight-on and unadorned, generally avoiding flowery phrases or broad philosophizing.

In a rare television interview recently, he said one of his strengths as chief justice is that he has "a relatively passive nature," meaning he has "a very high boiling point," allowing him to be effective in maintaining good civil relations among justices even when they disagree on issues.

But just as no one mistakes the Court's stately profile for meaning it isn't at least equal in power to the presidency or Congress, no one mistakes Rehnquist's stately profile for meaning he isn't a major figure in shaping the Court.

Rehnquist can be called conservative in several senses of the term. It is certainly on target in describing his legal, social, and political views.

His personal style—except for a few things such as adding four gold stripes to each arm of his judicial robe a few years ago—is conservative.

And the steadiness with which he has held his views across his life, going back at least to college days at Stanford, can be called conservative. People who know him professionally and personally say he has changed little.

Tall and soft-spoken, he walks slowly and somewhat stooped over, but is believed to be in generally good health. He has learned to live with a bad back that troubled him more than 20 years ago and with the impact of tearing a leg muscle when he fell down some stairs in 2002.

In that recent television interview with PBS' Charlie Rose, Rehnquist said it would be "silly" if someone who was 79 said he doesn't think about retirement, but he has given no indication that he plans to take such a step soon—especially not now with the presidential election coming up. Observers assume no justice will retire before the election, but that either Republican President Bush or Democratic challenger John Kerry will have several appointments in the next term, most likely including Rehnquist's seat.

With 32 years on the Court, and almost 18 as chief justice, Rehnquist is already among the longest-serving justices in U.S. history (he would need about four more years to top William O. Douglas, but he says that is not a goal for him). He is the third longest-serving chief justice among only 17 people who have held the title.

The Rehnquist Court

Periods in Supreme Court history are usually known by the name of the chief justice, so the current Court is often referred to as the Rehnquist Court. To what degree is that so?

In any decision, the chief justice gets the same one vote as the other eight justices, and there is little indication that Rehnquist's power of persuasion has won over justices to his point of view very often.

Furthermore, Rehnquist is neither the most assertive conservative on the Court these days—Justices Antonin Scalia and Clarence Thomas are—nor is his vote the most closely watched. In a Court that often divides 5–4 in key cases, eyes are usually on Justice Sandra Day O'Connor, who frequently casts the swing vote.

On the other hand, the fact that Rehnquist presides not only when the Court hears arguments but in the justices-only conferences when cases are actually decided does give his role real weight. He also generally gets to decide who writes the opinions in a case.

A strong argument for calling this the Rehnquist Court is the way his view of how the Court should operate has come to dominate. He is much more efficient and less pompous than his predecessor, Warren Burger, and the Court sticks to its schedule much more. Furthermore, it takes fewer cases than it used to, down to 75 to 100 a year, compared with 125 to 150 under Burger.

But the main reason to call this the Rehnquist Court is simply because, whether directly his doing or not, the Court's decisions have moved in his direction over the years.

Rehnquist says he doesn't think much about his legacy, but when he amplifies on the subject, it appears that he, those who admire him, and those who criticize him are in substantial agreement on its main outlines:

He has a smoothly running Court where people get along and his views often prevail. He has played a big role in putting the brakes on many of the legal thrusts associated with the era of Chief Justice Earl Warren in the 1950s and 1960s—although the Court hasn't gone nearly as far to the right as some people either hoped or feared. And Rehnquist has led a movement to check some of the power of Congress to pass laws, favoring the notion that some subjects are better left to the states.

Highlights of Rehnquist's decades on the Court include his dissent in 1973 in the 7–2 *Roe v. Wade* decision that made abortion legal; his 1995 majority opinion in a 5–4 landmark decision that a federal law banning guns near schools was unconstitutional because the states, not Congress, had the power to control such activity; his majority opinion in a 5–4 decision in 2000 that the Boy Scouts of America was within its rights when it expelled an adult Scout leader because he was gay; and his majority opinion in the 5–4 decision in 2002 that found that private school voucher programs such as the one in Milwaukee are constitutional.

And, of course, in 2000, there was *Bush v. Gore*. When the battle over recounting the vote in Florida ended up in the Supreme Court, a 5–4 decision settled the issue in favor of Bush, with Rehnquist backing the president's position that the count should be terminated.

In addition, Rehnquist—the only current justice who was never a judge prior to joining the Court—presided over the impeachment trial in the U.S. Senate of President Bill Clinton.

Wisconsin Roots

Rehnquist's known penchant for placing small bets with friends on Packers and Badgers football games is one of his few ties these days to the state where he grew up. Since his mother died in 1988, he has returned to the Milwaukee area rarely, most recently in 2002 when he was honored by Shorewood High School 60 years after his graduation.

Rehnquist's father was head of the Milwaukee sales office of a medical equipment and supplies company. Rehnquist went to Shorewood's Atwater School and Shorewood Junior and Senior High School; he graduated in 1942, 11th in a class of 234.

Rehnquist never lived in Milwaukee after leaving to attend Stanford University in California. His time at Stanford was interrupted by three years in the Army Air Force. He received both bachelor's and master's degrees in 1948.

From there, he went to Harvard, where he received a master's degree in political science. He then returned to Stanford, graduating first in his law school class in 1952 (with Justice O'Connor a few slots behind him).

From Stanford, he became a clerk for then-Justice Robert Jackson, his first exposure to the Supreme Court.

While in Washington, Rehnquist met Natalie Cornell, a native of San Diego and then a CIA employee. They married in 1953 and had three children, a son and two daughters. Natalie Rehnquist died of cancer in 1991; Rehnquist remains single and says spending time with his children and 11 grandchildren is one of his main interests outside work.

Rehnquist moved to Phoenix in 1953 to go into private practice. Over the next 16 years, he became active in conservative politics and close personally with then–U.S. Sen. Barry Goldwater.

In 1969, when another Arizona Republican, Richard Kleindienst, became a top official in the Justice Department of the new administration of President Richard Nixon, Rehnquist was offered a position as head of the Justice Department's Office of Legal Counsel.

Rehnquist got onto the Court almost as an impulse pick by Nixon in October 1971 after others ran into opposition before they were nominated. Rehnquist, then 47, didn't know he was being considered until the day before Nixon announced the choice.

According to John Dean, the Nixon aide involved in the selections who later became famous in the Watergate scandal, Nixon preferred a Supreme Court nominee who was a woman and a Southerner.

Rehnquist was confirmed on a 68–26 Senate vote after contentious hearings that focused on such things as his views on racial issues, including a memo he wrote for Justice Jackson in 1952 on why the Supreme Court's 1896 decision that "separate but equal" facilities for black and white people should remain the law. Rehnquist argued that the memo was meant to outline a legal position and did not give his personal view, although some highly doubted his claim.

In 1986, when Warren Burger announced that he was retiring as chief justice, President Ronald Reagan nominated Rehnquist to head the Court.

In his early years on the Court, Rehnquist was often the lone dissenter in 8–1 decisions. But the six people who followed him to the Court were nominated by Republican presidents, and the Court moved decidedly more in line with Rehnquist's views.

On the other hand, the Court has not been either as conservative or as predictable as some expected. Many of the Warren- and Burger-era decisions on subjects such as affirmative action, abortion, freedom of speech, and criminal rights have been modified but still stand.

Overall, the Court has moved in a conservative direction—but done it conservatively, case by case, bit by bit.

In a 1985 interview in the *New York Times*, he said, "I don't know that a court should have a sense of mission. I think the sense of mission comes best from the president or the House of Representatives or the Senate.

"The Supreme Court and the federal judiciary are more the brakes that say, 'You're trying to do this, but you can't do it that way.'"

In reality, the Court has been frequently in the position of telling the country this is the way it is going to go—all the more reason to regard Rehnquist as a major figure of the times.

In the recent session with Charlie Rose, Rehnquist recounted how he intended, when he enrolled in graduate school in political science at Harvard in 1948, to become a professor of government.

But he decided first to take an occupational aptitude test funded by the GI Bill.

"It said I should be a lawyer," Rehnquist recalled.

More than a half-century later, he said, "I've obviously found my niche."

Timeline: William H. Rehnquist

1942: Graduates from Shorewood High School 11th in his class of 234.

1943–'46: Serves in U.S. Army Air Force during World War II.

1948: Receives bachelor's and master's degrees from Stanford University in California.

1949: Receives master's degree from Harvard.

1952: Graduates first in his law school class at Stanford.

1952–'53: Is clerk for U.S. Supreme Court Justice Robert Jackson.

1953–'69: Private law practice in Phoenix, becomes active in conservative politics, close friend of then–U.S. Sen. Barry Goldwater.

Aug. 8, 1953: Marries Natalie Cornell; son, James, born in 1955, daughters, Janet, born in 1957, and Nancy, in 1959.

1969: Joins the U.S. Justice Department in Washington as assistant attorney general in charge of the Office of Legal Counsel.

October 1971: Nixon unexpectedly nominates Rehnquist, then 47, and Lewis Powell Jr. to fill two vacancies on the Supreme Court.

January 1973: Rehnquist is one of two dissenters (the other is Byron White) in 7–2 *Roe v. Wade* decision legalizing abortion.

June 17, 1986: Chief Justice Warren Burger announces his retirement. President Ronald Reagan nominates Rehnquist to be chief justice and Antonin Scalia to replace Rehnquist.

Sept. 17, 1986: Rehnquist is confirmed as chief justice after contentious confirmation process.

1999: Presides over the Senate trial of President Bill Clinton on impeachment articles related to the Monica Lewinsky scandal.

2000: Votes with the 5–4 majority to end the election recount controversy in Florida, making George W. Bush president.

2002: Writes the main opinion in the court's 5–4 decision upholding the constitutionality of school voucher programs such as the one in Milwaukee.

Reviewing Rehnquist

BY RICHARD BRUST
ABA JOURNAL, MAY 2003

When it comes to changing people's minds about the Constitution, there have been few U.S. Supreme Court justices who espoused a philosophy and stuck with it as tenaciously as William H. Rehnquist. Sworn onto the bench in 1972, Rehnquist, an assistant attorney general under Richard Nixon, came with conservative credentials intact. He joined a Court that was still engaged in the ideals of the Earl Warren era: strong national government, deference to Congress, and a trail of historic civil rights cases.

In many opinions in the 1970s, Rehnquist was the lone dissenter on the right. But after being elevated to chief justice in 1986, he would help to usher in a change in legal thought that could rank him as among the most influential chief justices in the Court's history.

"Rehnquist is somebody with a long vision," says Duke law professor H. Jefferson Powell, a former deputy solicitor general. "His opinions oftentimes are prophetic of what's going to happen if he gets the votes."

Over the course of Rehnquist's tenure, lawyers, scholars, and other observers have analyzed the Court as if fitting together the pieces of a puzzle, case by case, anticipating where the next piece will come from, and trying to foretell what the picture might look like.

Now, with talk of his retirement becoming more audible, many are beginning to examine the assembled mosaic, taking in the chief justice's handiwork and assessing the Rehnquist Court as a movement.

"I think people are trying to step back," says Jed Rubenfeld of Yale Law School. "Since about 1995 the Court has been doing dramatic things in constitutional law, and we have gotten dramatic developments in different areas of doctrine. After a certain point, people say, 'Wait a second. Is there something that links these dramatic developments?' A lot of people are looking to see whether there is broader coherence."

A Defining Issue

Although the Rehnquist Court has come to be marked by rulings on such controversial issues as abortion, affirmative action and a presidential election, most observers identify federalism—the shift in power from the central government to states and private associations—as its hallmark.

Many agree that Rehnquist's emphasis on states' rights was apparent back in the 1970s. All anyone had to do then was to page through several opinions on relatively mundane matters and open to the dissent. There, under Rehnquist's name, was the blueprint for the idea that states deserve to be considered sovereign, far removed from the reach of Congress.

"It's quite clear that Rehnquist has been committed to enhancing states' rights ever since he was an associate justice," says Northwestern law professor Thomas Merrill.

"Rehnquist has been more skillful than most" in elucidating his philosophy, says Powell. "Some of the other justices think more on a case-by-case basis."

Powell's viewpoint is that Rehnquist detailed that philosophy soon after he joined the Court. One such case was *Fry v. United States*, 421 U.S. 542 (1975), a relatively run-of-the-mill ruling upholding wage and price controls imposed on states by the Nixon administration. Filing the lone dissent was the Court's junior member, but Rehnquist's argument outlined the philosophy that the Court would use in raising federalism to a defining principle.

To counter Congress' claim to authority under the commerce clause or the Fourteenth Amendment, wrote Rehnquist, states may assert an "affirmative constitutional defense," based on the idea that the framers intended a much greater degree of sovereignty.

In subsequent cases, Rehnquist persisted. The high-water mark was his 1976 opinion in *National League of Cities v. Usery*, 426 U.S. 833, which struck an early blow for state immunity from federal law—in this case the Fair Labor Standards Act, a treasured piece of New Deal legislation. A controversial decision, it was overruled less than a decade later in *Garcia v. San Antonio Metropolitan Transit Authority*, 469 U.S. 528 (1985).

Eleventh Amendment Emphasis

In 1979, Rehnquist got another opportunity to address his notion of federalism, *Nevada v. Hall*, 440 U.S. 410. In dissent, he wrote that "unconsenting states are not subject to the jurisdiction of the courts of other states."

Rehnquist's opinion in *Hall* highlights the Eleventh Amendment, which prohibits citizens of one state from suing another state in its courts. It also revives a 19th century case, *Hans v. Louisiana*, 134 U.S. 1 (1890), which expanded the Eleventh Amendment to bar a state's own citizens from suing their state in that state's courts. That ruling has informed some key federalism majorities of the last decade.

State immunity, Rehnquist wrote in *Hall*, stems from the "constitutional plan—the implicit ordering of relationships within the federal system necessary to make the Constitution a workable governing charter and to give each provision . . . the full effect intended by the framers."

That theme, with variations, has been replayed in the landmark cases that marked the last several terms, among them: *United States v. Lopez*, 514 U.S. 549 (1995) and *United States v. Morrison*, 529 U.S. 598 (2000), which limited Congress' authority under the commerce clause; *Alden v. Maine*, 527 U.S. 706 (1999), which held that Congress may not subject a state to suit in its own courts without the state's consent; and *Seminole Tribe v. Florida*, 517 U.S. 44 (1996), which further raised the importance of the Eleventh Amendment.

"Certainly, some of what were considered the more unusual [Rehnquist opinions] in the 1970s have come to pass," says Powell.

Now, in the waning years of Rehnquist's tenure, an emerging body of scholarship is scrutinizing how and why those decisions have come to pass. Experts see federalism emerging for different reasons and under different guises. For instance, Northwestern's Merrill, also a former deputy solicitor general, finds the source of the federalism movement in the sudden quiet from the Court's revolving door of justices.

According to Merrill, there really were two Rehnquist Courts: The first began in 1986 with Rehnquist's ascension to chief, the second around 1994, with the swearing in of Justice Stephen G. Breyer.

The difference can be described in one word: turnover. For the first eight years, the Court was in a state of flux, with the departure and subsequent replacement of six justices. By contrast, since 1994, the Court has experienced the longest interval without turnover since the early 1820s.

That transition is important, says Merrill. Among the consequences is a shift from cases dealing predominantly with social issues—religion, abortion, free speech, affirmative action—to those dealing with federalism.

"The emergence of these issues is not an accident," he writes in an article published this spring in the *Saint Louis University Law Review*. "The Court moved eagerly to put issues about federalism on the agenda."

Strength in Numbers

The reason for the shift might be described in an altered catch phrase: Familiarity breeds consent. With a consistent and predictable voting bloc in place, the second Rehnquist Court could get down to the business of advancing its judicial philosophy.

Merrill summons numbers to back his claim: From 1987–94, 17 cases dealt with social issues, 13 with federalism. From 1995–2002, nine cases could be classified as dealing with social issues, 25 dealt with federalism.

What's more, the number of 5–4 rulings gradually increased in the late 1990s, reaching an all-time high of 31 percent in the 2000 term, more than half of them by the dominant coalition that joined the chief justice: Justices Antonin Scalia, Clarence Thomas, Sandra Day O'Connor, and Anthony M. Kennedy.

But according to Merrill, the emergence of federalism is as much about group dynamics and the psychology of social bonding as it is about law.

With justices coming and going, the members of the first Rehnquist Court saw a need to test the newcomers and see where each stood. After all, congressional hearings revealed less and less about each nominee. Social issues cases were a way to prod a new justice and see what he or she was all about.

By the time the Court settled down in the mid-1990s, alliances had formed and held. Radical arguments on the left or right could not expect to find free-roaming allies anymore. Alignments coalesced and a core of justices began to feel more comfortable backing the chief's judicial philosophy.

"I don't think he has persuaded other justices that federalism is something they should be committed to," Merrill says in an interview. "It is something Rehnquist felt strongly about and he was able to get other justices on his side, but for their own particular reasons. It's a coalition based on mixed motives."

For Thomas, the motive was scorn for Congress and a deep belief in original intent, says Merrill. For Scalia, after years of lone stinging dissents, federalism was a platform he could hop on to lecture about other issues.

For Kennedy and O'Connor, sensitive to public opinion and accepting of precedent, the shift coincided with the Republicans' takeover of Congress. That afforded them the political cover to strike out, with greater confidence, in the direction of Rehnquist's federalism, according to Merrill.

Rehnquist's federalism philosophy allowed each justice a comfortable outlet for his or her ideas. "I don't really view Rehnquist as an intellectual leader," Merrill says. "He is an impresario. He is like the guy who deals the cards at a blackjack table. He's skilled at seeing where he has five votes."

Historic Parallel

For Northwestern law professor John O. McGinnis, the Rehnquist Court is less about wheeling and dealing than it is a return to early American life. In fact, says the former deputy assistant attorney general, the Rehnquist Court revives Alexis de Tocqueville's *Democracy in America*, the classic study read by every political science major about cultural life in the early republic.

Tocqueville, who arrived in 1831 from France, became fascinated with how and why American democracy worked. He identified a series of cultural and civic associations—groups that tempered raucous early American life and at the same time gave the smallest shopkeeper and community organizer a mouthpiece to contribute to the ongoing social conversation.

"Americans of all ages, all stations of life, and all types of disposition are forever forming associations," Tocqueville wrote. "In democratic countries knowledge of how to combine is the mother of all other forms of knowledge."

The motivation behind Rehnquist's federalism, McGinnis says, was to revitalize these groups and let them compete.

"These mediating institutions are still an important part of us," says McGinnis. The Court's agenda is a "revival of the markets" of competing ideas, he adds.

Nowhere is this better illustrated, says McGinnis, than in last term's school vouchers case, *Zelman v. Simmons-Harris*, 536 U.S. 639 (2002), which allows parents to use tuition vouchers for private schools, including religious schools. The upshot, says McGinnis, is the increase in competition among private associations.

"The voucher case is almost the most important case" last term, he says, "because it symbolizes competition in the crucible of education." And, he says, it "allows religion to come back in competitive influence."

Again, says McGinnis, in *Boy Scouts v. Dale*, 530 U.S. 640 (2000), the court invigorated what it called "expressive associations" by liberating groups from having to accept members whose views conflict with the association message. In this case, the Court upheld the Scouts' denial of membership to a gay individual.

Add state governments to the roster of competing associations, says McGinnis. That explains the Court's use of the Tenth and Eleventh Amendments to loosen the strings that tether states to Congress' will.

Not that states retain the same attachments today as in the early republic. "That notion of federalism is much less strong," McGinnis says. In fact, he says, he is "not at all sure federalism can be restored in its previous form." The associations that Tocqueville revered fulfill that purpose.

As distinct from McGinnis' historical interpretation of the Court's motives, Yale law professor Rubenfeld's interpretation is more critical. In fact, Rubenfeld sees the federalism debate as a mirage, a "trap" to ensnare the unsuspecting. The Court's real agenda, he says, is to reverse the steady march toward antidiscrimination law, a policy that Rubenfeld terms "anti-antidiscrimination."

"What struck me when I was looking at the groundbreaking cases of the last eight years was that you do see more innovative opinions," says Rubenfeld, a former assistant U.S. attorney in New York City. "But you didn't see a consistent federalism direction."

In fact, he says, "Sometimes a decision can sound like a federalism case, and be received and debated as a federalism case, without actually being a federalism case."

For Rubenfeld, the Court's federalism agenda is a stalking horse. Take, for example, the *Boy Scouts* case. The majority opinion, written by the chief justice, subjugates New Jersey's public-accommodations law to the Scouts' First Amendment right of expressive association.

Where, asks Rubenfeld, in the Constitution does one find a right to expressive association? Or is this an "unwritten constitutional right that felicitously pops up to prevent states from doing exactly what the Court has been supposedly telling us . . . that Congress cannot do without usurping state authority?"

That is, either the states are sovereign or they're not. And if not, then what is the Court's motivation? Says Rubenfeld, "The freedom of expressive association . . . is a right to discriminate." Period.

"What I saw," he says, "were two different kinds of cases." On the one hand, the Court has struck down federal laws because the Court saw its role as abiding by what the text of the Constitution says.

"But then," adds Rubenfeld, "you see *Boy Scouts*, where a state law was struck down, just the kind of law that the Supreme Court in its federalism decisions would uphold."

It's the flip side of McGinnis' concept of restoring Tocqueville's associations. "Antidiscrimination laws are nothing other than laws regulating association," says Rubenfeld, because most all associations engage in some kind of expression. Thus, the federalism trap.

Rubenfeld finds examples of such thinking up and down the line of the Court's canon of decisions that fall under the rubric of federalism.

"You know, there's this sense among lots of people that antidiscrimination law has gone too far," Rubenfeld says, referring to legal developments in sexual harassment and handicapped accommodation laws. "That's the core idea that might be uniting the Court."

Some See Bid for Supremacy

As for the idea of sovereignty, says New York University law professor Larry D. Kramer, the Rehnquist Court's legacy is less about state sovereignty than it is about judicial sovereignty, a bid for supremacy over the other two branches, especially Congress.

"These cases are less about political conservatism," Kramer maintains, "than they are about establishing the Court's own exclusive control over Congress."

In trimming back Congress' leeway to pass legislation, the Court has revealed its hand by lecturing the legislative branch in what it may or may not do under the Constitution, Kramer says.

The Court has gone so far as to admonish Congress for being remiss in not adopting the methods of fact-finding and analytical argument used by the judiciary.

Among other cases, Kramer cites *Morrison*, in which the Court struck down integral parts of the Violence Against Women Act as insufficiently supported by the commerce clause, among other reasons.

But, Kramer notes, despite the volumes of testimony from women who lost their jobs and required medical treatment, Rehnquist held that "the existence of congressional findings is not sufficient, by itself, to sustain the constitutionality of the commerce clause." The Court went on to criticize Congress' method of reasoning as "unworkable."

"Think of how Congress gathers information and makes a record," says Kramer. "It's different from the way courts do it, and we *want* it to be different."

For example, he says, "Judicial fact-finding is often about keeping things out of Court." Congress, on the other hand, strives to include as much information as possible.

Kramer's conclusion is that the Court is asserting its supremacy by insisting that Congress adopt the Court's language and customs. Hence, judicial sovereignty.

In addition, Kramer questions the notion favored by many contemporary conservatives that the federalism philosophy is based on the founding fathers' original intent. In a *Harvard Law Review* article two years ago, Kramer wrote that the founding generation never bothered to detail how the Court might review legislation, because it wasn't their intention that it do so.

"You just can't take these phrases out of context and understand them the way the founders understood them," says Kramer. The founders would have considered judicial review "repellent because it would have been tantamount to a monarchy. It was such a different world."

Whatever their approach, Kramer and others agree that the Rehnquist Court's federalism revival is revolutionary. "The doctrinal principles certainly are revolutionary," Kramer says.

Merrill concurs, and adds: "We are having a federalism revolution because, given the mix of motives and strategies among the nine justices, it is basically the only revolution to be had."

O'Connor's Legacy More Than a Mere Swing Vote

By Michael McGough
Toledo Blade (Ohio), July 3, 2005

Last Monday, likely her last day on the Supreme Court bench, Justice Sandra Day O'Connor served as the fifth vote for the Court's holding that two counties in Kentucky violated the First Amendment by posting the Ten Commandments, later augmented with secular documents, in their courthouses.

But in addition to signing the majority opinion of Justice David Souter, one of the Court's staunchest advocates of a strict separation of church and state, Justice O'Connor wrote a separate concurring opinion in which she emphasized that the Court was ruling as it did "for the same reason that guided the Framers—respect for religion's special role in society."

Justice O'Connor's role in the Ten Commandments case—providing the fifth vote for the majority while writing separately in softer tones—exemplified the influential role she has played in her 24 years on the Court.

It is a cliché that Justice O'Connor is a swing vote, sometimes voting with liberals, sometimes with conservatives, but she has been more than a whimsical wild card. Her case-by-case approach and penchant for separate concurrences have prevented the Court from embracing extreme positions, to the consternation of more ideological colleagues, especially Justice Antonin Scalia.

Justice O'Connor has become the arbiter of entire areas of constitutional law, including the role of religion in public life. She is the author of what is called the "endorsement test" for determining whether government involvement with religion violates the First Amendment. Under that test, the Court asks whether a "reasonable observer" would consider, say, a Nativity scene in a courthouse an endorsement of religion.

"O'Connor has been remarkably consistent and consistently influential," said Nancy Maveety, an associate professor of political science at Tulane University and the author of *Sandra Day O'Connor: Strategist on the Court*. Justice Maveety, who has analyzed Justice O'Connor's voting patterns over many years, described Justice O'Connor as "contextually conservative," which means that the justice is "comparatively restrained when it comes to revising or over-turning precedent and is likely to reason by exception when faced with a case not adequately covered by an existing rule."

Ms. Maveety described Justice O'Connor's approach to judging as "judicial accommodationism," and said that Justice O'Connor had made it a practice to join "minimum-winning collations" on the Court, enhancing her influence further by writing either "regular" concurring opinions (in cases in which she also signed the majority opinion) or "special" concurrences, in which she concurred only in the result.

The result of Justice O'Connor's "accommodationism," Ms. Maveety said, is that the Court as a whole often will embrace a "common-sense" position in tune with public opinion.

That's the problem, Justice O'Connor's critics have charged, accusing her of being unprincipled and of acting like the legislator she once was.

In reacting yesterday to her retirement, Derek Gaubatz, director of litigation of the Becket Fund for Religious Liberty, praised Justice O'Connor for her generous view of the First Amendment's Free Exercise Clause, but complained about Justice O'Connor's approach to another part of the First Amendment prohibiting the "establishment" of religion by government.

"She was stubbornly resistant to any sort of categorization." Mr. Gaubatz said. "Her 'reasonable observer' test for government display of religious symbols led the Court away from any principled interpretation of what counts as an 'establishment of religion' to a

Martin H. Simon-Pool/Getty Images

Associate Justice Sandra Day O'Connor, the first woman to sit on the Court, announced her retirement in July 2005.

subjective test that varied with the whims (including frequently Justice O'Connor herself) of the individual justices."

But the case-by-case approach that O'Connor's critics see as a vice is regarded as a virtue by some legal observers.

"In any given era you're likely to find someone occupying that middle position on the Court," said Edward B. Foley, a law professor at Ohio State University and a former Ohio state solicitor.

"Like Justice Lewis Powell [in the 1970s and '80s], Justice O'Connor was a balancer, and it's not surprising that a balancer ends up as a swing vote."

Ken Gormley, a professor of law at Duquesne University who is close to Justice O'Connor, offered a similar description. "I think she really made her name in recent years as a pragmatist," Mr. Gormley said. "She found practical solutions to impossible problems."

As would not be the case if it were Chief Justice William Rehnquist who had stepped down yesterday, a retirement that was widely expected because of Chief Justice Rehnquist's poor health, the Court's position on several issues could be up for grabs depending on the philosophy of the woman or man who succeeds Justice O'Connor.

"The stakes are much higher after an O'Connor retirement than after a Rehnquist retirement," said Michael Comiskey, associate professor of political science at Penn State's Fayette campus and the author of *Seeking Justices: The Judging of Supreme Court Nominees.* "If he chooses someone in the mold of Justice [Antonin] Scalia or [Clarence] Thomas, I think we would have another situation like the one involving Robert Bork," Mr. Comiskey added, referring to President Ronald Reagan's unsuccessful nominee for the Court in 1987. "On the other hand, if he chose someone who was perceived as only a moderate conservative confirmation would be easier."

Within hours of Justice O'Connor's announcement yesterday, e-mail Inboxes in Washington were filled with litanies of the decisions in which Justice O'Connor cast the crucial vote for a liberal position—holdings that might be undone by a more ideological successor.

Religion. In addition to her votes this week to strike down Ten Commandments monuments on public property in Kentucky and in Texas (where she was in the minority), Justice O'Connor was part of a 5–4 majority that ruled in the 1992 case of *Lee v. Weisman* that a prayer at a public school graduation was unconstitutional.

Abortion. Justice O'Connor joined the majority in the 1992 *Planned Parenthood of Southeast Pennsylvania v. Casey* decision that reaffirmed the essential holding of *Roe v. Wade* by a 5–4 vote. In 2000 she was part of a 5–4 majority in *Stenberg v. Carhart* striking down a Nebraska law banning so-called "partial-birth" abortions. A similar federal law is moving up the appeals process.

Affirmative action. Justice O'Connor wrote the majority opinion in the 2003 case of *Grutter v. Bollinger* upholding an affirmative action program at the University of Michigan Law School and reaffirming a principle first enunciated in the 1978 *Bakke* case that state universities may consider race as one factor in admissions.

Civil rights. Although critical in earlier cases of "racial gerrymandering" designed to maximize minority voting power, Justice O'Connor was part of a 5–4 majority in the 2001 case of *Hunt v. Cromartie* allowing legislators to take race into account in redistricting. Last year, in *Tennessee v. Lane*, Justice O'Connor joined with four liberal justices to uphold the right of disabled people to sue state governments under the Americans With Disabilities Act.

Although much attention yesterday was focused on swing votes in which Justice O'Connor supported a liberal result, she often swung in the conservative direction. Along with Justices Rehnquist, Scalia, Thomas, and Anthony Kennedy, Justice O'Connor was a member of the "Federalism Five," a bare majority that struck down part or all of two federal laws—the Gun-Free School Zones Act and the Violence Against Women Act—on the grounds that they infringed on states' rights.

Arthur Hellman, a law professor at the University of Pittsburgh, noted that Justice O'Connor remained an ardent supporter of states' rights through her final term. For example, she vigorously dissented from last month's 6–3 decision in *Gonzales v. Raich* upholding the right of the federal government to prosecute users of medical marijuana in California, despite the fact that the state allows the use of the drug by cancer patients. Mr. Hellman cited that dissent and Justice O'Connor's equally astringent dissent in last week's 5–4 *Kelo v. City of New London* decision upholding the use of eminent domain as evidence that she was "going back to her roots" this term and voting conservatively. In the marijuana and eminent domain cases, Mr. Hellman noted, Justice Kennedy, not Justice O'Connor, voted with liberals—as he did this term in a 5–4 vote striking down the death penalty for murderers under the age of 18.

Mr. Hellman added that the fact that Justice Kennedy also has been a swing vote might complicate any plans President Bush has to move the Court rightward.

"If Bush appoints someone quite conservative, I can see Kennedy moving more to the liberal camp," Mr. Hellman said.

V. The Future of the Court

Editors' Introduction

Prior to the announced retirement of Sandra Day O'Connor in July 2005 and the death of William Rehnquist in September 2005, the same nine justices had served on the bench for over a decade, one of the longest periods without a vacancy in the Supreme Court's over-200-year existence. However, familiarity has not bred ideological consensus. Indeed, the Court has been one of the most divided in history, with the reliably liberal justices John Paul Stevens, Ruth Bader Ginsburg, and Stephen Breyer joined by David Souter frequently pitted against the arch-conservatives William Rehnquist, Antonin Scalia, and Clarence Thomas, who usually had the support of Anthony Kennedy. This breakdown often left the less-predictable centrist conservative O'Connor the swing vote in important decisions. With O'Connor's impending departure, liberal groups had feared that President George W. Bush would appoint a doctrinaire conservative along the lines of a Scalia or Thomas, who would definitively tilt the Court's balance rightward, likely threatening such pillars of progressive orthodoxy as civil rights, abortion rights, gay rights, environmental protection laws, and the separation of church and state. With the stakes so high, few doubted that a cataclysmic confirmation battle was imminent.

Bush's nomination of U.S. Court of Appeals judge John G. Roberts Jr. to replace O'Connor and then to succeed Rehnquist as chief justice forestalled that anticipated clash, however. Though quite conservative, Roberts's thoughtful, even-tempered manner made it difficult for progressive groups to rally the public against his confirmation. Bush's unexpected selection of Harriet Miers to replace O'Connor similarly circumvented a divisive ideological confrontation. While many of the president's supporters expressed disappointment that he did not pick a more renowned and better credentialed conservative, the Democratic opposition in Congress initially did not scuttle Miers's candidacy: they merely characterized her as an undistinguished Bush "crony" who received the nomination in return for her years of loyal service to the commander in chief.

The articles in this chapter explore how the Court is likely to evolve in the years ahead, taking into account the impact the addition of Roberts and other anticipated changes may have. Drawing upon Roberts's writings and testimony before Congress, Charles Lane considers how the new chief justice will likely behave on the bench in the opening piece, "Roberts Was Influenced by Critics of the Warren Court." "Roberts," Lane argues, "has consistently espoused a clear view of federal judicial intervention: Less is more." That said, it remains an open question as to how Roberts will rule on some of the more divisive matters facing the judiciary, such as abortion and gay rights. As with Roberts, Miers's positions on these and other controversial issues is similarly uncertain. The subsequent piece, "Bush's Unconventional Choice," by Linda Feldmann, Warren Richey, and Gail Russell Chaddock, describes Miers's background but notes that her views are even less clearly defined than those of Roberts.

Alan J. Borsuk argues in "Stable Court Defied Forecasts" that with the departures of O'Connor and Rehnquist—as well as the advancing age of the liberally inclined John Paul Stevens—the delicate ideological balance that had existed on the Court will likely be upset. Given George W. Bush's political bent, Borsuk reasonably expects a more conservative Court; however, using David Souter as an example, he notes that there is always a degree of uncertainty as to how a justice will rule once on the bench.

In "Picking Judges a Disorderly Affair," Charlie Savage describes how the judicial confirmation process has changed over the past few decades, developing into a new front in the culture wars, with liberal and conservative groups lobbying the public, as well as like-minded politicians, so as to scuttle particular nominations.

Though one might not know it from the apocalyptic language often employed by political partisans, the Supreme Court rarely "turns on a dime," Tony Mauro argues in "High Court Reality Check." Thus liberal worries that a retirement or two could spell the end of legalized abortion and gay rights, among other things, are largely unfounded, Mauro claims.

Roberts Was Influenced by Critics of the Warren Court

By Charles Lane
The Washington Post, September 6, 2005

From his youthful days as a Reagan administration aide to his current job as a judge on the U.S. Court of Appeals for the District of Columbia Circuit, John G. Roberts Jr. has consistently espoused a clear view of federal judicial intervention: Less is more.

This same principle was held dear by the man Roberts served as a Supreme Court clerk, the late William H. Rehnquist—whose former position as chief justice of the United States is now suddenly within Roberts's grasp.

In the quarter-century since he served as Rehnquist's aide, Roberts has made an instinctual and deeply held conservatism plain at nearly every turn. As a young Reagan administration aide, he registered his skepticism toward Court-recognized "fundamental rights," such as the right to privacy. Earlier this year, Judge Roberts voted to permit President Bush to subject terrorism suspects to military trials at Guantanamo Bay.

The question—more urgent now since Bush nominated him yesterday morning to lead the high court—is where Roberts's vision of judicial restraint would lead him on the most volatile issues. The woman Roberts was originally tapped to replace, Justice Sandra Day O'Connor, sometimes displayed her conservatism by bowing to precedents on social issues—notably *Roe v. Wade*, which established a right to abortion rooted in a right to privacy. Rehnquist labored mightily to reverse some rulings on abortion and the rights of criminal defendants that he thought were wrongly decided in the first place.

To Roberts's supporters, his history suggests he will be a careful and principled leader of the federal judiciary, one who would restore the true constitutional balance of power between the courts and the people's elected representatives in Congress, the White House, and the states.

To his opponents, it suggests a willingness to leave the constitutional rights of women and minorities unprotected against violations by the more political branches of government.

What is unmistakable from Roberts's record, however, is that his essential philosophy about the role of courts in American life is strongly held. There is little prospect that the 50-year-old judge will be any less likely to press his beliefs in conference with colleagues on the Court than he was to promote them in memos to his elders in the Reagan administration.

Sounding very much like the 26-year-old aide who ghostwrote articles and speeches on judicial restraint for President Ronald Reagan's Justice Department, Roberts told the Senate firmly in a written submission last month that federal judges "do not have a commission to solve society's problems, as they see them, but simply to decide cases before them according to the rule of law."

The Primacy of Process

Roberts has said that defining the proper boundaries of judicial review is a "central problem" of American government. Few legal analysts of any ideological stripe would dispute that.

Throughout history, the Supreme Court has provoked controversy by using its power to declare laws unconstitutional in ways that critics saw as overstepping its authority.

Roberts has said that defining the proper boundaries of judicial review is a "central problem" of American government.

President Thomas Jefferson condemned the 1803 *Marbury v. Madison* decision that established the doctrine of judicial review.

The *Dred Scott* case of 1857—which declared that black people were "beings of an inferior order" and that congressional efforts to restrict slavery in northern territories were a violation of property rights—discredited the institution for a generation. A series of rulings striking down state and federal economic regulations provoked President Franklin D. Roosevelt's "Court-packing" plan, until the justices backed down and began upholding New Deal legislation.

In the 1950s and '60s, the Supreme Court looked at the country's problems and decided, time and again, that the federal judiciary should reform society and establish individual rights. Even today, long after the death of the chief justice, Earl Warren, who led the Court during that period, and long after a majority of the Court has been named by Republican presidents who opposed the Warren Court's innovations, the Court continues to recognize such Warren-like concepts as a "fundamental right" to privacy that protects abortion and private consensual homosexual conduct.

The Warren revolution remains a model for many people of how the Court must act as a guarantor of individual and minority rights. Roberts, however, was one of those who recoiled from the Warren Court's activism.

Roberts grew up in a mostly white Indiana suburb where his father's steel company was touched by federal court battles over affirmative action, and he attended Harvard College and Harvard Law School as Boston was grappling, sometimes violently, with court-ordered school desegregation.

Mark Wilson/Getty Images

Chief Justice John G. Roberts Jr.

But his gravitation to concepts of judicial restraint probably reflected the natural bent of his orderly, traditionalist mind, rather than the controversies swirling outside the academic setting in which he spent most of the 1970s.

Asked by a senator in 2003 to name the legal text that most influenced him, Roberts chose the 1973 edition of Hart & Wechsler's *The Federal Courts and the Federal System*, a 1,657-page legal textbook used in Harvard's class on federal courts. It has always been "within reach of my desk" since law school, he told the Senate. And, indeed, he has often cited it in his writings since Cambridge.

Unknown to most Americans, the Hart & Wechsler volume is instantly recognizable to law professors as an exhaustive, sophisticated—and deeply skeptical—treatment of the Warren Court revolution.

It is considered a virtual Bible of a postwar legal movement known as the Legal Process School, especially influential at Harvard, whose leading figures were liberals and conservatives who professed concern not so much for the results the court was reaching as for the damage its overreaching might do to the judiciary's own legitimacy.

Roberts's choice of the book is "extremely revealing," said Cass Sunstein, a professor of law at the University of Chicago.

For the Legal Process School, it was a given that "judges in solving legal problems are not doing the same thing that legislators are doing in solving political problems," says Todd Rakoff, a professor of law at Harvard.

The strength of Legal Process was its insistence that courts adhere to neutral principles, that they "should not become champions of particular causes or litigants," as Dennis J. Hutchinson, a professor of law at the University of Chicago, puts it.

Yet Legal Process has lost influence in more recent years, under attack from a new generation of law professors who fault it for ignoring the political power relationships embedded in the law—that its insistence on identifying neutral principles is unrealistic.

> *To many, Roberts's intellectual pedigree marks him as a careful "lawyer's lawyer."*

"The question about legal process," Rakoff says, "is 'Is it true that there are legal answers that aren't political answers?'"

A Closet Activist?

That, in essence, is the critique liberals are raising about Roberts's jurisprudence today: that his insistence on a limited role for the federal courts is a cover for conservative policy preferences.

Announcing its opposition to Roberts, the Alliance for Justice said that Roberts supports "weakening women's rights and civil rights laws, cutting back the vital role of our courts in enforcing legal protections and restricting the ability of the people's democratically elected representatives to enact crucial, nationwide worker, anti-discrimination and environmental safeguards."

Court conservatives such as Rehnquist and Justices Antonin Scalia and Clarence Thomas have also espoused judicial restraint. Yet that has not prevented them from striking down many federal and state statutes, often on the basis of a states'-rights doctrine that dissenting justices on the court have criticized as too loosely based in constitutional text.

The accusation that Roberts is capable of his own brand of activism has not come exclusively from liberal advocacy groups.

On the D.C. Circuit, he wrote an opinion for a 2 to 1 majority in which he interpreted a law to deny a former Amtrak employee the right to sue the government-subsidized railroad in federal court for allegedly spending taxpayer money on defective railroad cars.

Judge Merrick Garland wrote in dissent that Roberts's opinion "falls back on policy considerations" but "the policy [sic] on which the court relies are not those of the Congress of the United States."

But to many, Roberts's intellectual pedigree marks him as a careful "lawyer's lawyer," with a healthy recognition of the courts'—and his own—fallibility.

"Of all the people Bush could have nominated, this is a guy who is actually telling the truth when he says he can't decide a case until he's seen the facts and the briefs," says Jonathan Macey, a professor of law at Yale University.

St. John's University law professor John Barrett, noting that Roberts has named legal craftsmen such as Justices Felix Frankfurter and Robert Jackson as the Supreme Court members he most admires, suggests that he "may end up disappointing President Bush."

If he remains true to the legal view embodied by the Legal Process School, Barrett said, "he'll shy from agenda-driven decision making" and respect long-established precedents, even those, such as *Roe v. Wade*, of which he may disapprove.

"A kind of continuity of judicial decision-making is a value in the process world," Barrett said. "Moderation, deference, continuity, caution, candor—it's not swing for the fences judging."

Another crucial influence on Roberts's judicial philosophy was Henry J. Friendly, a judge on the U.S. Court of Appeals for the 2nd Circuit in New York, for whom Roberts worked as a law clerk in 1979–1980, just after graduating from Harvard.

Friendly, a Rockefeller Republican who served on the 2nd Circuit from 1959 until his death in 1986, is widely regarded as the most talented appeals court judge of his generation. He was a longtime private-sector lawyer who wrote his own rigorous opinions, as well as many influential law review articles.

He regularly plucked top students from Harvard, where he had studied, to be his aides. Roberts, whose credentials as a prize-winning undergraduate majoring in history and managing editor of the *Harvard Law Review* matched Friendly's own, got his clerkship without even having to be interviewed, according to Richard J. Lazarus, Roberts's close friend.

Friendly could be a stern taskmaster. "Sometimes the clerk thought he had something interesting to say, and sometimes the judge would disagree," said Macey, also a former Friendly clerk.

Roberts loved him. His esteem is evident not only from his frequent citations of Friendly's work in his own writings, including six of his 49 opinions on the D.C. Circuit, but also from the fact that he corresponded with the judge throughout his time as a Reagan aide.

In one letter, dated Nov. 4, 1981, Roberts told Friendly that it was "an exciting time to be at the Justice Department, when so much that has been taken for granted for so long is being seriously reconsidered." He continued: "You assist us down here every day through the articles and opinions that so often light the way."

Friendly's views on many issues paralleled those of the Legal Process School, says Rakoff, a former Friendly clerk. The 1988 edition of the Hart & Wechsler book is dedicated to him.

Friendly felt that the Warren Court's 1966 *Miranda v. Arizona* ruling, which created the "right to remain silent," was misguided. In a famous 1970 article, Friendly attacked the Warren Court for opening up state criminal convictions to wide-ranging federal court review.

Friendly felt that a state conviction should usually be challengeable in federal court only when the prisoner also had a strong claim of innocence, rather than wasting the courts' time on technical issues raised by guilty defendants.

But the Warren Court had expanded access to the federal courts as a remedy for what it considered the widespread abuse of rights by state criminal justice systems, especially in the South.

Friendly thought state courts were just as capable of protecting federal constitutional rights as federal courts were.

On Nov. 12, 1981, Roberts offered then–Attorney General William French Smith his unsolicited critique of the Warren Court's decisions, in a memo that cited Friendly's article seven times and the Hart & Wechsler book once.

"The current availability of federal habeas corpus"—the legal term for post-conviction constitutional challenges—"particularly for state prisoners, goes far to making a mockery of the entire criminal justice system," he wrote.

In April 2003, Roberts, sitting before the Senate Judiciary Committee as a nominee to the U.S. Court of Appeals for the D.C. Circuit, offered similar comments in response to a question by Sen. Russell Feingold (D-Wis.) about the death penalty—a major source of habeas corpus petitions in federal court.

Roberts replied that "it's not certain, it's not definite, and there doesn't seem to be any reasonable time limitation. The effectiveness, if you believe in capital punishment, the effectiveness of capital punishment diminishes if the crime was committed 30 years ago. And if it takes that long to get through the system, it's not working, whether you're in favor of the death penalty or against it."

In the meantime, however, conservative critiques of federal habeas had become the law of the land. In 1996, the Republican Congress passed, and President Bill Clinton, a Democrat, signed a bill that sharply restricted access to federal habeas corpus.

Nevertheless, petitions for habeas corpus from state prisoners continue to occupy much of the Court's time—far more than higher-profile issues such as abortion and school prayer.

Bush's Unconventional Choice

By Linda Feldmann, Warren Richey, and Gail Russell Chaddock
The Christian Science Monitor, October 4, 2005

From a reputed short list of potential U.S. Supreme Court nominees crowded with conservative judicial stars, President Bush has selected a woman he knows well personally and trusts—but who brings to the table little public record on which to assess her views.

Harriet Miers, the White House counsel, has never been a judge and is not a recognized expert on constitutional law, in sharp contrast to the new chief justice, John Roberts.

Still, she has diverse experience, including many years in private law practice, and political experience that none of the sitting justices has, both as a member of the Dallas City Council and, for the past five years, as a member of Mr. Bush's White House inner circle. Before being named counsel 10 months ago, Ms. Miers had served as assistant to the president, staff secretary, and deputy chief of staff.

As the replacement for the retiring Sandra Day O'Connor, the first woman justice, Miers would maintain the presence of two women on the Court, and perhaps also present a counterweight to the liberal Ruth Bader Ginsburg.

In announcing her nomination Monday morning, Bush said she "stood out as exceptionally well suited to sit on the highest court of our nation."

Reaction to Miers's selection was swift and varied, from across the political spectrum. Some conservatives expressed enthusiasm; others moaned that she is unqualified and, more troubling, a stealth nominee who cannot be counted upon to side with the conservatives, especially on incendiary social issues such as abortion, gay rights, and the church-state divide.

From the left, the cries of cronyism were equally piercing, aimed at a president under fire of late for placing appointees of questionable qualifications in central positions, such as federal emergency management and immigration. Miers's selection also harks back to Bush's naming of Dick Cheney as his running mate in 2000, when Mr. Cheney headed up the Bush team's veep vetting process.

But just as striking were the words of encouragement from a key Democrat, Senate minority leader Harry Reid. Senator Reid, in fact, acknowledges that he recommended Miers for the nomination. In a statement after Bush's announcement, Reid said, ". . . the Supreme Court would benefit from the addition of a justice who has real experience as a practicing lawyer."

Miers now faces the daunting challenge of following John Roberts to the witness chair in the Senate Judiciary Committee. Chief Justice Roberts came to the table with a golden résumé and no questions over qualifications, just over judicial philosophy. Miers will need to show enough senators that she has the legal chops to merit lifetime appointment to the nation's ultimate appeals court.

Democrats are going see her as "someone who has distinguished herself purely through political appointments," says Michael Gerhardt, a law professor at the University of North Carolina and a judicial confirmation expert. "It is hard to look at her career and think that the next logical step for her from White House counsel is to be on the Supreme Court of the United States."

With little hard evidence that Miers will take positions that please the activist base of the Republican Party, Bush is essentially saying to his party, "Trust me," says Professor Gerhardt.

> ### *Miers's selection . . . may point to a reluctance by Bush to tempt the possibility of a filibuster in the Senate.*

Miers's selection over the many other long-mentioned candidates—with lengthier paper trails—may point to a reluctance by Bush to tempt the possibility of a filibuster in the Senate. If Senate Democrats were to engage in endless debate, Bush and his Republican allies would then face a decision over whether to go "nuclear" by changing the rules and allowing his nominee to pass with a simple majority. To some analysts, Bush's selection of a nominee who does not trigger automatic, fierce partisan opposition in the Senate is a sign of his weakened political position.

But now Bush is facing qualms from his right flank. "Many conservatives today will view this as the most unqualified nominee since Abe Fortas," says Manuel Miranda, chairman of the Third Branch Conference, a coalition of libertarian and conservative organizations and a former counsel on judicial nominations to Senate majority leader Bill Frist. "It's exactly the opposite of what we were looking for . . . to undo the need for stealth nominees."

Questions were raised about Mr. Fortas's nomination because of his friendship with President Lyndon Johnson.

Conservative activist lawyer Jay Sekulow, a stalwart in backing White House judicial nominees and an emissary to religious conservatives, backs Miers fully. She represents "the conservative mainstream of judicial philosophy of interpreting the Constitution, not rewriting it," he said in a statement, touting as one example Miers's leadership in opposing the American Bar Association decision to come out in support of *Roe v. Wade*, the abortion rights precedent. He does not address the issue of her donations to Democratic political candidates, including Al Gore in 1988.

Miers is not the first high Court nominee to lack judicial experience. Former Chief Justice William Rehnquist had never been a judge prior to donning the robes of a justice. Lewis Powell, a member of the high court from 1972 to 1987, was one of the nation's most respected lawyers but had no prior service on the bench.

Likewise, Chief Justices John Marshall and Earl Warren were not jurists before joining the court.

Harriet Miers File

- Born in 1945, in Dallas.
- Degrees in mathematics (1967) and law (1970) from Southern Methodist University.
- Joined Dallas law firm in 1972; by 1985, was first woman president of Dallas Bar Association.
- Member, Dallas City Council, 1989–1991.
- Chairwoman of Texas lottery commission from 1995 to 2001, when she joined the White House. She has been counsel to President Bush since February 2005.
- Named by *National Law Journal* as one of the nation's 100 most powerful attorneys.
- Has worked with multiple charities, including the Young Women's Christian Association, Childcare Dallas, Goodwill Industries, Exodus Ministries, Meals on Wheels, and the Legal Aid Society.
- Single; no children.

White House Press Release, Associated Press

Stable Court Defied Forecasts

By Alan J. Borsuk
Milwaukee Journal Sentinel, September 6, 2005

By one measure, the death of Chief Justice William H. Rehnquist ends the most stable period for the U.S. Supreme Court in more than 180 years. Until this year, Aug. 3, 1994, was the last time a justice left the Court—a run of 11 years and one month with no change in the roster of the nine justices.

By another measure, the Court's Rehnquist years were a period of unpredictability in which major issues often were decided by 5–4 votes and justices in the middle held great power.

The liberal days of the 1960s under Chief Justice Earl Warren were over, but conservative justices, starting with Rehnquist, never quite got a solid lock on the Court.

Things conservatives most wanted and liberals most feared, such as wholesale overturning of decisions made in the Warren era and reversal of the *Roe v. Wade* abortion-rights decision of 1973, didn't come to pass.

Whether that second period also is at an end is a question that will fuel the actions of both conservatives and liberals as they tackle the nomination of U.S. Appeals Judge John Roberts to succeed Rehnquist immediately, and as they look to deal with a nomination for a successor to Justice Sandra Day O'Connor at some point.

The timing of President Bush's move Monday to switch Roberts' destination from O'Connor's chair to Rehnquist's was a surprise; it came less than 36 hours after Rehnquist's death and before the chief justice's funeral.

But it was not a surprise that Bush turned to Roberts when he has such major problems staring him in the face, the Iraq war and the aftermath of Hurricane Katrina in particular.

Roberts, who was nominated in July, generally has been well received. There will be opposition as his nomination goes before the Senate, but Roberts is almost certain to be sitting in the center seat on the Court soon, likely even by Oct. 3, when the Court's term begins.

Substituting Roberts, who once was a clerk for Rehnquist, for Rehnquist does not really change the balance of power on the Court—or, more accurately, the uncertainty about the balance of power.

Rehnquist was a reliable conservative vote during his 33 years on the bench and never wavered in opposing abortion, among several issues. Roberts is likely to have a similar voting pattern, which means the forecast is for not much change in the votes from the chief justice's seat.

> *It is a good rule of thumb that unpredictability about the Court's future grows as the time frame grows.*

But Bush's decision on Roberts means the president will have a second shot at filling O'Connor's seat, and she has been the most significant swing vote on the Court in recent years, the justice most likely to be the fifth vote in a 5–4 decision. For example, she can be looked at as the person who has kept affirmative action alive in the country in recent years. Filling her position is actually a bigger deal than filling Rehnquist's when it comes to counting votes.

The battle over filling O'Connor's position might be all the more intense. A second nominee from Bush, particularly if the nominee is someone without the credentials and political ability of Roberts and with more adamant conservative stands, could face much stiffer opposition than Roberts has faced.

Pivotal Choices

The outcomes for the two seats will affect the Court for decades. Logically, it will lead to solidifying a conservative majority on the Court. Furthermore, the most liberal member of the Court, John Paul Stevens, also is the oldest member of the Court; he's 85. He's in good health, but the chance for more change on the Court favorable to conservatives before the end of Bush's second term can't be ignored.

Yet it is a good rule of thumb that unpredictability about the Court's future grows as the time frame grows.

With his quick action Monday, Bush greatly reduced the uncertainty about what is going to happen on the Court in the next few weeks. Most likely, there will be only a very brief interim period without a chief justice.

But Bush did much less to reduce the unknown elements of the next few months.

Will he nominate someone to succeed O'Connor quickly? If so, whom? Will the nominee win Senate confirmation? Or will O'Connor end up staying on the Court for the entire term, which ends next summer? Her retirement announcement in June was worded so that her retirement doesn't take effect until her successor is confirmed.

Think of Souter

And as for the unknown elements of the Court's future for the next few decades, consider two things.

Souter has become a code word for conservatives. Nominated by President George H. W. Bush in 1990, Justice David Souter has turned out to be a moderate to liberal justice and not the conservative many expected.

Conservatives want to do all they can to avoid putting someone on the Court who looks conservative but will turn out to be not quite so.

And seven of the nine justices during the last 11 years of the Rehnquist Court were nominated by Republican presidents. There ought to have been a reliable majority that Republicans liked in recent years. But Court decisions have upset Republicans just about as often as Democrats—more often than Democrats, some would say—in recent years.

Rehnquist himself said in recent years that changing the Court was like turning a battleship, something done in gradual steps and not abruptly.

The Court, he said, isn't like Congress, in which members can pick an issue, throw a bill in the hopper, and launch a campaign. It is much more influenced by precedent, and it moves in increments so gradual that it might take years to see new patterns.

Bush clearly is in a position to make powerful decisions on the future of the Court. He acted with that knowledge Monday.

No president since Richard Nixon in 1971 has had such a condensed opportunity to change the Supreme Court. But that doesn't mean things will turn out just the way Bush hopes.

Presidents try to steer the Court with their appointments, yet as historians and justices have said, the Court tends to steer itself once the justices are seated.

The long run of stability in Court membership is over. It's a different thing to predict that the long run of unpredictability also is at an end.

Picking Judges a Disorderly Affair

By Charlie Savage
The Boston Globe, May 8, 2005

To her friends in Texas, Priscilla Owen, President Bush's appeals court nominee, is a woman who grew up on a farm with her widowed mother, aced the bar exam, sings in her church choir, and trains guide dogs in her spare time. But in the nation's capital, Owen is known only by rival slogans.

To the liberal People for the American Way, Owen is an "extremist" who would "overturn more than 100 Supreme Court precedents affecting the environment, civil rights, privacy and reproductive rights, and religious liberty."

To the conservative Committee for Justice, she is "a restrained and principled jurist" who denies that "judges legitimately can interpret statutory language to reflect their own political and ideological commitments."

Those competing caricatures are the products of an escalating message war between well-funded liberal and conservative legal activist groups who have played an increasingly influential role in judicial fights over the past two decades.

As the Senate returns this week from recess to confront a simmering dispute over Democratic efforts to block Owen and a handful of other conservative judicial nominees, such sloganeering will reach a fever pitch.

Conservative groups are urging Republicans to act in the next two weeks to end a longstanding Senate filibuster rule that allows a bloc of 40 senators to delay votes on nominees, a step that would forever change the nature of the Senate. Liberal groups are urging Democrats not to back down. For the professional ideological purists on both sides, there can be no compromise.

Decades ago, the selection of judges was a far more orderly affair. Presidents and home-state senators from both parties quietly consulted with each other about acceptable prospects, whose qualifications were then reviewed by the American Bar Association before a nomination was made public.

Today, presidents of both parties systematically examine nominees for their ideology, even as they claim to have no litmus tests on abortion. The ABA's role has been thrown out. And when a nominee is announced, interest groups unleash a torrent of researchers who pore over their every past writing and speech, looking for fragments that can be extrapolated into definitive denunciations of their alleged bias.

"I was here when [President] Nixon was going down, and the atmosphere then was not as poisonous as it is now," said Robert Bork, whose derailed Supreme Court bid in 1987 was a milestone in Beltway rancor. "These outside groups have a lot to do with it. They are highly ideological and quite far to the left. And they have a lot of influence because they have a lot of fund-raising capacity."

Democrats and left-wing activists make essentially the same claim, but blame right-wing ideologues for enveloping the process in political gamesmanship.

"Right-wing anger and interest in judicial nominations predated Robert Bork, and it is part of a very well-orchestrated Republican strategy," said Nan Aron, president of the liberal Alliance for Justice. "The one issue that a Republican president can deliver to appease and nurture the right wing of his base is judges, and so Republican presidents play this issue."

> *"Many perceive the judicial nomination process as broken."*— John R. Lott Jr., American Enterprise Institute

But many political analysts agree that both factions have contributed to the escalating brinkmanship.

"Many perceive the judicial nomination process as broken," John R. Lott Jr. of the conservative American Enterprise Institute wrote in a study indicating that the success rate of nominations has fallen steadily over the past two decades. "Neither Democrats nor Republicans have 'clean hands' in this debate and . . . the problem has been getting progressively worse over time."

The origins of the struggle trace back to the explosive growth of the power of the federal judiciary that began with the Supreme Court decision to end segregation in 1954 and climaxed with its 1973 declaration of a constitutional right to an abortion. A wave of class-action lawsuits and litigation over new environmental and antidiscrimination laws added to the expanded judicial scope.

Amid this rise in the political clout of the judiciary came the first nomination crisis of the modern era. When Chief Justice Earl Warren retired in 1968, President Lyndon B. Johnson tried to elevate Associate Justice Abe Fortas. But Republicans and conservative Southern Democrats launched a filibuster to prevent a vote, and Fortas withdrew himself from consideration.

Johnson's term ended and Richard Nixon entered the White House, successfully nominating Warren Burger to become chief justice.

After Ronald Reagan's victory in 1980, his counselor Edwin Meese, seeking what he later termed "a jurisprudence of original intention," set out to systematically screen nominees and put conservatives on the bench.

But by the time of Reagan's reelection in 1984, liberals had decided to take sharp actions of their own. The Alliance for Justice, representing major civil rights and abortion rights groups, formed a "Judicial Selection Project" to pore over the past writings and speeches of nominees, looking for ammunition.

At the same time, People for the American Way, a liberal group founded in 1981 to counter the religious right, launched a public-relations campaign against some of Reagan's nominees, accusing him of trying to pack the courts with extremists. Its paid advertisements marked a major escalation in how judicial battles would be fought.

In 1987, after Democrats had retaken control of the Senate, Reagan nominated Bork to the Supreme Court. Liberal groups declared war, unleashing snippets from long-past testimony and decades-old articles to pressure lawmakers to reject Bork not because he was unqualified, but because of his "hard-right" ideology on issues like affirmative action and abortion.

The memory of that defeat and the bruising 1991 confirmation fight over Supreme Court Justice Clarence Thomas, who pronounced himself the victim of a "high-tech lynching" amid accusations of sexual harassment still rankles conservatives today.

"The hardball tactics were pioneered by the Democrats," argued Sean Rushton of the Committee for Justice. "We weren't responsible for ratcheting things up with Bork and Thomas."

The tables turned when Bill Clinton was president. After Republicans took control of Congress in 1995, they slowed his confirmations down, all but stopping them during the 1996 campaign. But Clinton won reelection, galvanizing a new era of opposition by conservative groups who denounced Senate Judiciary chairman Orrin Hatch, Republican of Utah, for not trying hard enough to stop the president's judicial nominees.

Foremost among them was Tom Jipping, director of the new Judical Selection Monitoring Project. Adopting the tactics pioneered by groups like People for the American Way a decade earlier, Jipping launched a $1.4 million fund-raising campaign that included direct-mail letters and a video featuring Bork, asking recipients to help bring down "activist liberal judges."

Jipping's group had great success. Hatch slowed the process down. Dozens of Clinton's nominees never received a vote, leaving numerous vacancies across the federal bench for the winner of the 2000 presidential election to fill.

One of the blocked nominees from the Clinton era was Sam Paz, a civil rights lawyer who shut down his practice and lived off savings for 18 months after Clinton nominated him to a district judgeship.

Paz, who said he was "vilified" because he had represented victims of police brutality, withdrew after it became clear that he would never get a vote.

"I ended up not working that period of time, and it was extremely stressful on my relationship with my ex-wife[;] we got a divorce during that period because I was worried about how I was going to support my family," Paz said.

The disputed 2000 election, when George W. Bush became president despite losing the popular vote, led both factions to dig in ever deeper.

Bush eliminated the longstanding rule that the ABA should review the qualifications of candidates, arguing that it was too liberal.

Meanwhile, the minority Democrats decided to filibuster 10 of Bush's appeals court nominees whom they, with help from outside groups, decided to target as extremists.

One was Owen, a Texas Supreme Court justice. A People for the American Way analysis found that she tended to side with businesses when they were sued. Most notably, the analysis held that she was opposed to abortion rights.

This claim is based on a dispute about how to interpret a 1999 Texas statute that required parental notification before a minor could get an abortion. The statute contained an exception for a minor who was sufficiently well informed about the choices. Owen interpreted that exception more narrowly than other justices.

For that, and her affiliation with a conservative legal fraternity called the Federalist Society, Owen has been denounced as a regressive who would work for the rest of her life to dismantle all the civil and constitutional rights that have been created since the New Deal.

A multimillion-dollar lobbying campaign trying to make that argument, and another to fight against it, have ensued. And if those efforts are fraying the political fabric of Washington, neither faction blames itself.

"Have we vilified people? I don't believe we have," said Aron. "I think we're doing a great service for the country. . . . Given that judges serve lifetime appointments, it's critically important that Americans across this country understand how judges' decisions affect their daily lives and why it's important for them to weigh in on the decision as to who becomes a judge."

Bork said: "The immediate future looks like it's going to be rancorous, polarized, and venomous, but the Supreme Court has made itself a political institution, and it's culturally to the left of the American public. The fight is that the Democrats want to maintain that, because it's the only branch of government they have on their side right now."

High Court Reality Check

By Tony Mauro
USA Today, November 18, 2004

When George W. Bush is sworn in for a second term on Jan. 20, the absence of a key participant may dampen the celebration. It may be the first time in more than 40 years that a president is sworn in by someone other than the chief justice of the United States.

Chief Justice William Rehnquist, 80, is battling thyroid cancer. He had to miss November's public sessions of the Court, though he is working from home. But participating in the outdoor inauguration, on what almost invariably turns out to be a frigid D.C. day, may be more than he should take on.

The reality of an ailing chief justice who may leave the Court in the near future is sad. It is also starting to make people crazy, and that is also sad—and unnecessary.

The beating Sen. Arlen Specter, R-Pa., has taken from conservatives in the past two weeks is one sign of the silliness that is beginning, even before there is a Supreme Court vacancy. Right after the election, Specter, who supports abortion rights, said an anti-abortion candidate nominated to the Court would have a tough time being confirmed by the Senate. For the sin of stating an undeniable truth, Specter was treated as though he had invited Osama bin Laden over for dinner. Critics launched a fierce campaign to keep him from taking over as chair of the Judiciary Committee, which will review any nominees. Specter seems to have survived, but just barely.

But hysteria is breaking out on all sides of what undoubtedly will be a battle royal over the next nomination to the Supreme Court. Liberals warn that America is "one vote away" from losing precious rights. Conservatives respond in kind, energizing supporters with the tantalizing prospect that reversing liberal doctrines is within easy reach. Rumors about who will replace Rehnquist race across Washington. The latest: President Bush will appoint Justice Clarence Thomas as chief justice.

It's doubtful anyone knows, so before Washington and the nation are consumed with confirmation madness, here is a reality check on issues that will be raised in the coming weeks and months:

- **Court Makeovers**. Sorry to disappoint, but the Supreme Court rarely turns on a dime. Adherence to precedent is a highly cherished value that envelops and tames even those justices who arrive with an "agenda" in hand. Some scholars suggest that the security of lifetime appointment, among other factors, makes conservatives move to the left over time, or at least to the middle. Justices Sandra Day O'Connor and Anthony Kennedy, both Reagan appointees, are good examples.

- **Abortion**. *Roe v. Wade*, the 1973 decision that declared an abortion right, was upheld by a 1992 decision written by justices O'Connor, Kennedy, and David Souter, Republican appointees all. They wrote that "an entire generation has come of age" relying on the right to an abortion. The 1992 ruling was a 5–4 decision, but the majority has since been bolstered by Clinton appointees. So it would take two or three committed abortion opponents, replacing justices such as O'Connor and John Paul Stevens—who show no interest in leaving—to uproot abortion rights. A Bush-appointed replacement for Rehnquist would cause no change.

- **Affirmative Action**. The Court's 2003 vote on the issue, upholding a University of Michigan policy, was also 5–4. Does that mean that just "one more vote" is needed to kill affirmative action? Not really. A Bush replacement for Rehnquist is likely to vote just as Rehnquist did—in the four-vote minority. No shift there. More substantively, O'Connor, who authored the ruling, wrote it for the ages. Even affirmative-action supporters think her endorsement of another 25 years of such programs will help insulate it from reversal.

- **Gay Rights**. The Court, this time by a 6–3 vote, struck down sodomy laws in 2003 with a sweeping declaration of the right of all Americans to a substantial measure of personal privacy and dignity. Reversing that decision would require four or more new justices who are deeply opposed to the right to privacy and nonchalant about the importance of precedent, says lawyer Paul Smith, who won the gay-rights case. That's not going to happen.

- **Chief Justice Thomas**. Before the election, the nightmare scenario for many liberals was the possibility that Thomas would become chief justice. But Thomas' supporters note that as chief justice he would wield the same basic power he has as an associate justice: one vote. Liberal veterans of past confirmation battles say if Thomas is elevated, the real danger may lie with the nominee Bush picks to replace Thomas as associate justice.

To be sure, even one new justice changes the Court's dynamics, and even entrenched precedents can be eroded. Vigilance during the nomination process is warranted; today's appointees will influence the law for decades. But as divided as it can be, the Supreme Court tends to rule from the middle. Unless most or all of the Court's moderate-to-liberal justices head for the exit door in the next four years, that centrist tradition will continue.

Appendix

A Brief Overview of the Supreme Court

The Supreme Court of the United States
One First Street, NE, Washington, DC 20543 Phone: 202-479-3211

Members:
Chief Justice of the United States: John G. Roberts
Associate Justices: John Paul Stevens, Sandra Day O'Connor, Antonin Scalia, Anthony M. Kennedy, David H. Souter, Clarence Thomas, Ruth Bader Ginsburg, Stephen G. Breyer

The Supreme Court consists of the Chief Justice of the United States and such number of Associate Justices as may be fixed by Congress. The number of Associate Justices is currently fixed at eight (28 U. S. C. §1). Power to nominate the Justices is vested in the President of the United States, and appointments are made with the advice and consent of the Senate. Article III, §1, of the Constitution further provides that "[t]he Judges, both of the supreme and inferior Courts, shall hold their Offices during good Behaviour, and shall, at stated Times, receive for their Services, a Compensation, which shall not be diminished during their Continuance in Office."

Officers:
Administrative Assistant to the Chief Justice: Sally M. Rider
Clerk: William K. Suter
Librarian: Judith A. Gaskell
Marshal: Pamela Talkin
Reporter of Decisions: Frank D. Wagner
Director of Budget and Personnel: Cyril A. Donnelly
Court Counsel: Scott Harris
Curator: Catherine Fitts
Director of Data Systems: Donna Clement
Public Information Officer: Kathleen L. Arberg

Court Officers assist the Court in the performance of its functions. They include the Administrative Assistant to the Chief Justice, the Clerk, the Reporter of Decisions, the Librarian, the Marshal, the Director of Budget and Personnel, the Court Counsel, the Curator, the Director of Data Systems, and the Public Information Officer. The Administrative Assistant is appointed by the Chief Justice. The Clerk, Reporter of Decisions, Librarian, and Marshal are appointed by the Court. All other Court Officers are appointed by the Chief Justice in consultation with the Court.

Constitutional Origin. Article III, §1, of the Constitution provides that "[t]he judicial Power of the United States, shall be vested in one supreme Court, and in such inferior Courts as the Congress may from time to time

From the official Web site of the Supreme Court of the United States, *www.supremecourtus.gov*, 2005.

ordain and establish." The Supreme Court of the United States was created in accordance with this provision and by authority of the Judiciary Act of September 24, 1789 (1 Stat. 73). It was organized on February 2, 1790.

Jurisdiction. According to the Constitution (Art. III, §2):

"The judicial Power shall extend to all Cases, in Law and Equity, arising under this Constitution, the Laws of the United States, and Treaties made, or which shall be made, under their Authority;—to all Cases affecting Ambassadors, other public Ministers and Consuls;—to all Cases of admiralty and maritime Jurisdiction;—to Controversies to which the United States shall be a Party;—to Controversies between two or more States;—between a State and Citizens of another State;—between Citizens of different States;—between Citizens of the same State claiming Lands under Grants of different States, and between a State, or the Citizens thereof, and foreign States, Citizens or Subjects.

"In all Cases affecting Ambassadors, other public ministers and Consuls, and those in which a State shall be Party, the supreme Court shall have original Jurisdiction. In all the other Cases before mentioned, the supreme Court shall have appellate jurisdiction, both as to Law and Fact, with such Exceptions, and under such Regulations as the Congress shall make."

Appellate jurisdiction has been conferred upon the Supreme Court by various statutes, under the authority given Congress by the Constitution. The basic statute effective at this time in conferring and controlling jurisdiction of the Supreme Court may be found in 28 U. S. C. §1251 et seq., and various special statutes.

Rulemaking Power. Congress has from time to time conferred upon the Supreme Court power to prescribe rules of procedure to be followed by the lower courts of the United States. See 28 U. S. C. §2071 et seq.

The Building. The Supreme Court is open to the public from 9 A.M. to 4:30 P.M., Monday through Friday. It is closed Saturdays, Sundays, and the federal legal holidays listed in 5 U. S. C. §6103. Unless the Court or the Chief Justice orders otherwise, the Clerk's Office is open from 9 A.M. to 5 P.M., Monday through Friday, except on those holidays. The Library is open to members of the Bar of the Court, attorneys for the various federal departments and agencies, and Members of Congress.

The Term. The Term of the Court begins, by law, on the first Monday in October and lasts until the first Monday in October of the next year. Approximately 8,000 petitions are filed with the Court in the course of a Term. In addition, some 1,200 applications of various kinds are filed each year that can be acted upon by a single Justice.

Members of the Supreme Court of the United States

Name	State App't From	Appointed by President	Judicial Oath Taken	Date Service Terminated
Chief Justices				
Jay, John	NY	Washington	(a) Oct. 19, 1789	June 29, 1795
Rutledge, John	SC	Washington	Aug. 12, 1795	Dec. 15, 1795
Ellsworth, Oliver	CT	Washington	Mar. 8, 1796	Dec. 15, 1800
Marshall, John	VA	Adams, John	Feb. 4, 1801	July 6, 1835
Taney, Roger Brooke	MD	Jackson	Mar. 28, 1836	Oct. 12, 1864
Chase, Salmon Portland	OH	Lincoln	Dec. 15, 1864	May 7, 1873
Waite, Morrison Remick	OH	Grant	Mar. 4, 1874	Mar. 23, 1888
Fuller, Melville Weston	IL	Cleveland	Oct. 8, 1888	July 4, 1910
White, Edward Douglass	LA	Taft	Dec. 19, 1910	May 19, 1921
Taft, William Howard	CT	Harding	July 11, 1921	Feb. 3, 1930
Hughes, Charles Evans	NY	Hoover	Feb. 24, 1930	June 30, 1941
Stone, Harlan Fiske	NY	Roosevelt, F.	July 3, 1941	Apr. 22, 1946
Vinson, Fred Moore	KY	Truman	June 24, 1946	Sep. 8, 1953
Warren, Earl	CA	Eisenhower	Oct. 5, 1953	June 23, 1969
Burger, Warren Earl	VA	Nixon	June 23, 1969	Sep. 26, 1986
Rehnquist, William H.	VA	Reagan	Sep. 26, 1986	Sep. 3, 2005
John G. Roberts	MD	Bush, George W.	Sep. 29, 2005	
Associate Justices				
Rutledge, John	SC	Washington	(a) Feb. 15, 1790	Mar. 5, 1791
Cushing, William	MA	Washington	(c) Feb. 2, 1790	Sep. 13, 1810
Wilson, James	PA	Washington	(b) Oct. 5, 1789	Aug. 21, 1798
Blair, John	VA	Washington	(c) Feb. 2, 1790	Oct. 25, 1795
Iredell, James	NC	Washington	(b) May 12, 1790	Oct. 20, 1799
Johnson, Thomas	MD	Washington	(a) Aug. 6, 1792	Jan. 16, 1793
Paterson, William	NJ	Washington	(a) Mar. 11, 1793	Sep. 9, 1806
Chase, Samuel	MD	Washington	Feb. 4, 1796	June 19, 1811
Washington, Bushrod	VA	Adams, John	(c) Feb. 4, 1799	Nov. 26, 1829
Moore, Alfred	NC	Adams, John	(a) Apr. 21, 1800	Jan. 26, 1804
Johnson, William	SC	Jefferson	May 7, 1804	Aug. 4, 1834
Livingston, Henry Brockholst	NY	Jefferson	Jan. 20, 1807	Mar. 18, 1823
Todd, Thomas	KY	Jefferson	(a) May 4, 1807	Feb. 7, 1826
Duvall, Gabriel	MD	Madison	(a) Nov. 23, 1811	Jan. 14, 1835
Story, Joseph	MA	Madison	(c) Feb. 3, 1812	Sep. 10, 1845
Thompson, Smith	NY	Monroe	(b) Sep. 1, 1823	Dec. 18, 1843
Trimble, Robert	KY	Adams, J. Q.	(a) June 16, 1826	Aug. 25, 1828
McLean, John	OH	Jackson	(c) Jan. 11, 1830	Apr. 4, 1861
Baldwin, Henry	PA	Jackson	Jan. 18, 1830	Apr. 21, 1844
Wayne, James Moore	GA	Jackson	Jan. 14, 1835	July 5, 1867
Barbour, Philip Pendleton	VA	Jackson	May 12, 1836	Feb. 25, 1841
Catron, John	TN	Van Buren	May 1, 1837	May 30, 1865
McKinley, John	AL	Van Buren	(c) Jan. 9, 1838	July 19, 1852
Daniel, Peter Vivian	VA	Van Buren	(c) Jan. 10, 1842	May 31, 1860
Nelson, Samuel	NY	Tyler	Feb. 27, 1845	Nov. 28, 1872

* Elevated

From the official Web site of the Supreme Court of the United States, *www.supremecourtus.gov*, 2005.

Name	State App't From	Appointed by President	Judicial Oath Taken	Date Service Terminated
Woodbury, Levi	NH	Polk	(b) Sep. 23, 1845	Sep. 4, 1851
Grier, Robert Cooper	PA	Polk	Aug. 10, 1846	Jan. 31, 1870
Curtis, Benjamin Robbins	MA	Fillmore	(b) Oct. 10, 1851	Sep. 30, 1857
Campbell, John Archibald	AL	Pierce	(c) Apr. 11, 1853	Apr. 30, 1861
Clifford, Nathan	ME	Buchanan	Jan. 21, 1858	July 25, 1881
Swayne, Noah Haynes	OH	Lincoln	Jan. 27, 1862	Jan. 24, 1881
Miller, Samuel Freeman	IA	Lincoln	July 21, 1862	Oct. 13, 1890
Davis, David	IL	Lincoln	Dec. 10, 1862	Mar. 4, 1877
Field, Stephen Johnson	CA	Lincoln	May 20, 1863	Dec. 1, 1897
Strong, William	PA	Grant	Mar. 14, 1870	Dec. 14, 1880
Bradley, Joseph P.	NJ	Grant	Mar. 23, 1870	Jan. 22, 1892
Hunt, Ward	NY	Grant	Jan. 9, 1873	Jan. 27, 1882
Harlan, John Marshall	KY	Hayes	Dec. 10 1877	Oct. 14, 1911
Woods, William Burnham	GA	Hayes	Jan. 5, 1881	May 14, 1887
Matthews, Stanley	OH	Garfield	May 17, 1881	Mar. 22, 1889
Gray, Horace	MA	Arthur	Jan. 9, 1882	Sep. 15, 1902
Blatchford, Samuel	NY	Arthur	April 3, 1882	July 7, 1893
Lamar, Lucius Quintus C.	MS	Cleveland	Jan. 18, 1888	Jan. 23, 1893
Brewer, David Josiah	KS	Harrison	Jan. 6, 1890	Mar. 28, 1910
Brown, Henry Billings	MI	Harrison	Jan. 5, 1891	May 28, 1906
Shiras, George, Jr.	PA	Harrison	Oct. 10, 1892	Feb. 23, 1903
Jackson, Howell Edmunds	TN	Harrison	Mar. 4, 1893	Aug. 8, 1895
White, Edward Douglass	LA	Cleveland	Mar. 12, 1894	Dec. 18, 1910*
Peckham, Rufus Wheeler	NY	Cleveland	Jan. 6, 1896	Oct. 24, 1909
McKenna, Joseph	CA	McKinley	Jan. 26, 1898	Jan. 5, 1925
Holmes, Oliver Wendell	MA	Roosevelt, T.	Dec. 8, 1902	Jan. 12, 1932
Day, William Rufus	OH	Roosevelt, T.	Mar. 2, 1903	Nov. 13, 1922
Moody, William Henry	MA	Roosevelt, T.	Dec. 17, 1906	Nov. 20, 1910
Lurton, Horace Harmon	TN	Taft	Jan. 3, 1910	July 12, 1914
Hughes, Charles Evans	NY	Taft	Oct. 10, 1910	June 10, 1916
Van Devanter, Willis	WY	Taft	Jan. 3, 1911	June 2, 1937
Lamar, Joseph Rucker	GA	Taft	Jan. 3, 1911	Jan. 2, 1916
Pitney, Mahlon	NJ	Taft	Mar. 18, 1912	Dec. 31, 1922
McReynolds, James Clark	TN	Wilson	Oct. 12, 1914	Jan. 31, 1941
Brandeis, Louis Dembitz	MA	Wilson	June 5, 1916	Feb. 13, 1939
Clarke, John Hessin	OH	Wilson	Oct. 9, 1916	Sep. 18, 1922
Sutherland, George	UT	Harding	Oct. 2, 1922	Jan. 17, 1938
Butler, Pierce	MN	Harding	Jan. 2, 1923	Nov. 16, 1939
Sanford, Edward Terry	TN	Harding	Feb. 19, 1923	Mar. 8, 1930
Stone, Harlan Fiske	NY	Coolidge	Mar. 2, 1925	July 2, 1941*
Roberts, Owen Josephus	PA	Hoover	June 2, 1930	July 31, 1945
Cardozo, Benjamin Nathan	NY	Hoover	Mar. 14, 1932	July 9, 1938
Black, Hugo Lafayette	AL	Roosevelt, F.	Aug. 19, 1937	Sep. 17, 1971
Reed, Stanley Forman	KY	Roosevelt, F.	Jan. 31, 1938	Feb. 25, 1957
Frankfurter, Felix	MA	Roosevelt, F.	Jan. 30, 1939	Aug. 28, 1962
Douglas, William Orville	CT	Roosevelt, F.	Apr. 17, 1939	Nov. 12, 1975
Murphy, Frank	MI	Roosevelt, F.	Feb. 5, 1940	July 19, 1949
Byrnes, James Francis	SC	Roosevelt, F.	July 8, 1941	Oct. 3, 1942
Jackson, Robert Houghwout	NY	Roosevelt, F.	July 11, 1941	Oct. 9, 1954
Rutledge, Wiley Blount	IA	Roosevelt, F.	Feb. 15, 1943	Sep. 10, 1949
Burton, Harold Hitz	OH	Truman	Oct. 1, 1945	Oct. 13, 1958
Clark, Tom Campbell	TX	Truman	Aug. 24, 1949	June 12, 1967
Minton, Sherman	IN	Truman	Oct. 12, 1949	Oct. 15, 1956
Harlan, John Marshall	NY	Eisenhower	Mar. 28, 1955	Sep. 23, 1971

Name	State App't From	Appointed by President	Judicial Oath Taken	Date Service Terminated
Brennan, William J., Jr.	NJ	Eisenhower	Oct. 16, 1956	July 20, 1990
Whittaker, Charles Evans	MO	Eisenhower	Mar. 25, 1957	Mar. 31, 1962
Stewart, Potter	OH	Eisenhower	Oct. 14, 1958	July 3, 1981
White, Byron Raymond	CO	Kennedy	Apr. 16, 1962	June 28, 1993
Goldberg, Arthur Joseph	IL	Kennedy	Oct. 1, 1962	July 25, 1965
Fortas, Abe	TN	Johnson, L.	Oct. 4, 1965	May 14, 1969
Marshall, Thurgood	NY	Johnson, L.	Oct. 2, 1967	Oct. 1, 1991
Blackmun, Harry A.	MN	Nixon	June 9, 1970	Aug. 3, 1994
Powell, Lewis F., Jr.	VA	Nixon	Jan. 7, 1972	June 26, 1987
Rehnquist, William H.	AZ	Nixon	Jan. 7, 1972	Sep. 26, 1986*
Stevens, John Paul	IL	Ford	Dec. 19, 1975	
O'Connor, Sandra Day	AZ	Reagan	Sep. 25, 1981	
Scalia, Antonin	VA	Reagan	Sep. 26, 1986	
Kennedy, Anthony M.	CA	Reagan	Feb. 18, 1988	
Souter, David H.	NH	Bush, G.	Oct. 9, 1990	
Thomas, Clarence	GA	Bush, G	Oct. 23, 1991	
Ginsburg, Ruth Bader	NY	Clinton	Aug. 10, 1993	
Breyer, Stephen G.	MA	Clinton	Aug. 3, 1994	

Notes:
The acceptance of the appointment and commission by the appointee, as evidenced by the taking of the prescribed oaths, is here implied; otherwise the individual is not carried on this list of the Members of the Court. Examples: Robert Hanson Harrison is not carried, as a letter from President Washington of February 9, 1790 states Harrison declined to serve. Neither is Edwin M. Stanton who died before he could take the necessary steps toward becoming a Member of the Court. Chief Justice Rutledge is included because he took his oaths, presided over the August Term of 1795, and his name appears on two opinions of the Court for that Term.

The date a Member of the Court took his/her Judicial oath (the Judiciary Act provided "That the Justices of the Supreme Court, and the district judges, before they proceed to execute the duties of their respective offices, shall take the following oath . . .") is here used as the date of the beginning of his/her service, for until that oath is taken he/she is not vested with the prerogatives of the office. The dates given in this column are for the oaths taken following the receipt of the commissions. Dates without small-letter references are taken from the Minutes of the Court or from the original oath which are in the Curator's collection. The small letter (a) denotes the date is from the Minutes of some other court; (b) from some other unquestionable authority; (c) from authority that is questionable, and better authority would be appreciated.

Timeline of Landmark Cases

1803

Marbury v. Madison: The Court established its authority over judicial review, asserting its right to strike down acts of Congress that it found unconstitutional.

1819

McCulloch v. Maryland: The justices found that the same Constitutional provision that enabled Congress to enact laws that it deemed "necessary and proper" also gave it the right to charter a national bank.

1819

Trustees of Dartmouth College v. Woodward: The Court ruled that a private college's charter could not be amended at will by the state, a decision that would later be applied to business contracts as well.

1824

Gibbons v. Ogden: This verdict determined that Congress had final authority over the regulation of interstate commerce.

1857

Dred Scott v. Sandford: In addition to ruling that the Missouri Compromise, which had already been repealed, was unconstitutional, the Court declared that slaves were not citizens of the United States nor of any specific state but were instead the private property of their owners and thus could not sue for freedom simply by crossing into a free state.

1896

Plessy v. Ferguson: The Court affirmed a state law that required separate facilities for white and non-white railroad passengers, declaring that this statute violated neither the interstate commerce clause nor the Thirteenth and Fourteenth Amendments.

1904

Northern Securities Co. v. United States: When two competing railroad corporations merged by forming a state-chartered holding company, the Court ruled them in violation of the Sherman Antitrust Act after finding that the deal restrained trade and led to unfair competition.

1908

Muller v. Oregon: This decision upheld an Oregon law that prohibited women from working more than a certain number of hours.

1911

Standard Oil Co. of New Jersey et al. v. United States: The Justices ordered the break-up of the Standard Oil Trust after ruling that the company had unfairly restricted trade.

1919

Schenck v. United States: The right of the government to restrain freedom of speech and the press in the Espionage Act of 1917 was affirmed, especially if "the words used . . . create a clear and present danger."

1925

Gitlow v. New York: The justices concluded that the freedom of speech enshrined in the First

Amendment extends to the states as well and thus cannot be unduly curtailed by state governments; however, particular types of speech, if they threaten public safety, can be legally restrained.

1935

Schechter Poultry Corp. v. United States: The Court ruled the National Industrial Recovery Act unconstitutional after determining that through it Congress had ceded much of its power to regulate interstate commerce to the president.

1937

National Labor Relations Board (NLRB) v. Jones & Laughlin Steel Corp.: In another interstate commerce decision, the Court upheld the National Labor Relations Act, ruling that Congress could regulate labor relations.

1951

Dennis et al. v. United States: The justices upheld convictions under the Smith Act of 1940 (an antisedition initiative) of individuals found guilty of trying to overthrow the government by promoting Communist ideology.

1954

Brown v. Board of Education of Topeka, Kansas: The Court declared the fundamental inequality of separate public schools for black and white students and decided that such state-sanctioned segregation violated the Fourteenth Amendment's promise of equal protection. The case led states to eliminate previously lawful segregation in other types of facilities as well.

Bolling v. Sharpe: The justices found that the District of Columbia's segregated public school system violated the Fifth Amendment's due process clause affirming personal liberty.

1957

Roth v. United States and *Alberts v. California*: In these two obscenity cases, the Court ruled that certain offensive material was't protected by the First Amendment and established the definition of obscene subject matter as "utterly without redeeming social value," containing content which the average person would deem "prurient." Later, in *Miller v. California* (1973), the views of the "local community," rather than the individual, were determined to be the measure by which material was judged obscene.

1961

Mapp v. Ohio: Evidence obtained by criminal investigators in violation of the Fourth Amendment prohibition of unlawful search and seizure was found to be inadmissable in both state and federal trials.

1962

Engel v. Vitale: This ruling declared that the recitation of a prayer—especially one composed by the state—in public schools was unconstitutional and would be considered an attempt to establish an official religion.

Baker v. Carr: The Court determined that federal courts could address claims of unequal voter distribution among a state's legislative districts.

1963

Gideon v. Wainwright: State and federal courts were ordered to appoint and, if necessary, pay for an attorney for anyone charged with a serious crime who could not afford a lawyer.

1964

New York Times Co. v. Sullivan: The Court found that, in accordance with the First Amendment, the press cannot be successfully sued for defamation of character by a public official unless that official could prove that the writer of the story in question demonstrated "reckless disregard" for the truth and had malicious intent.

1965

Griswold v. Connecticut: Though a right to privacy is not specifically enumerated in the Constitution, the Court ruled that taken together various Amendments imply this right; consequently, a law prohibiting the distribution of material or counsel related to contraception violates a couple's right to marital privacy.

1966

Miranda v. Arizona: The justices decreed that a suspect must be informed of his or her right to an attorney and to remain silent when arrested by law enforcement officials.

1972

Furman v. Georgia: The Court determined that a death sentence imposed for a homicide inadvertently committed during the commission of a lesser crime—burglary, for example—constitutes "cruel and unusual punishment."

1973

Roe v. Wade: The justices, by a 7–2 margin, overturned a Texas law prohibiting abortion except to save the life of the mother, declaring that a woman had the legal authority to terminate her pregnancy by virtue of the right to privacy implied by the Fourteenth Amendment; however, the Court held that the states could impose certain restrictions on abortions sought in the second and third trimesters of pregnancy.

Doe v. Bolton: This decision struck down a Georgia statute that restricted a woman's access to an abortion; the Court ruled that abortion must be available to preserve the health of the mother, but defined health as including the woman's familial and emotional well-being in addition to her physical condition.

1974

United States v. Nixon: In a unanimous judgment, the Court rejected President Richard Nixon's argument citing "executive privilege" as the basis for his refusal to comply with subpoenas seeking materials relating to his involvement in the Watergate Hotel break-in and cover-up.

1976

Gregg v. Georgia, *Profitt v. Florida*, and *Jurek v. Texas:* Through these three cases, the Justices found that capital punishment did not necessarily constitute cruel and unusual punishment.

1978

Regents of University of California v. Bakke: In a complicated and closely decided verdict, the justices determined that racial quota systems in higher education ran afoul of the Civil Rights Act of 1964, but that race could nevertheless be used as a factor in admissions.

1986

Bowers v. Hardwick: Declaring that the Constitution does not guarantee the right to homosexual intercourse, the justices upheld a Georgia anti-sodomy statute, the same type of law they would overturn in 2003 in *Lawrence and Garner v. Texas*.

1990

Cruzan v. Director, Missouri Department of Health: By a 5–4 margin, the justices upheld a Missouri law mandating that mentally incompetent patients not be removed from life support unless there was a clear indication that the patient no longer wanted the treatment.

1995

Adarand Constructors v. Peña: In a dispute over a U.S. Department of Transportation policy that gave preferential treatment to contractors who hired disadvantaged minority-owned subcontractors, the Court ruled that race alone does not determine economic disadvantage, and thus strict scrutiny must be employed to ensure that equal protection standards are met.

U.S. Term Limits Inc. v. Thornton: The Court declared state-imposed congressional term limits unconstitutional, reasoning that the Constitution alone determines congressional qualifications.

1997

Clinton v. Jones: The justices unanimously declared that President Bill Clinton was not immune from civil litigation resulting from events prior to his assumption of his office, in this case his alleged harassment of Paula Jones.

City of Boerne v. Flores: The Court overturned the Religious Freedom Restoration Act (RFRA), which limited state government interference in the free expression of religion, on the grounds that it exceeded Congress's mandate by encroaching on powers granted to the states and the judiciary.

Reno v. ACLU: The justices nullified the Communications Decency Act controlling the transmission of explicit material over the Internet, finding that the statute violated the right to free speech enshrined in the First Amendment.

1998

Clinton v. City of New York: This 6–3 verdict struck down the Line-Item Veto Act, which allowed the president to remove selected parts of a piece of legislation, stating that under the Constitution the president is allowed only to sign or veto—not edit—a bill passed by Congress.

Faragher v. City of Boca Raton: By a margin of 7–2, the justices determined that an employer can be held responsible if a supervisor creates a hostile working environment through a pattern of sexual harassment.

Burlington Industries, Inc. v. Ellerth: The Court ruled 7–2 that an employer who does not act promptly and conscientiously to correct sexually harassing behavior by members of its staff remains liable for damages if an employee is repeatedly harassed even if he or she suffers no career-related consequences, such as those relating to pay or promotion.

1999

Department of Commerce v. U.S. House: The justices found that the planned use of statistical sampling rather than a direct count to determine the population of congressional districts during the 2000 census violated aspects of the Census Act.

Alden v. Maine; *Florida Prepaid v. College Savings Bank*; and *College Savings Bank v. Florida Prepaid:* These three 5–4 verdicts held that the states, by virtue of the sovereignty granted them by the Eleventh Amendment, were immune from certain forms of litigation.

2000

Troxel v. Granville: The justices voted 6–3 to overturn a Washington law that permitted a litigant to apply for court-mandated child-visitation rights, even over the objections of the child's guardians, if a court deemed it in the child's best interests.

Boy Scouts of America v. Dale: The Court ruled 5–4 that a New Jersey law prohibiting discrimination against homosexuals by groups using public accommodations violated the Boy Scouts of America's right to "freedom of association"; thus the Scouts could legally bar gays from their organization.

Stenberg v. Carhart: The Court struck down a Nebraska law barring so-called partial-birth abortions except to save the life of the mother, deciding in a 5–4 verdict that the law in question placed an "undue burden" on a woman's right to an abortion as established in *Roe v. Wade* and did not take into account pregnancies that threatened the health, if not the mortality, of the mother.

Bush v. Gore: The justices determined by a 7–2 margin that aspects of a Florida Supreme Court ruling requiring a manual recount of disputed ballots throughout the state in the 2000 presidential election violated the Constitution's Equal Protection Clause; then, by a 5–4 vote, they found that there was no acceptable way for a constitutional recount to proceed.

2001

Easley v. Cromartie: The Court found that the crafting of an oddly shaped North Carolina congressional district with a Democratic majority was not an unconstitutional racial gerrymander simply because the populace happened to be disproportionately African American.

Good News Club v. Milford Central School: In a 6–3 ruling, the justices found that a New York school district that barred a religious club from using public school facilities after hours violated the group's freedom of speech rights, even though the policy was motivated by a desire to adhere to the Constitution's Establishment Clause prohibiting state endorsement of a particular religion.

2002

Atkins v. Virginia: A convicted murderer diagnosed as mentally retarded was spared the death penalty when the Court ruled 6–3 that the execution of the mentally infirmed constituted "cruel and unusual punishment" and thus violated the Eighth Amendment.

Ring v. Arizona: By a 7–2 margin the justices struck down an Arizona statute whereby a judge, having found that aggravating circumstances were involved, could sentence a convicted murderer to death; the statute in question was found to violate a defendant's Sixth Amendment right to a trial by jury by transferring the fact-finding authority normally reserved to the jurors to the judge.

Zelman v. Simmons-Harris: The Court decided in a 5–4 verdict that an Ohio program providing tuition assistance vouchers to families with students in private schools, many of them religiously affiliated, did not violate the Constitution's Establishment Clause barring the government's endorsement of a particular church.

Federal Maritime Commission v. South Carolina State Ports Authority: When the South Carolina State Ports Authority (SCSPA) refused docking privileges to a gambling ship, the company owning the vessel petitioned the Federal Maritime Commission to overrule the SCSPA, which it subsequently did. The Court, however, decided in a 5–4 ruling that the SCSPA acted properly, since the federal government did not have the power to decide cases between a state and a private party, based on the sovereignty granted the states by the Eleventh Amendment.

2003

Lawrence and Garner v. Texas: Overturning *Bowers v. Hardwick*, the Court declared that the Constitution's Due Process Clause gave homosexuals the freedom to conduct their intimate lives without the interference of the government.

Bibliography

Books

Bayer, Linda. *Ruth Bader Ginsburg*. Philadelphia: Chelsea House Publishers, 2000.

Breyer, Stephen G. *Active Liberty: Interpreting Our Democratic Constitution*. New York: Knopf, 2005.

Clinton, Robert Lowry. Marbury v. Madison *and Judicial Review*. Lawrence, Kan.: University Press of Kansas, 1989.

Cushman, Claire, and Melvin I. Urofsky, eds. *Black, White, and* Brown*: The Landmark School Desegregation Case in Retrospect*. Washington, D.C.: Supreme Court Historical Society/CQ Press, 2004.

Ely, James W., Jr., et al., eds. *The Oxford Companion to the Supreme Court of the United States*. New York: Oxford University Press, 2005.

Foskett, Ken. *Judging Thomas: The Life and Times of Clarence Thomas*. New York: Morrow, 2004.

Friedman, Leon, and Fred L. Israel. *The Justices of the United States Supreme Court, 1789–1995: Their Lives and Major Opinions*. New York: Chelsea House Publishers, 1997.

Greenberg, Jack. *Crusaders in the Courts: How a Dedicated Band of Lawyers Fought for the Civil Rights Revolution*. New York: BasicBooks, 1994.

Hall, Kermit, ed. *The Oxford Guide to United States Supreme Court Decisions*. New York: Oxford University Press, 1999.

Hartman, Gary R., Roy M. Mersky, and Cindy Tate Slavinski. *Landmark Supreme Court Cases: The Most Influential Decisions of the Supreme Court of the United States*. New York: Facts on File, 2003.

Hilliard, Bryan. *The U.S. Supreme Court and Medical Ethics: From Contraception to Managed Health Care*. St. Paul, Minn.: Paragon House, 2004.

Irons, Peter. *A People's History of the Supreme Court*. New York: Viking, 1999.

Keck, Thomas M. *The Most Activist Supreme Court in History: The Road to Modern Judicial Conservatism*. Chicago: University of Chicago Press, 2004.

Klarman, Michael J. *From Jim Crow to Civil Rights: The Supreme Court and the Struggle for Racial Equality*. New York: Oxford University Press, 2004.

Lazarus, Edward. *Closed Chambers: The Rise, Fall, and Future of the Modern Supreme Court*. New York: Penguin, 2005.

Levin, Mark R. *Men in Black: How the Supreme Court Is Destroying America*. Washington, D.C.: Regnery Pub., 2005

Lewis, Anthony. *Gideon's Trumpet*. New York, Random House, 1964.

Maroon, Fred J. (photographer), and Suzy Maroon (text). *The Supreme Court of the United States*. New York: Thomasson-Grant & Lickle, 1996.

McGuire, Kevin T. *Understanding the U.S. Supreme Court*. Boston, MA: McGraw-Hill, 2002.

Nelson, William E. Marbury v. Madison: *The Origins and Legacy of Judicial Review*. Lawrence: University Press of Kansas, 2000.

O'Brien, David M. *Storm Center: The Supreme Court in American Politics*. New York: W. W. Norton, 2005.

O'Connor, Sandra Day. *The Majesty of the Law: Reflections of a Supreme Court Justice*. New York: Random House, 2003.

Ogletree, Charles J., Jr. *All Deliberate Speed: Reflections on the First Half Century of* Brown v. Board of Education. New York: W. W. Norton & Co., 2004.

Paddock, Lisa. *Facts About the Supreme Court of the United States*. New York: H. W. Wilson, 1996.

Rehnquist, William. *The Supreme Court*. New York: Vintage Books, 2002.

————. *The Supreme Court: How It Was, How It Is*. New York: Morrow, 1987.

Ring, Kevin A. *Scalia Dissents: Writings of the Supreme Court's Wittiest, Most Outspoken Justice*. Washington, D.C.: Regnery Pub., 2004.

Ryden, David K. *The U.S. Supreme Court and the Electoral Process*. Washington, D.C.: Georgetown University Press, 2002.

Samuels, Suzanne Uttaro. *First Among Friends: Interest Groups, the U.S. Supreme Court, and the Right to Privacy*. Westport, Conn.: Praeger, 2004.

Scalia, Antonin. *A Matter of Interpretation: Federal Courts and the Law: An Essay*. Princeton, N.J.: Princeton University Press, 1997.

Schwartz, Bernard. *A History of the Supreme Court*. New York: Oxford University Press, 1993.

Spaeth, Harold J., and Jeffrey A. Segal. *Majority Rule, or, Minority Will: Adherence to Precedent on the U.S. Supreme Court*. New York: Cambridge University Press, 2001.

Starr, Kenneth W. *First Among Equals: The Supreme Court in American Life*. New York: Warner Books, 2002.

Stuart, Gary. Miranda: *The Story of America's Right to Remain Silent*. Tuscon: University of Arizona Press, 2004.

Tushnet, Mark. *A Court Divided: The Rehnquist Court and the Future of Constitutional Law*. New York: W. W. Norton, 2005.

Urofsky, Melvin I., ed. *The Supreme Court Justices: A Biographical Dictionary*. New York: Garland Pub., 1994.

Waltenburg, Eric N., and Bill Swinford. *Litigating Federalism: The States Before the U.S. Supreme Court*. Westport, Conn.: Greenwood Press, 1999.

Yarbrough, Tinsley E. *David Hackett Souter: Traditional Republican on the Rehnquist Court*. New York: Oxford University Press, 2005.

Web Sites

Readers seeking additional information about the Supreme Court of the United States may wish to refer to the following Web sites, all of which were operational as of this writing.

American Law Sources On-line

www.lawsource.com/also/usa.cgi?us1

American Law Sources On-line (ALSO!) features links to various online legal resources, including recent and historical rulings of the Supreme Court.

FindLaw U.S. Supreme Court Center

supreme.lp.findlaw.com

FindLaw.com is the nation's leading provider of online legal information for legal professionals, businesses, and the public. FindLaw's U.S. Supreme Court Center features an index of Court cases, as well as Court briefs, decisions, schedules, and rules.

Jurist Legal Intelligence

jurist.law.pitt.edu/issues/issue_scotus.htm

Maintained by faculty and students of the University of Pittsburgh School of Law, Jurist tracks developments in legal affairs and strives to publish them quickly and fairly. In addition to covering recent events on the Supreme Court, Jurist includes links to past decisions, as well as biographies of the justices and other resources.

Legal Information Institute Supreme Court Collection

straylight.law.cornell.edu/supct/index.html

This non-profit organization at Cornell University Law School provides information about all U.S. Supreme Court opinions handed down since 1992, as well as synopses of selected landmark cases up to that year. It also includes more than a decade of opinions issued by the New York Court of Appeals and other resources, including a glossary of "legalese" and all Supreme Court rules.

The Oyez Project

www.oyez.org

Begun in the late 1980s, the Oyez Project seeks to provide a "multi-media Supreme Court experience." The Project's online component includes over 2,000 hours of audio. Researchers can listen to all the oral arguments made before the Court since 1995, as well as certain earlier selections. The Oyez Project also features a wealth of other information, including biographies of the justices and a virtual tour of the Court grounds.

The Supreme Court Historical Society

www.supremecourthistory.org

A private, nonprofit organization, the Supreme Court Historical Society is dedicated to the collection and preservation of the history of the Supreme Court. The Society's Web site offers an in-depth overview of the Court's history and procedures.

The Supreme Court of the United States

www.supremecourtus.gov

This is the official Web site of the Supreme Court. Visitors can access a variety of essential information, including historical articles; biographies of the justices, both past and present; arguments made before the Court, as well as the eventual rulings; and the Court's upcoming schedule.

Supreme Court Zeitgeist

judgejohnroberts.com

This Web site—*not* affiliated with Chief Justice John G. Roberts, despite its URL—contains recent news, links, and blogs about the U.S. Supreme Court.

United States Supreme Court Monitor

www.law.com/jsp/scm/index.jsp

A component of Law.com, one of the most respected online legal resources, the United States Supreme Court Monitor charts the latest Court-related news.

Web Guide to U.S. Supreme Court Research

www.llrx.com/features/supremectwebguide.htm

Maintained by the Dickinson School of Law, the Web Guide to U.S. Supreme Court Research provides links to the most authoritative legal Web sites dealing with specific aspects of the Court and its work.

Additional Periodical Articles with Abstracts

More information about the Supreme Court and related subjects can be found in the following articles. Readers who require a more comprehensive selection are advised to consult the *Readers' Guide Abstracts*, *Social Sciences Index*, and other H.W. Wilson Publications.

The *Lawrence* Legacy. *The Advocate*, p38 January 20, 2004.

Although the Supreme Court has put an end to sodomy laws, the writer says, it could be years before the full implications of the decision are realized. In its June 26 ruling in the case of *Lawrence v. Texas*, the U.S. Supreme Court rendered invalid the 13 state sodomy laws that are still on the books. Just four months after the ruling, however, a local judge in Virginia Beach, Virginia, allowed a prosecution on sodomy charges to proceed against a gay man named Joel Singson. Legal experts say that the time-related disparity between the Supreme Court ruling and the judicial system in some parts of the nation comes as no surprise, the writer declares.

The Court Begins to Shift. *The Chronicle of Higher Education*, p1 July 15, 2005.

The *Chronicle* writer speculates that Justice Sandra Day O'Connor's recently announced retirement from the U.S. Supreme Court may initiate profound changes in the Court's jurisprudence that will have major repercussions for the country as a whole and for higher education in particular. O'Connor's departure from the Court could destabilize higher-education law and leave it more vulnerable than ever to the strong political cross-currents that have unsettled the Supreme Court for much of the period during which William Rehnquist has been chief justice.

Brown v. Board of Education: An Axe in the Frozen Sea of Racism. Jack Greenberg. *Dissent*, v. 51 pp67–73 Fall 2004.

The decision taken by the Supreme Court in the 1954 *Brown v. Board of Education* case to abolish school desegregation was the beginning of the end of all forms of segregation in the U.S., claims Greenberg. The Court's decision had powerful implications, because it created a legal and moral imperative to achieve equality, and because it defined equality as a human right. The decision also led to the development of national measures of equality, Greenberg writes, and sparked the creation of a people's movement that supported desegregation.

How to Judge Future Judges. Sandford Levinson. *Dissent* v. 49 pp63–68 Fall 2002.

In considering nominees for the membership of the U.S. Supreme Court, writes Levinson, the crucial question that senators must decide upon is what they believe the Constitution, as interpreted by the Supreme Court, should look like in the future. Senators must ask if nominees offer compelling visions of what the constitutional order truly is, Levinson declares, as the good and evil done by persons appointed to the Court will live long after they leave it.

The War That Never Ends. *The Economist*, v. 366 pp24–26 January 18, 2003.

The writer explains that abortion in the U.S. is still a controversial issue—30 years after the Supreme Court declared abortion a constitutional right in 1973—because of the way in which the U.S. went about creating its legislation. The declaration of abortion as a constitutional right enraged opponents because it denied them their say, according to the writer, and supporters of abortion were left relying on the precarious balance of power in the Supreme Court. Legalization of abortion in the U.S. did not have the legitimacy of majority support, and instead it rested on a very controversial interpretation of the Constitution. In Europe, countries went down the legislative route and so managed to neutralize the debate. The future of abortion politics in the U.S. is uncertain, the writer says, because the situation in 2003 marks the first time since the Supreme Court made its ruling that the president, the leader of the Senate, and the leader of the House have all been against abortion.

Pledge Stays Intact As Justices Dismiss Atheist's Challenge. Caroline Hendrie. *Education Week*, v. 23 pp1+ June 23, 2004.

Hendrie reports that the U.S. Supreme Court has overturned a highly controversial ruling by the U.S. Court of Appeals for the Ninth Circuit that would have barred public schools in nine Western states from reciting the Pledge of Allegiance because it contains the words "under God." The Court ruled that the plaintiff, Dr. Michael A. Newdow, lacked the legal standing to bring the case because at the time, he did not have legal custody of his daughter, whose right not to say the Pledge Newdow was fighting to gain. However, the ruling did not address the merits of the church-state complaints against the Pledge, leaving the way open for similar legal challenges in the future.

Decisions That Have Shaped U.S. Education. Perry A. Zirkel. *Educational Leadership*, v. 59 pp6–12 December 2001/January 2002.

Zirkel discusses U.S. Supreme Court decisions that have shaped education. Made during the past six decades, these rulings relate to equality in education, specifically desegregation, special education, and the accommodation of disabilities; freedom of expression, particularly the saluting of the flag, per-student expenditure, students with limited English proficiency, student speech, censorship, teachers' speech, and school libraries; school discipline as it pertains to school safety, student suspensions, and expulsions, corporal punishment, searches of students, random drug tests, sexual harassment, and disruptive students in special education; and the role of religion in education, specifically government aid to religious schools and prayer at school events.

The Supreme Court Rules: 2004. Michael M. Uhlmann. *First Things*, pp17–26 October 2004.

Uhlmann examines how the U.S. Supreme Court dealt with the charge that President Bush was making unfounded claims about the reach of presidential war power. In an election year, liberals were hoping that the Supreme Court would rebuke the president for his actions in the war on terrorism. They have been sorely disappointed, however, writes Uhlmann, as the Court's decisions have sustained presidential discretion in wartime even as they placed procedural limits on the manner of its exercise. Two of the cases that the Court heard concerned constitutional claims asserted by American citizens; the third involved similar claims asserted by foreigners. Central to all of them, Uhlmann says, was the tension between national security and civil liberties in a time of war.

Bending Before the Storm: The U.S. Supreme Court in Economic Crisis, 1935–1937. William F. Shugart, III. *Independent Review* (Oakland, Calif.) v. 9 pp55–83 Summer 2004.

The dynamics of the switch in attitude, from opposition to support, by the Supreme Court for President Franklin D. Roosevelt's "New Deal" legislation during the U.S. economic crisis between 1935 and 1937 are explored by Shugart. He notes that the nine members of the Supreme Court, known as the "Nine Old Men," were strongly against Roosevelt's initiatives to greatly expand the government's regulatory powers until February 5, 1937, when the president announced his plan to appoint six new justices in order to remove any obstacles that the judiciary had put in the way of his policy proposals. Shugart concludes that, fearing for their positions, the Supreme Court justices subsequently upheld virtually all of Roosevelt's economic regulatory policies and bent to his political will.

Making Sense of the Michigan Affirmative Action Cases: *Grutter v. Bollinger*. Vikram David Amar. *Insights on Law & Society*, v. 4 pp11–13 Fall 2003.

Amar examines how the U.S. Supreme Court upheld the value of educational diversity in two University of Michigan affirmative action cases. In *Grutter v. Bollinger*, Justice O'Connor's majority opinion upheld the University of Michigan Law School's program that used race in admissions. At the same time, in *Gratz v. Bollinger*, the Court struck down the university's program for undergraduate admissions for using race too formulaically and mechanically. The

Grutter case clarified that racial diversity can be pursued only if race is seen as one aspect of the person, explains Amar.

Faith and Freedom. Dale McDonald. *Momentum* (Washington, D.C.), v. 34 pp78–79 November/December 2003.

The intersection of freedom and faith has generated fierce debate in the public forum and U.S. Supreme Court for much of the nation's history, writes McDonald. Current significant issues in this area include the withdrawal of a state college scholarship from a student who declared a major in theology in preparation for religious ministry and the right of religiously affiliated service providers to compete fairly with their secular counterparts for federal grants that support social service programs administered by federal, state, or local government. McDonald discusses each of these issues.

Brown at 50. Eric Foner and Randall Kennedy. *The Nation*, v. 278 pp15–17 May 3, 2004.

Foner and Kennedy recount how, on May 17, 1954, the U.S. Supreme Court ruling in *Brown v. Board of Education* overturned state laws requiring or allowing racial segregation in public primary and secondary schools. Such laws, the Court held, violate the equal protection clause of the Fourteenth Amendment. Simultaneously, in *Bolling v. Sharpe*, the Court held that the due process clause of the Fifth Amendment prevented the federal government from racially segregating students in the District of Columbia. The rulings reflected and encouraged developments that would soon ignite the civil rights movement. According to the writers, *Brown* and *Bolling* derived from an extraordinary campaign of social reform litigation principally led by black lawyers who had themselves suffered cruel deprivations imposed by segregation. These decisions proved that at least some elements of the white establishment were willing to begin cautiously to challenge open, unembarrassed, official discrimination against blacks and other minorities. The writers discuss the legacy of the decisions on the development of race legislation and future jurisprudence.

No Blank Check. David Cole. *The Nation*, v. 279 pp4–5 July 19–26, 2004.

Cole reports that the Bush administration sustained major losses in a pair of historic Supreme Court decisions that were issued on June 28 on its asserted power to detain "enemy combatants." The Court ruled that foreign nationals detained at Guantanamo Bay are entitled to file *habeas corpus* petitions in federal court to challenge the legality of their detentions. In the case of U.S. citizen Yaser Hamdi, it also ruled that U.S. citizens are entitled to at least a fair hearing on whether they are "enemy combatants" before they can be held over a sustained length of time. According to Cole, the magnitude of the administration's loss is evident by comparison with earlier Supreme Court decisions during periods of war. The Court has historically shown extraordinary deference to claims of national security, but this time, Cole says, the Court pointedly refused to defer to the administration during wartime.

Chief Among Equals: Selecting a New Chief Justice. *National Review*, v. 57 p14 May 23, 2005.

In considering a replacement for ailing chief justice William Rehnquist, who is expected to retire in the near future, the Bush administration should be looking for a chief justice outside the current Court, the writer argues. The ideal candidate would respect the text of the Constitution as it was understood by the ratifying public, respect the Court's precedents, and be prepared to overrule those precedents when they are seriously out of line with the constitutional text. According to the writer, the willingness to do so is particularly important in an era in which the Court has taken on so many responsibilities and faces few effective checks.

Brown v. Board of Education at 50: Where Are We Now? Charles R. Hancock and Janine Hancock Jones. *The Negro Educational Review*, v. 56 pp91–98 January 2005.

The writers review recent research into the achievement of the aims and vision of the landmark desegregation ruling in *Brown v. Board of Education of Topeka, Kansas*. This research, they claim, indicates that the U.S. remains in a state eerily and arguably similar to the pre-*Brown* era of segregation.

Divide and Rule: Supreme Court Decisions on Terrorism. Jeffrey Rosen. *The New Republic*, v. 231 pp11–13 July 26, 2004.

Rosen claims that the Supreme Court's recent decisions repudiating the Bush administration's demand that the courts stay out of the war on terrorism were neither minimalist nor outrageously activist. Although simultaneously lauded as an example of judicial restraint and excoriated as the activism of an imperial judiciary, the decisions were actually an expression of pragmatism, says Rosen. They were the opinion of justices who were unwilling to accept the executive's claims of unreviewable authority but who wanted to give the president enough flexibility to descend from his imperious perch. Unfortunately for the White House, the Court's patience may soon run out, according to Rosen, at which time five legalistic justices seem set to rule that the president lacks authority to detain U.S. citizens indefinitely on American soil. Ultimately, Rosen argues, that would be the best outcome for civil liberties because it would compel Bush to get congressional approval for the detention procedures that neither judges nor presidents should invent.

Immodest Proposal. Jeffrey Rosen. *The New Republic*, v. 229 pp19–21 December 22, 2003.

When the U.S. Supreme Court struck down sodomy laws in *Lawrence v. Texas* in June 2003, writes Rosen, critics predicted that the unnecessarily broad opinion would reignite the culture wars by encouraging the lower courts to establish a right to gay marriage before the public was prepared to accept it. On November 18, 2003, in *Goodridge v. Department of Public Health*, the Massachusetts Supreme Judicial Court vindicated the critics' worst fears, expansively citing *Lawrence* to justify its decision to redefine marriage to encompass same-sex unions. According to Rosen, the Massachusetts Supreme Judicial Court could have followed the example of Vermont by backing civil unions but not same-sex marriage. The writer argues that the Massachusetts decision was both constitutionally unconvincing and politically naive.

Armies Ready for Court Battle But Are Unable to Find a Fight. Elisabeth Bumiller. *The New York Times*, pp1+ July 24, 2005.

Ed Gillespie, the White House adviser in charge of the effort to have Judge John G. Roberts confirmed as a Supreme Court justice, has settled in his office with an army at hand but no one to fight, Bumiller observes. The nomination of Judge Roberts has not sparked the kind of partisan uproar that other nominees might have. Still, according to Bumiller, both Democrats and Republicans are poised for a battle, with millions of dollars ready to be spent.

In His Opinions, Nominee Favors Judicial Caution. Adam Liptak. *The New York Times*, ppA1+ July 22, 2005.

Analyzing 49 opinions that Judge John G. Roberts wrote while sitting on the Federal Appeals Court in Washington, Liptak concludes that Roberts is a thoughtful conservative who favors limitations on federal power, a cautious judiciary, and individual responsibility.

O'Connor Leap Moved Women Up the Bench. Adam Liptak. *The New York Times*, ppA1+ July 5, 2005.

President Ronald Reagan's nomination of Sandra Day O'Connor as the first female Supreme Court justice in 1981 opened the way for women on the bench, Liptak writes. Justice O'Connor was a midlevel appellate court judge when she was elevated from that role. It was a first in the history of the Court, and she opened up a set of opportunities that would not have existed without her, Liptak argues. In 1981, Mr. Reagan's first year in office, there were only 48 women federal judges, some of them semi-retired. Today, there are 201 women and 622 men among active federal judges, according to the Federal Judicial Center.

Center Court. Jeffrey Rosen. *The New York Times Magazine*, pp17–18 June 12, 2005.

It seems that the views of a majority of Americans are better represented by the moderate majority on the Supreme Court than by the polarized party leadership in the Senate, Rosen claims. A recent CBS News poll found that 68 percent of respondents said that Congress "does not have the same priorities for the country" as they do. By contrast, a survey conducted by Quinnipiac University found that a 44-percent plurality approved of the way the Supreme Court is doing its job. The most obvious reason why this situation has come about, argues Rosen, is the partisan gerrymandering that removes the incentive for Democrats and Republicans in Congress to court the moderate center in general elections while they cater to their own ideological bases, thereby creating very polarized parties.

The Evolution of a Justice (adapted from *Becoming Justice Blackmun*). Linda Greenhouse. *The New York Times Magazine*, pp28–33 April 10, 2005.

Justice Harry A. Blackmun, the author of *Roe v. Wade*, is lauded today as a great proponent of women's rights, reports Greenhouse, but his recently unsealed papers demonstrate that this was not always the case. The Library of Congress, in line with Blackmun's instructions, opened his papers to the public in March 2004, on the fifth anniversary of his death. During the 32 years since the Court decided *Roe v. Wade*, Greenhouse says, the right to abortion has become so entwined, both in political debate and in the public mind, with women's rights in general that it is easy to assume that the middle-aged men who voted in 1973 to overturn state abortion laws believed that they were striking a blow for women's equality. Blackmun's papers reveal a more complex reality, however, highlighting what turns out to be a highly tenuous connection between the abortion cases and the cases on women's equality that came before the Court simultaneously in the early 1970s. Greenhouse discusses Blackmun's attitude toward *Roe v. Wade*.

Supreme Confidence: Justice A. Scalia. Margaret Talbot. *The New Yorker*, v. 81 pp40+ March 28, 2005.

Talbot's profile of Justice Antonin Scalia describes, among other things, how Scalia often stresses the deep and redeeming religiosity of the American people, revels in intellectual combat, delivers conservative judgments on social issues, has little confidence in social progress, has a narrow view of what judges ought to be trusted to do, and interacts aggressively with lawyers.

***Marbury v. Madison*, Rightly Understood.** Peter Schotten. *Perspectives on Political Science*, v. 33 pp134–141 Summer 2004.

Schotten discusses the *Marbury v. Madison* ruling of 1803, which established the authority and legitimacy of the U.S. Supreme Court. In *Marbury*, Chief Justice John Marshall established the Court's authority to exercise national judicial review. However, according to Schotten, the ruling should not be viewed as simply a judicial power grab but as an attempt to avoid political crises between Federalists and Republicans. By helping to ensure the stability of a fragile Republican regime, promoting the concept of national sovereignty, and trying to promote the cause of an energetic national government, Marshall advanced the founders' vision, Schotten writes.

Unpacking the Court: The Case for the Expansion of the United States Supreme Court in the 21st Century. Jonathan Turley. *Perspectives on Political Science*, v. 33 pp155–162 Summer 2004.

Turley proposes expanding the U.S. Supreme Court from nine to 19 members. After discussing the origins of the modern Supreme Court and historic fluctuations in its size, he examines the danger of judicial autocracy on a nine-member court. The writer then delineates the advantages of an expanded 19-member court, suggesting that it would reduce the relative authority and predictability of individual justices, increase the workload of the Court and allow justices to sit by designation, increase the rate of turnover for Court membership, eliminate "double duty" problems and remove the chief justice from circuit supervision, and reduce confirmation controversies.

The U.S. Presidential Election and the *Bush v. Gore* Supreme Court Decision. Gerald R. Webster. *Political Geography*, v. 21 pp99–104 January 2002.

The 2000 presidential election produced over two dozen different lawsuits including two separate decisions by the U.S. Supreme Court. In this essay, Webster examines the most important of these decisions, *George W. Bush v. Albert Gore, Jr.*, highlighting its logic and geographic implications.

Marbury v. Madison: How John Marshall Changed History by Misquoting the Constitution. Winfield H. Rose. *PS, Political Science & Politics*, v. 36 pp209–214 April 2003.

In writing his opinion on *Marbury v. Madison* (5 U.S. 137 1803), Chief Justice John Marshall seriously misquoted the relevant part of Article III of the Constitution, and he did so intentionally to serve his own purpose, Rose argues. The Constitution had given Congress the power to adjust the original and appellate jurisdictions of the Supreme Court, but Marshall removed that power in order to avoid a confrontation with President Jefferson on the one hand, and on the other to establish judicial review, Marshall's greatest legacy. According to Rose, Marshall's arguments were smart artifices to extricate himself and the Court from a political dilemma and to establish the Court as a truly equal third arm of government. Marshall had the nerve and the courage to misquote the Constitution for his own purpose, says Rose, and he was skilled enough to do it in such a manner that it has been largely unrecognized for 200 years.

Supreme Court Senility: Interview with D. J. Garrow. Jesse Walker. *Reason*, v. 37 pp44–46 July 2005.

Historian David J. Garrow's articles suggest, writes Walker, that the Supreme Court is a closed society with its own customs. In "Mental Decrepitude on the U.S. Supreme Court," which appeared in the fall 2000 issue of the *University of Chicago Law Review*, he demonstrated in uncomfortable detail that the Court is an institution not just of laws but of men, revealing that, since the 18th century, some of the justices have suffered from senility, severe depression, and drug addiction. In "The Brains Behind Blackmun," which appeared in the May/June 2005 *Legal Affairs*, he uncovered the story of a judge who ceded to his law clerks much greater control over his official work than did any of the other justices from the last half-century whose papers are publicly available. In an interview, Garrow discusses his views on the Court and its culture.

Landmark Ruling Paves the Way for Vouchers. Stephen Phillips. *The Times Educational Supplement*, p18 July 5, 2002.

The U.S. Supreme Court has narrowly approved a controversial program that offers poor urban students in Cleveland, Ohio, vouchers to attend private schools. Phillips writes that the decision clears the way for public funding of private religious schools, and it has been described as the most momentous legal ruling on education since the 1954 ban on segregation.

Index